WRITING
EDUCATIONAL
BIOGRAPHY

3 U N

CRITICAL EDUCATION PRACTICE
VOLUME 13
GARLAND REFERENCE LIBRARY OF SOCIAL SCIENCE
VOLUME 1098

WRITING EDUCATIONAL BIOGRAPHY

EXPLORATIONS IN QUALITATIVE RESEARCH

EDITED BY
CRAIG KRIDEL

GARLAND PUBLISHING, INC.
A MEMBER OF THE TAYLOR & FRANCIS GROUP
NEW YORK AND LONDON
1998

1944 7787

Library of Congress Cataloging-in-Publication Data

Writing educational biography : explorations in qualitative research /
    edited by Craig Kridel.
            p.   cm. — (Garland reference library of social science ; v. 1098.
    Critical education practice ; v. 13)
        Includes bibliographical references (p.   ) and index.
        ISBN 0-8153-2294-1 (hardcover) (alk. paper)
        ISBN 0-8153-2296-8 (paperback)
        1. Education —Research.   2. Educators—Biography.   3. Education—
    Biographical methods.   I. Kridel, Craig Alan.   II. Series: Garland reference
    library of social science ; v. 1098.   III. Series: Garland reference library of
    social science. Critical education practice ; vol. 13.
    LB1028.W75   1998
    370'.7—dc21   97-38260
                                                                         CIP

Paperback cover design by parlour.

Printed on acid-free, 250-year-life paper
Manufactured in the United States of America

for Robert V. Bullough, Jr.
whose 1981 biography *Democracy in Education: Boyd H. Bode*
represents the significance of educational biography
for our postmodern society

for Maxine Greene
whose writings,
from *The Public School and the Private Vision*
to *Releasing the Imagination,*
display the importance of the humanities
for educational research and scholarship

and

for Louis M. Smith
whose research portrays the scholar's
love and enthusiasm
for the adventure of biography

Table of Contents

Preface

Writing Educational Biography grew out of conversations and presentations of the Archival and Biographical Research Special Interest Group (SIG) of the American Educational Research Association (AERA). Sessions at this annual meeting permitted the contributors to discuss concerns and topics related to educational biography. The Museum of Education at the University of South Carolina continued this dialogue throughout the years with invited speakers, conferences and award presentations for distinguished work in biography. This compilation of essays emerged from these events.

As *Writing Educational Biography* explores an increasingly popular dimension of qualitative research in education, I have been greatly aided by the work of others examining the possibilities of biographical work. I drew lessons from many fine periodicals and book series: *Biography: An Interdisciplinary Quarterly* with its emphasis upon biographical studies in the humanities; *Vitae Scholasticae* and its concern with biography in the foundations of education; the *JCT: An Interdisciplinary Journal of Curriculum Studies*, which often focuses on cultural-postmodern critique; *The Narrative Study of Lives* drawing primarily from a tradition of psychology; and the *Journal of Narrative and Life History* and Sage's *Qualitative Research Methods* series with their emphases on the social sciences.

I also found the prolific work currently underway in the fields of teacher education and curriculum theory quite helpful—the many examples of first year teacher research, teacher lore and teacher narrative (Bullough and Gitlin, 1995; Bullough, Knowles and Crow, 1991; Goodson and Walker, 1991; Schubert and Ayers, 1992; Ducharme, 1993; Clandinin and Connelly, 1995). Similarly, the International Society for Educational Biography, now in its second decade, has pioneered opportunities for educators involved in the study of disparate biographical subjects, and the annual *JCT* "Bergamo" conferences have provided an important venue for the exploration of narrative. In all of this work, I saw that a significant strand of research and writing was underway—distinct from social science life-writing and narrative—one that sought to reconcile a more traditional concept of "fact and truth" with emerging postmodern and poststructuralist perspectives. Such a reconciliation could serve to blend the humanities and social sciences in a constellation of traditional and postmodern sensibilities. Such hopes and this prospect gave impetus to this collection.

I thank Marie Ellen Larcada of Garland Publishing and Critical Studies in Education editors Shirley Steinberg and Joe Kincheloe who chose to support a collection of essays on biographical research. I appreciate the thoughtfulness of William Pinar who brought this collection to their attention. Victoria Kalemaris of the McKissick Museum of Education, University of South Carolina, and Mary Bull of the South Carolina State Library assisted in obtaining fugitive details. Other colleagues who provided advice include Robert V. Bullough, Jr., Herbert J. Hartsook, Paul R. Klohr, William H. Schubert, Wayne J. Urban, Alan Wieder and Kenneth Wollitz. Lastly, this collection was inspired by Louis M. Smith's "Biographical Method" entry in the *Handbook of Qualitative Methods* (Denzin and Lincoln, 1994). He concluded that his essay there will be a success if he "intrigued any of you who have never done life histories or biographies, or those of you who have never read Bowen, Clifford, or Edel, among others" (p. 302). I wish the same and hope these essays serve as more inducement to read in biographical theory and to undertake research ventures in education.

Craig Kridel, January 1997

Writing
Educational
Biography

Introduction

> The growing public fascination with biography and the increasing number of academic studies of the genre seem to have coincided in the last two decades. Scholars from many different disciplines have been attracted to biography as a way of dealing with social, political, cultural, and psychological issues and of reaching an audience of readers far larger than the one available to them in the academy.
> Carl Rollyson (1992, p. 1).

The study of biography is slowing emerging as a significant development in the field of educational research. Such a development has promise as a way of bridging critical relationships among the balkanized research realms that characterize the study of education in the postmodern world. "Good biographies deal with the ways people faced living—tell how they met problems, how they coped with big and little crises, how they loved, competed, did the things we all do daily—and hence these studies touch familiar chords in readers" (Vandiver, 1983, p. 16). We need little convincing of such "touched chords" as we see teachers and researchers discuss and share case studies and other educational narratives. Indeed, biography and life-history, in a variety of forms, are basic to qualitative research. Academics write biographies of university presidents and increasingly construct narratives and case studies of teachers and students. Introductory qualitative research textbooks often include treatments of life-history writing, and societies for educational biography are now well established. Various educational research conferences have included biography sessions, and several publishers now offer

journals and collected essays on life-history writing in education. The past few years have seen a phenomenal growth and
resurgence of interest in life writing with numerous allusions
and references to biography permeating this literature.

Much of the current writing in the field of education,
however, draws upon the important work in the social sciences
and attends primarily to matters of narrative, life-history, story
telling, voice and autobiography. Psychology, feminist studies,
critical theory, anthropology and sociology are all well represented with only marginal reference to the humanities. Of
course, one expects the field of education, most commonly
conceived of as an applied social science, to align itself within
its broader research tradition. The insights that have evolved
from all of these various areas, as well as from those arising
from current postmodern sensibilities, have greatly refined
and expanded our conceptions of educational research and
inquiry.

Still, as dimensions of narrative and life-history writing per-
meate current qualitative research, a substantial body of literature—writings that constitute a well-defined and burgeoning
field of biographical theory—seems yet to have entered fully
into the educational discourse. Such work is often overlooked,
if not ignored. This is not to suggest that education writers
must pepper their essays with references from the works of
various distinguished biographers—Lytton Strachey, Leon
Edel, Catherine Drinker Bowen and James Garraty. Yet, these
and other writers offer insights that promise to illuminate educational discourse. While distinctions and definitions among
the various forms of life-writing often seem needlessly
complex and sometimes confusing, a distinct tradition of biography exists. This body of thought compels further exploration in the field of education as part of the re-examination of
educational research methods prompted by postmodernism.
Biographical inquiry provides a fresh perspective on and new
possibilities and dimensions for education—new ways to
examine how one describes the behavior of others, new ways
to appraise the impact of the pedagogical process on students
and teachers, new ways to explain how educational policy
manifests itself in the lives of individuals.

Intent of the Collection
In the spirit of adventure and exploration, I set out to compile this collection of essays, extending an invitation to educators who seek to expand our understanding of qualitative research and explore aspects of biographical inquiry applicable to the field of education. I would be pleased if readers were inspired to undertake the writing of a biography after reading this collection though, of course, such an outcome would be somewhat unusual. Rather, the purpose of this collection is to portray many pervasive influences of biographical inquiry in education and to emphasize that the self-examination of a biographer—those typical documentary, interpretive and literary concerns of biography—can enhance and enrich the practice of educational research.

I have made a special effort to avoid duplicating the work of others. Although various contributors in this collection discuss biography's potential for providing insights in educational research, I saw little need to focus exclusively upon the importance of biography. Such justifications serve as supplemental reading to this collection and are found in James Garraty's *The Nature of Biography* (1957), Leon Edel's *Writing Lives: Principia Biographica* (1959), Carolyn G. Heilbrun's *Writing a Woman's Life* (1988), *Composing a Life* (1989) by Mary Catherine Bateson, and Linda Wagner-Martin's *Telling Women's Lives* (1994), as well as in various collections: *Telling Lives: The Biographer's Art*, edited by Marc Pachter (1981); *The Biographer's Gift*, edited by James Veninga (1983); *Between Women*, edited by Ascher, DeSalvo and Ruddick (1984); *Biography as High Adventure*, edited by Stephen Oates (1986); *Contesting the Subject*, edited by William Epstein (1991); *The Challenge of Feminist Biography*, edited by Alpern, Antler, Perry and Scobie (1992); and *The Art of Literary Biography*, edited by John Batchelor (1995). These and many other books constitute an important set of readings in biographical theory and offer a rich collection of thoughtful, literary reflections for those eager to learn about the nature of biographical inquiry.

Similarly, this book is not a primer for the act of writing biography in education, though certain essays in the collection accept this pedagogical role. Such didactic guides for novice biographers have already been prepared, most notably *The Biographer's Craft* by Milton Lomask (1986), *From Puzzles to Portraits* by James L. Clifford (1970), and aspects of "Biographical Method" by Louis M. Smith and "Personal Experience Methods" by D. Jean Clandinin and F. Michael Connelly, both chapters in the *Handbook of Qualitative Methods* (Denzin and Lincoln, 1994, pp. 286-305, 413-427). Other method books addressing components of life writing abound including those that focus on interpretive biography (Denizen, 1989), archival techniques (Hill, 1993), oral history (Yow, 1994), memoirs and lifestories (Ledoux, 1993), local school history (Butchart, 1986), and even biography for children (Hannabuss and Marcella, 1993) and secondary school students (Fleming and McGinnis, 1985). In short, "how-to" primers are well represented in the literature. Finally, in preparing *Writing Educational Biography*, I wanted to avoid assembling a variety of biographical essays and "life-portraits." These collections typically focus on the biographical subject to the exclusion of research issues and methods. For example, *Lives in Education* (L. G. Smith and J. K. Smith, 1994) and *Teachers and Mentors* (Kridel, Bullough and Shaker, 1996), a compilation of biographical and pedagogical vignettes, attend more to biographical content than to research methods. Such collections, while indicative of the growing interest in educational biography, do not offer (nor did they set out to provide) a discourse and exploration of method.

Instead, I was convinced that there was a place in the literature for authors to discuss aspects of biography and to consider the biographer's art and craft within the context of being educational researchers. A balance between theoretical discourse and "how-to" primer has been difficult to maintain; however, I encouraged the contributors to draw upon their work so as to provide context for methodological issues and insights. In so doing I was generally unconcerned with the delegation of topics and themes—I did not assign specific topics but, instead, grouped chapters as the drafts arrived. The complexity of biography is therefore well-represented, and agreements (with some inevitable overlapping) among our contributors are readily apparent. Significant diversity also appears; such is the status of current biographical research, thus it is well represented within this collection. I asked the contributors to examine their work as researchers and to reflect upon a broader set of issues that generally constitute the tenets of biographical theory. In effect, I asked them to engage in middle-range theorizing, and the result is a collection of essays that acknowledges biography's presence in education, discusses some methodological issues from the perspective of veteran and novice biographers, underscores some caveats when one begins archival work and, most importantly, displays the complexity and distinctiveness—the sense of exploration—that accompanies such scholarly endeavors. In effect, *Writing Educational Biography* serves as a beginning, as a micrologos—a little knowledge—for those who wish to explore the possibilities of biographical research in education.

Definitions and Approaches in Biographical Research

Biography itself lives a cursed and blessed life—"a disease of English literature" to George Eliot, or "the most delicate and humane of the branches of the art of writing" to Lytton Strachey. W. H. Auden viewed biography as "usually in bad taste" and, to Coleridge, it was the "cravings of worthless curiosity." Biographers themselves do not go unscathed. Bernard DeVoto describes the harassed researcher as one who "sweats out life in courthouses, record-offices, newspaper morgues and family attics." Jon Stallworthy calls the biographer a "postmortem exploiter." And one must not overlook the archives—the primary workplace of a biographer—which Edel sees as "great clutter of masses of papers." Other comments, however, suggest the universality and value of this literary form; Emerson stated, "There is properly no history: only biography," and Yeats said, "Nothing exists but a stream of souls, that all knowledge is biography." In short, descriptions abound. What eludes us is any consensus on a definition.

In fact, building a comprehensive, all-inclusive definition of biography seems fruitless and futile, especially once placed in juxtaposition with the various areas of life-history writing, life-writing, biography, psychobiography, narratology or narrative lives. Perhaps the most succinct way to define the term "biography" is to quote the opening sentence in James Garraty's (1957) *The Nature of Biography*: "Biography, to begin with a very simple definition, is the record of a life" (p. 3). This description fails, however, to anticipate the complexity of issues, traditions, concerns and problems biographers inevitably face—complexities that serve as the real content for discussions on biographical method.

The term "educational biography" can be just as elusive and is used in this collection merely to represent works of biographical subjects from the field of education. The term "literary biography," while at times alluding to its own artistic aspects and literary qualities, typically refers to biographies of literary figures; similarly, this is typically the case with the terms "political biography" or "military biography" meaning the study of political or military figures. This collection uses "educational biography" in this same manner—that is, to refer to biographical research that examines the lives of those individuals who worked or work in the field of education, broadly conceived. Perhaps more important than definition is the tradition from which a writer speaks—history or literature, humanities or social sciences, art or craft, or a variety of such subspecialties as feminist biography, psychobiography, prosopography (group biography), or "new" biography à la postmodernism. Those working in the broadest conception of educational biography—namely, those involved in telling the life of another whose career falls within the field of education—draw from all disciplines.

One looks in vain for clearly delineated categories of biographical research. Many such categories exist, yet none enjoys a general allegiance. Nonetheless, a collection that calls itself *Writing Educational Biography* must provide some conceptual structure, some framework, for those who wish to examine biographical works. Perhaps the simplest yet most comprehensive framework for biographical research—biographical types—is described by Stephen Oates in *Biography as High Adventure* (1986) and *Biography as History* (1991). Oates mentioned three approaches to biography: the scholarly chronicle, the critical study and the narrative biography. All three approaches have their merits, and aspects of each may appear within one work. The *scholarly chronicle* reflects the biographer's quest for objectivity and consists primarily of "a recitation of facts." The writing is detached, informative and comprehensive. Such biographies provide an important service through their detail, meticulousness and expansive examination of documents and materials related to the biographical subject. *The Life and Mind of John Dewey* by George Dykhuizen (1973) well represents a scholarly chronicle from the field of education. The contents follow a cradle-to-grave organization with the book's final illustration consisting of a photograph of the Dewey Memorial at the University of Vermont. While Harold Taylor's "Introduction" poignantly describes Dewey's life and work, Dykhuizen's text presents a straightforward, orderly exposition. As Taylor (1973) stated, "Dykhuizen has been painstaking and indefatigable in his own way in putting together the present book and in giving his readers access to information available only in a book of this kind" (p. xvii). In the 324 pages, Dewey's birth is reported on page 2 and his cremation on page 321. An incredible array of facts and details are reported in between while the biographer maintains an ever-objective stance in relation to the subject.

Oates' second category is the *critical study* or what could be construed as an author's analysis of subject—at times called an "intellectual biography." The biographer "analyzes his subject with appropriate detachment and skepticism, comparing his subject with similar lives in other eras, offering judgments about significance and consequence, . . . perhaps dazzling the audience with his erudition and argumentative force" (Oates, 1986, p. x). Robert Westbrook's *John Dewey and American Democracy* (1991) could be viewed in this category. The literary, scholarly and artistic aspects of the work are staggering; the emphasis, however, addresses aspects of intellectual context and interpretation. As Richard Rorty (1991) described Westbrook's work, "This splendid book will do a great deal to make Dewey more available and plausible, and to help his writings shape the imagination of a new generation of Americans" (Rorty, 1991, p. 15). Few comments could be more gratifying to a biographer of a critical study.

Oates' third category is *narrative biography*, which certainly does not exclude aspects of the previous two types.

Oates pointed out that "There is no such thing as a good narrative biography that is unanalytical. The process of selection, study, and interpretation is entirely analytical" (Oates, 1991, p. 11). Yet, the narrative biography seeks to wed scholarly, critical perspective with a story in narrative form that, as Oates has described, elicits "from the coldness of paper, the warmth of a life being lived." While few examples of educational biography can be cited for this third category, *John Dewey and the High Tide of American Liberalism* by Alan Ryan (1995) comes close. Whether this specific work falls into the category is, of course, open to speculation (as is the case with Dykhuizen's and Westbrook's works), yet this and the other two categories offer a useful direction for understanding the range of biographical writing. Moreover, the identification of specific educational biographies provides examples from which to begin constructing a conceptual framework for contrasting methodological approaches.

Other biographical approaches exist. Nonetheless, Oates' tripartite configuration provides a helpful introduction to biographical research. Perhaps one of the more interesting aspects of biography—if not one of its greatest attributes—is the actual blurring of genres, combining areas, topics and paradigms.

Hopes for Educational Biography

> It is time . . . to invent biographical forms that resist legitimating competition, domination, and an ethos of self-absorption.
> Rob Wilson (1991, p. 183)

Ours is a postmodern age where educators clearly recognize the importance of personal narrative, the power of stories, and the significance of whose perspective is being expressed and whose is being heard. Authoritative knowledge becomes antiquated with the emergence of multifaceted research methodologies embodying interpretive, naturalistic inquiry. As interest in biographical research grows in the academic community, methodology becomes increasingly complex. Denzin and Lincoln (1994) noted that the "means for interpretive, ethnographic practices is still not clear, but it is certain that things will never be the same. We are in a new age where messy, uncertain, multi-voiced texts, cultural criticism, and new experimental works will become more common, as will more reflexive forms of fieldwork, analysis, and intertextual representation" (p. 15). The implications for biography emerge as one struggles with such problems and issues. Answers are elusive. Yet, as the field of education further explores various forms of qualitative research—ethnographies, case studies, life histories, interpretive practice, participative inquiry, narratives and "narrative reasoning," and teachers' stories—biographical work clearly has much to offer as researchers feel their way along and seek to shed light on this complex phenomenon we call education.

Biography can help as we attempt to understand the role of researchers and the academy in a postmodern society. For as postmodern inquiry underscores and emphasizes the plurality, fragmentation and "fractured totality of everyday experience," the call for community becomes ever more compelling. "Otherwise," as Richard Bernstein (1992) wrote, "we are threatened by a new form of tribalism in which difference and otherness are reified, and where there is a failure to seek out commonalties and solidarities" (p. 313). Biographers, while maintaining allegiance to the concepts of "intended, shared meaning," "facts and recognized truths," "common humanity" and "interpretation of human character," offer one way to establish discourse among the varied, often polarized communities of our era. Such efforts do more than merely collect facts and preserve information. The researching of life-histories, the writing of personal narratives, and the collection of documents (and other materials) in archival settings permit biography "to inspire comparison. Have I lived that way? Do I want to live that way? Could I make myself live that way if I wanted to?" (Rose, 1984, p. 5). This is when biography transcends the bounds of qualitative research and brings together the disparate communities in education so that we can consider the universal in a single human life. This is when the sweeping gestures of the biographer, the force of the narrative, enter the field of education with great promise and power.

This is the context within which I invited the contributors to examine various aspects of their work and its relation to educational biography, and this is the hope that I have for *Writing Educational Biography*, a beginning for the growing interest in biographical inquiry in education.

PART ONE

Qualitative Research and Educational Biography

Introduction

With biography's immense and growing popularity, we have already noted its modest representation in the field of education—especially in relation to such other forms of qualitative work as ethnography, narrative and storytelling. Biographies of educators are scarce, although numbers and tallies can mislead if one relies solely on bibliographic computer searches. Biography becomes better represented in education when one recognizes aspects of biographical inquiry in our work as educational researchers. I invited scholars from the areas of teacher education, ethnography, history of education, and curriculum theory to describe the incidental presence of biographical research in their work. They were instructed not to identify differences between biography and their fields of study. Drawing such distinctions entices yet beguiles the aspiring biographer; would not all researchers wish to confirm differences between a biography and a case study or biography and ethnography? Such distinctions, however, would be artificial at best and serve to contradict a premise of this collection—namely, that biographical research brings together rather than separates the disparate strands of educational inquiry.

Our contributors did not set out to speak for their field; I asked them to explore the biographical literature and to consider their research in relation to biography. Initially, they found such relationships easy to identify, but, as they worked further, they sought to explore new ground and to speculate on how biographical inquiry enhances their work and their field.

¶   Robert Bullough, Jr. discusses biography as it relates to case studies in teacher education. The connections are numerous as can been seen in his work—a "first year teacher" case study—documenting the pedagogical life of Kerrie Baughman. Bullough underscores the purpose of such research—namely, to reveal meaning as a way to provide understanding. Moreover, he is struck by biography's potential for teacher training: not in the businesslike efficiency that purports to correspond to professionalism in the classroom but, instead, in the complexity and thoughtfulness that appear whenever one takes a biographical perspective. He states that "Storytelling and life writing, in their various forms, provide powerful means for collecting future lives, for determining who we are, where we fit in the scheme of things, and where we want to head. Readers of biography know this well." Bullough also notes an aspect of teacher stories not always discussed—the difficulties caused by learning of a disconcerting past. Yet, such stories only serve to portray biography's crucial role of assisting one to better understand students. As Bullough notes, "[L]ike other teacher educators I have found when seeking to explain why something happened in a classroom, increasingly the road to understanding takes a biographical turn, not a detour."

Corrine Glesne's musings explore what biography brings to the study of ethnography and the contrasting aspects between these two types of research. Her experience with the biographical literature is quite similar to that of other contributors; all have been intrigued with traditional biographical theory as well as the "new biography" critiques. She recognizes her interests as both practical and theoretical: "One reason for this increasingly biographical orientation is practical: When conducting thorough interviews with a few, I can take my time, fitting their lives into my own. A major reason is, however, theoretical: I no longer desire disembodied information, but rather realize how much I need to know about the life of one person in order to understand something as complex as leadership. Categorizing may help me manage data, but probing the depths of people's respective stories kindles my imagination." As Glesne explores biography and its implications for ethnography, she accentuates its literary aspect (also noted by Bullough): "After reading about writing biography, I want to return to reading biography, knowing that now I will be observing, as I read, how authors shape data, what writing techniques they use, and how they join fact with imagination."

Biography as a form of historical research is a well-defined tradition even though such inquiry within the field of educational history is not extensive. Barbara Finkelstein emphasizes that biographical studies constitute "four otherwise indispensable entrees into the doing of history," and she proceeds to illustrate the possibilities of a particular genre of biography—literacy narratives—and how this form of inquiry enhances her research: "Through the lens of biography, historians have constructed creative windows through which one can glimpse several otherwise undiscoverable realities. Indeed, biography constitutes a unique form of historical study that enables education scholars to explore intersections between human agency and social structure." Biographical research, in one sense, becomes an alternative to the grand historical interpretations of education. Finkelstein concludes, "biographical studies, life histories and historical memoirs provide documentary reminders that historical processes are inevitably more complex than our capacity to define and understand them."

Postmodern curriculum theory calls into question the concept of "authentic representation" and greatly extends the role and place of the autobiographical voice in education. While biographical voice has yet to extend fully into this theoretical discourse, William Pinar and Anne Pautz examine the importance of this emerging role: "Just as the autobiographical voice is choral, so the biographical voice must be heard with an ear attuned to its different strands. And so biography intertwines with the life history of the writer to reveal aspects of both the writer and the subject—different people whose merged and separated voices collaborate to form a complex text: biography." As autobiography provides new understandings of the lived experience of teachers and students, Pinar and Pautz see biography as offering theorists an illumination of the complex layers of society, culture and politics through the lives of others. Possibilities abound as these contributors note the present and emerging role of biography in educational research.

Note

Robert V. Bullough delivered a presentation version of his chapter at the 1994 keynote session of the Archival and Biographical Research Special Interest Group of the American Educational Research Association. Barbara Finkelstein delivered a presentation version of her chapter at the 1995 keynote session of the Archival and Biographical Research SIG of AERA.

Chapter One

Musings on Life Writing: Biography and Case Studies in Teacher Education

Robert V. Bullough, Jr.

While I tell stories and write case studies, mostly of beginning teachers, I am hardly a biographer in any formal sense. A biographical aspect to case study research has, however, come to play an increasingly larger role in my thinking about teaching and teacher development. First, I must confess that my approach to writing a life is far from pure, and my motives for writing often elusive, discovered if at all after the fact when justifications are required. Some stories and the lives that inform them intrigue me; others do not. I have rarely set out to prove anything through my writing, but then case studies never prove anything. They help us to understand how and why something transpired; they illuminate action and reveal meaning.

I write this "musing" in the belief that many of the issues biographers struggle with are ones case study researchers confront, although often in a different form, and that case study researchers can benefit from the long experience of biographers as they seek to elevate the status of and refine their craft. I also write because like other teacher educators I have found when seeking to explain why something happened in a classroom, increasingly the road to understanding takes a biographical turn, not a detour. Increasingly, case study research blends biography with social science. I begin by considering this turn in teacher education and teacher education research.

A Biographical Turn

Researchers only recently discovered that teachers and teacher education students have lives—personal histories that demand attention because they influence how they interpret the world and determine what is learned in teacher education (Carter, 1993; Connelly and Clandinin, 1990). This may be a shocking omission and admission, but it is hardly surprising. Until recently, research in teacher education has been dominated by a logical-scientific approach to research, what Bruner (1986) called the "paradigmatic" mode, where the aim is to control and predict outcomes. In such work, individual life stories have no place, but more than the chill of numbers and the pallid lifelessness of law-like statements are at issue here. The prototype teacher, the virginal *Our Miss Brooks,* had no private life to speak of, certainly not one of compelling interest to researchers, and not just because hers seemed a boring life devoted to service, a life swallowed up by others. From the perspective of teacher education and until fairly recently, a teacher's life had importance as an unacknowledged source of such personal characteristics or qualities (e.g., being well organized) that are associated with obtaining student compliance and performance. Freudian influences aside, the presence of these characteristics or qualities, not their origin, commanded most of the interest. Since the time of Horace Mann, the task of teacher educators has been to admit only virtuous students to programs and to encourage the modeling of high moral standards while students learned a bag of teaching-related tricks.

The quest for professional status has also diverted attention from teacher biography. Perhaps as a reaction to meddlesome patronizing and a virulent case of status deprivation, modern teachers vigorously separate their public and private lives. Teachers no longer belong to the communities they serve, and parents and students know little about them as people, except indirectly. Professionals keep their distance. Yet, the public and private cannot so easily be separated in teaching. As Thomas (1993) noted, "It is difficult to separate, convincingly and reliably, self from professional persona. It seems . . . to be in the nature of teaching, that the mask of the role player is likely to slip. . . ." (p. 239). The person comes through when teaching. I have a lingering suspicion that one of the reasons teacher biography and autobiography did not capture the imagination of teacher educators and researchers earlier is that as students we also failed to see our teachers as persons; we could not see that behind the role that presented "life as tedious as a twice-told tale," was an interesting subject. Yet, to understand classroom events, researchers must understand the meaning of teacher and student actions, the conceptual basis upon which teachers act. To educate, then, is to influence the grounds upon which teachers make decisions, or put differently, to influence their beliefs. This work necessitates both knowing what beliefs underlie teacher or student interpretations and knowing something about their experimental origins. Enter biography. Enter autobiography.

Growing up the son of a junior high school art teacher, I knew teachers had private lives and I knew something about them, particularly about their financial struggles. My parents could not afford the three-speed racer I coveted in elementary school, and we ate a lot of macaroni and cheese. Teaching and working two part-time jobs must have affected my father's ability to plan his classes and invest his time in his students' development. But this insight came much later.

I recall more than just fleeting glimpses into teachers' lives and problems behind the professional personae. One of my teachers, a particularly attractive young woman, let it slip during class one morning that she was soon to be married. I think we were studying the religions of the world at the time. Probably Hinduism. Her slip explained why she had been so perky, why she giggled a bit too much for a teacher. I remember being titillated by the wicked thought that soon she would be having sex, but I shoved that idea from mind. She was *my* teacher.

I recall the glee-club teacher I watched wander daily through my teacher's classroom toward their shared office. One day he was gone, and no one mentioned his departure. But I overheard some talk: He was an alcoholic, had fallen off the wagon one too many times, and would not be helped aboard again.

In a moment of exquisite honesty, my favorite history teacher, a man of deep moral conviction, spoke his mind about the Vietnam War and the arms race. I shall never forget what he said, or how he said it. Years later, I visited him at school. He had changed. He seemed tired and a bit gloomy. With my graduate degree in education, I immediately recognized the problem: burnout. No doubt about it, the kids had worn him down. But later, in a hushed conversation, another teacher told me his beloved son had been killed in a farming accident, and since then he had lost the bounce in his step. An impending marriage, a destructive disease, a war and then a child's death—each profoundly affected what these teachers did in the classroom, how they responded to their students, and what and how they taught.

If the aim of teacher education is to produce effective "businesslike" teachers as many methods books say, we have little reason to attend to student biography or to the myths of self our students bring with them to our programs. Nor need we be concerned with teacher biography. The tenets of professionalism require teachers to set aside their private worlds and non-teaching selves upon entering the classroom. Yet, thankfully they still sneak through.

Each year my teacher education students remind me of this, and in so doing, underscore the importance of life writing in learning to teach. Biography and autobiography have the power to touch "our hearts as well as our minds" (Oates, 1986, p. xi). The touch is often soft, inevitably private, and occasionally profound. Sometimes I find myself wishing I did not know so much. Sometimes, after reading my students' life writing, I feel as though I am supposed to do something, take the kind of action empathy and decency require. But I do not know what, so I read on. Consider the words of one of my students:

> I was born in Yorkshire, England. . . . I was a perfectly normal baby until I was three days old. A growth was discovered under my upper lip making bottle feeding impossible. I was spoon fed, difficult for a baby of that age . . . open, oozing sores spread on the top of my mouth and couldn't be stopped. After a year the doctors decided to use a fairly new treatment, radium. These sores were injected with needles. It stopped the growth but caused the skin to deteriorate immensely (and necessitated) a series of operations as I grew older up to the

time of my freshman year in college. It's amazing how something so small and seemingly insignificant can affect one's life, thinking and relationships. But the place, on my face, made it something for all to see. People's reactions to my scars have caused much pain and made me the way I am. Mean, unthinking comments by others have not only been a part of my young life, but a part of my adult life as well. This has caused me to be shy, self-conscious, have low self esteem, and have a great need for acceptance. These things affect the way I teach. Meeting me you probably would never know these things, because I try very hard to respond in class and be outgoing.

The first time I read this paper my heart ached; it aches still. But after a few months in class seeing her work with young people, I realized my student's story would have a happy ending. As Erik Erikson (1958) suggested in *Young Man Luther*, we are all victims, vehicles and ultimately resolutions of the cultural dilemmas of an era. Some resolutions require remarkable courage and come at a high price. This was a courageous beginning teacher. In the classroom her personal struggle manifested itself in subtle ways that made her special, different from most others in class. She touched lives of often-ignored children. She recognized the signs of suffering and seemed instinctively to know how and when to respond. Students often sought her just to talk. Doing for others what she may have longed to have done for herself, she built students up, praised them, and openly and enthusiastically celebrated their accomplishments. The scars remain, but somehow they are difficult to see; the radiance of the person blocks them from view.

I know the life histories my students write, like all life writing, are partial, the results of "selective omission" (Barth, 1994, p. 68), and contingent, like the lives they portray, upon transformation through reinterpretation. Memory, too, is selective and "Our memories of feelings . . . are even more selective than our memories of events" (Marder, 1993, p. 227). Censorship increases partiality, but this is yet another reason for my awe at the intensity and integrity with which some of my students speak and write of themselves. Some utterances are too sacred to speak, however, especially to secular priests wielding red-pencil scepters. And some things simply cannot be said; there is no way to utter them without taunting truth: "Human speech is like a crazy kettle on which we can only beat out tunes fit to charm a dancing bear, when all the while we would fain conjure the wandering stars and make them weep for us" (Flaubert, n.d., p. 227).

A biographical turn clearly requires that educators look beyond teacher education as technology, as a quest for mastery of discrete teaching skills. "So often," Robert Coles (1989) wrote of his mentor William Carlos Williams, "he pointedly reminded me, students soon to become doctors, lawyers, architects, businessmen, teachers, or engineers are understandably preoccupied with their performing selves, with matters of technique, of knowledge—even though, he insisted, 'it is your response to the ethical questions that will make you what you are'" (p. 118). In teaching, the medium is the message, and the message is who and what the teacher is as an embodied human being, a person trying to make sense of a life while simultaneously helping others to make their own way.

Teachers teach themselves; they testify. This is important knowledge because as Polkinghorne (1988) wrote, "Self . . . is . . . a configuring of personal events into a historical unity which includes not only what one has been but also anticipation of what one will be" (p.150). Self is a narrative configuration, a telling, an "unfolding and developing story" without which we shatter, crumble and are lost to ourselves and to others (Glass, 1993). Through this story and its plot, we make sense of our ongoing experiences. They serve as the basis for acting in the classroom and elsewhere. Thus, to understand educational events, one must confront biography.

Comparing Biographical and Case Study Research

> A case study is an empirical inquiry that investigates a contemporary phenomenon within its real-life context; when the boundaries between phenomenon and context are not clearly evident; and in which multiple sources of evidence are used.
>
> Robert Yin (1989, p. 23)

Case studies might focus on decision making, organizations, programs, neighborhoods, institutions and processes, but in each instance, what matters is what people do, feel, believe and think. When the focus of a case study is on living a life—on the "cosmos of a single being" (Kendall, 1965, p. 4)—rather than, say, on institutional change, case study research and biographical writing have much in common. Both are narratives, and both face the challenge of untangling, telling and emplotting a life:

> The web of our life is of a mingled yarn, good and ill together: our virtues would be proud, if our faults whipped them not; and our crimes would despair, if they were not cherished by our virtues. (Shakespeare, *All's Well That Ends Well*, IV. iii. 83)

Both require the creation of a story line that connects the threads of one's life events into a single narrative. "It is the plot which shows the part an individual action contributes to the whole experience." It involves creation of a "pattern from a succession, and it involves a kind of reasoning that tacks back and forth from the events to the plot until a plot forms that both respects the events and encompasses them in a whole . . . a meaningful story" (Polkinghorne, 1988, pp. 18, 131). Both biographers and case study researchers ask and seek to answer the question, What is the story? The story gives meaning and invites meaning making.

As part of its appeal, biography encourages boundary crossing. When we read biographies, written and lived stories often connect and we "realize that we are not alone; we can live with another human being in another age; we can identify with his or her journey through the vicissitudes of life" (Oates, 1991, p. 7). Good case studies have a similar appeal and invite personal reflection (Jalongo and Isenberg, 1995). But the power of good stories does not wholly reside in the universality of themes. Each life, as Coles (1989) stated, speaking of George Eliot, "has its own nature, spirit, meaning, and rhythm. . . ." (p. 90). While similarities invite boundary crossing, differences in themes encourage boundary stretching and inspire considerations of alternative ways of being in the world, even with a class of fifth graders.

The power of case study research flows from the power of narrative: "Although principles are powerful, cases are memorable, and lodge in memory as the basis for later judgments" (Shulman, 1986, p. 32). The memorable stories tend to be well written. I must confess, I sometimes find myself reading case studies and wishing that we researchers had sharper ears for the rhythm of language, greater respect for the meaning of words, and better understanding of the narrative form that includes beginnings and endings and that flows temporally.

I also find myself yearning for more interpretative humility, recognizing that statements of causality are fundamentally, as James Hillman (1983) once remarked, "fictions." Certainly better and worse, more or less interesting, more or less compelling fictions exist and, while most fictions can help us understand why something transpired, no writer ever speaks of truth from a burning bush. In biography this problem manifests itself in a subtle way. Case study researchers often speak forthrightly of their reliance on social science categories to make sense of a life, although they do not always acknowledge being "heir to a given lineage of conceptualization" (Erikson, 1975, p. 145). Their explicitness about the interpretive schemes they use can invite a reader's criticism and skepticism. But for case study researchers, failing to be explicit creates serious ethical problems. On their part, biographers frequently shun or mask such categories, yet as Erikson (1958) noted speaking of the place of psychology in biographical writing, "there is always an implicit psychology behind the explicit anti-psychology" (p. 36). Humility may follow honesty about the tools one uses for interpreting a life.

The relationship between biographer and subject is, of course, complex and dynamic. Proximity presents puzzling problems tied to the interpretative need to get inside another's life while simultaneously not getting lost, or worse, without settling the other person's life space with our own characters. Case study researchers face roughly similar dangers, but perhaps with fewer checks. When writing of prominent lives, biographers inevitably sense someone looking suspiciously over their shoulders ready to take issue, determined to make certain the study is "true to a life" (Kendall, 1965, p. 8). In teacher education case study research, the lives told generally belong to current and former students known only to those directly involved in the study. Data are not public and are often generated by the researcher. Too easily and unwittingly, plot protection may masquerade as grounded theory; we invest in and are then blinded by a particular telling, ours or someone else's, we find compelling.

An informant or subject can check a researcher's commitment to a plot and offer potentially corrective insights while simultaneously causing the researcher to share more fully in the process. Corrections or adjustments in interpretations must be negotiated, however, because self-transparency—the belief that individuals can "comprehend their true nature and role" —is limited; one finds no genuine life narrative to which one can appeal for certainty (Fay, 1987) and motives are "always partially unconscious—that is, resistant to our very reason" (Erikson, 1975, p. 173). In my own case study work I share all that I write with those whose experience and views I seek to understand. Better interpretations often, but not always, result despite my understandable reluctance to open my thinking and my attempts to capture a moment of a life to this scrutiny.

Ironically, case study researchers ask their subjects or informants to open their lives to study when, in fact, we often hesitate to reveal our own thoughts and feelings—our bases for interpretation—to them. We believe we must keep our distance, even as we foster a one-sided intimacy that tugs at and invites a closer relationship. We hide behind the researcher's role and avoid confronting our "principled selfishness." A loss of humility can easily result, a prideful blindness. With this matter, biographers certainly have more experience: "Life-telling [is] an intimate act" (Pachter, 1981, p. 14). For the biographer, however, a different problem arises. Potential subjects protect themselves from the other side; anticipating invasion, they burn letters and seal documents for a century (Pachter, 1981). I first encountered this problem when I discovered while researching my dissertation that Boyd H. Bode's wife had destroyed his voluminous correspondence. A shared question arises: How much of a life should one tell, how much of the story? Lately, partaking of the spirit of daytime talk shows, popular biographies often tell more than I want or need to know. The biographer of a prominent person

cannot hide, however, and lawyers wait to follow up on threats
of libel when the victims are living, and sometimes when they
are dead. Generally, however, the dead rest, silently if not
necessarily in peace. Case study researchers have a different
recourse, subject anonymity: what readers don't know
supposedly won't hurt them, much.

In my work with Kerrie Baughman and the "First Year
Teacher" research (Bullough, 1989; Bullough with Baughman, 1993; Bullough and Baughman, 1995a, 1995b, 1997),
Kerrie insisted on being known, and I am glad for it. As our
relationship evolved over the years, and the work became
more collaborative, she became increasingly open about the
relationship between her public and private lives, and our answers to the "why" question became increasingly powerful
and interesting, even while they remain forever tentative. In biography, the dead have no such opportunity; and the living
often provide "authorized" biographies or employ ghost
writers to tell their stories as they want them told. What we lose
in both instances is the chance to negotiate meaning, from
which we can learn a great deal.

Case study researchers use the phrases "grounded
theory" and "constant comparison" to describe the process
of "emplotment," the quest for a story line that will "in-form
. . . a thousand thousand otherwise disparate facts and make
them dance together" (Mariani, 1984, p. 23). Somehow, out
of the mass of data, a story emerges that incorporates the relevant "facts" in productive ways. Under the influence of social
science and the quest for both reliable and valid conclusions,
the process of emplotment in case study research has lost
some of its mystery, being bounded by a technical scaffolding
and discussed in a decidedly technical jargon. Part of what is
lost is the wonder the biographer feels when he or she has
"got it," when the plot first begins to emerge, then pours
forth, and the elements suddenly flow together and make
sense:

> [F]inally, after writing and rewriting chapter after chapter of a
> person's life, after having lived for so long with the pale
> voices of the dead and perhaps with the still-insistent voices of
> the living who think that they were there, to suddenly feel

> something like light come streaming into the head, and to feel
> then the dust of all those words we call "facts" begin to take
> form, like the shape of the rose . . . emerging out of the steel-
> dust particles when a magnet has been placed beneath their
> surface. (Mariani, 1984, p. 18)

I have felt this same wonderful sensation after spending
months sitting in a classroom, reading my notes, and thinking
about my observations while trying to understand why a
teacher did what she did and how she understood her world
and the worlds of her students. Each time it happens, I feel a
profound sense of relief; the threat of chaos has retreated once
again, and I understand more clearly a truth, not a reality. I
have something valid and reliable finally to say.

Case study researchers under the influence of social
science find validity and reliability lively issues. They also are
issues for biographers. As Polkinghorne (1988) argued for
narrative research, answering the claims of validity and
reliability requires a return to the pre-scientistic definition of
each term—where validity is satisfied if conclusions are well
grounded (including demonstrating why alternative conclusions are not compelling) and reliability is satisfied when
data are dependable (p. 176). Bruner (1990) perhaps best
described this challenge, one that ultimately implies the moral
charge to exercise "interpretative caution":

> "[T]he-story-of-a-life" as told to a particular person is in some
> deep sense a joint product of the teller and the told. Selves,
> whatever metaphysical stand one takes about the "reality," can
> only be revealed in a transaction between a teller and a told,
> and as Mishler reminds us, whatever topic one approaches by
> interviewing must be evaluated in the light of that transaction.
> That much said, all that one can counsel is the exercise of a
> certain interpretative caution. (pp. 125-124)

Standards of validity and reliability remind us that we cannot
write just anything we wish, that interpretations, however
tentative, must be disciplined by data, and that we must
proceed cautiously and carefully before proclaiming a plot.

Many psychologists and historians take pains to let biographers know their work is of a baser kind—it's not quite

serious scholarship (Kendall, 1965). Case study researchers have received similar responses from the wider education research community, at least until recently. Some months ago, a colleague and friend passed along a xeroxed page from a teachers' magazine. In black ink he had circled this line: "Why study biography? I may quote William Butler Yeats: All knowledge is biography." Alongside, he wrote, "See, Bob, you were right after all." I chuckled, but it was no ordinary joke. Only yesterday I had defended my work, and in particular my increasing emphasis on teacher and student lives, as legitimate scholarship. For the most part, I found my argument reluctantly received until David Berliner—a genuine researcher whose opinions mattered, who had the power to vindicate or condemn— remarked in a chance conversation with my administrator that he was impressed with *First Year Teacher*.

Like biographies, case studies serve multiple purposes and come in different forms—for example, exploratory, descriptive and explanatory (Yin, 1989, pp. 15-16). The type of case depends on the nature of the questions, as well as the extent to which the investigator controls events. In my own work, the overlap is most evident in my desire to understand better how one becomes a teacher, a question that both biography and case study research can illuminate. Another interest is to help beginning teachers become part of the wider educational community, to help with their socialization which means becoming narratively grounded in teaching. Here, too, I find overlap, in the sense that my students need to become part of the story of American education, a story they will live, and in the living help invigorate and even rewrite. Subtexts to the story appear, tales of the first year of teaching, for instance. In the telling, beginning teachers begin to think more richly and deeply about their own experience and entertain alternative ways of being with young people. This kind of thinking—what Van Manen (1994) calls "narrative reasoning"—plays a crucial role in teacher development and identity formation. Becoming a teacher requires becoming part of the discursive teaching community. As "creatures of language" (Coles, 1989, p. 97) beginning teachers must learn the lore. Teacher life writings—biography and autobiography and case studies—are repositories of teacher lore and can help beginning teachers understand who they are and what they might become.

Concluding Comments

Storytelling and life writing, in their various forms, provide powerful means for collecting future lives, for determining who we are, where we fit in the scheme of things, and where we want to head. Readers of biography know this well. Becoming narratively situated is to know who we are and what we stand for. With collecting comes coherence and, in time, beginning teachers add to the tales.

Long ago, Dewey (1916) pointed out that we "never educate directly, but indirectly by means of the environment. Whether we permit chance environments to do the work, or whether we design environments for the purpose makes a great difference" (p. 22). I have spent a lot of time trying to design environments that invite teacher education students to reconsider and perhaps reconstruct their narratives of experience, their self-narratives, the tales they tell to themselves and others (Bullough and Gitlin, 1995) and then to provide contexts within which they can productively encounter and consider the teaching lore. This work requires means for helping students to confront themselves, their stories and the meanings embedded in those stories safely and constructively. The difficulty posed by change underscores the importance of this work. As Lortie (1975) suggested, the process of becoming a teacher and how we think of ourselves as teachers begins long before the decision to enter a teacher-education program. It begins at home, where teaching is a common occurrence and continues throughout the student years as part of "an apprenticeship of observation." In this work, life writing can play a central part and is for me a crucial element of instructive case studies.

As I said, I am a biographer in no formal sense, but I have come to appreciate the educational power and possibilities of life writing. Reading biographies and well-written case studies —those that blend humanities and social science—can usefully inform both beginning and experienced teachers. Stories are memorable; they encourage boundary crossing; and they invite and sometimes inspire comparison and reflection. When

well told, they challenge thinking and invite the consideration
of alternative possibilities; sometimes they produce a much
appreciated confirmation of beliefs; and they help us to know
who we are and where we fit into the scheme of things. In
teacher education, the study of educational biography and
case studies that include strong biographical components and
life writing represent, to my way of thinking, the most promising development in recent years. Certainly the recent turn
toward biography represents a direct and welcomed challenge
to traditional, skills-centered approaches to teacher education.
This said, the work has only just begun.

Chapter Two

Ethnography with a Biographic Eye

Corrine E. Glesne

> Nothing exists but a stream of souls.
> W. B. Yeats

I imagine "webs" of souls, but they are souls all the same—the colorful connections of people who live and have lived, whether in California or Kalimantan. Poets may attribute souls to swans and the pinon pine, but anthro-centric biographers and ethnographers are caught up with human souls. Interested in individuals—their connections and contexts—ethnographers and biographers research and write the lives of people. In reading about writing biography, I begin to consider ethnography with biographic eyes and to speculate on ways in which a biographic perspective might enhance ethnographic work.

As an ethnographer, I struggle with many of the same issues as biographers. We draw upon many of the same data sources—interviews, documents, archives. Participant observation, a tool of the ethnographers trade, is used by biographers who visit the places where their subjects worked and lived, observing such small but context-setting details as which window first caught the morning sun during the short days of December. Biographers and ethnographers make decisions about breadth and depth—the numerical questions of how many, how long, how many times. The ethnographer may narrow her study from several schools to one school to one classroom. The biographer may narrow his focus from the events of every year of a life to the later years, using broad strokes to fill in earlier years. Both biographers and ethnographers become so immersed in their work that they see it everywhere. They run for pen and paper when Terry Gross interviews on National Public Radio a classical musician whose words suddenly apply to the ethnographer's research on educational experiences of women or the biographer's work on the life of Paulo Freire.

Biographers and ethnographers must systematically manage their data. Books, documents, photocopies, five-by-eight notecards, and computer-generated paper blanket tables and floors. Then, with all the data collected and tentatively organized, both biographers and ethnographers select which pieces, which chunks, to use and which to file as rich refusals for future consultation. With selection comes the play of imagination as ethnographer and biographer begin to interpret, make sense of, give form to data. Although the form re-presents data as they never before appeared, research participants exclaim, "You're right. That's how it is!" and readers will recommend the article or book to their neighbors or colleagues.

A biographic approach is hardly foreign to ethnographers, a truism well treated by Langness and Frank (1981) and L. M. Smith (1994). In 1981, Marjorie Shostak published *Nisa: The Life and Words of a !Kung Woman*. Unlike traditional anthropological monographs, this book re-presented the culture of the !Kung primarily through Shostak's edited interview transcripts with one woman, Nisa. Similarly, Ruth Behar (1993) constructed her book *Translated Woman: Crossing the Border with Esperanza's Story* primarily from her interviews with Esperanza, a woman of Mexico. Shostak's and Behar's ethnographies focus on one person's words and life; more commonly, ethnographies with biographical leanings include shorter portraits of several people. For example, in Barbara Myerhoff's (1978) *Number Our Days: Culture and Community among Elderly Jews in an American Ghetto*, one chapter focuses on the tailor and wise man Schmuel, another on Jacob Koved who died at his 95th birthday party. These more biographical chapters further exemplify the community and cultural themes Myerhoff develops. They also connect the reader more closely to the community through identification and care for particular individuals. Anna Lowenhaupt Tsing

(1993) also used character development in her book *In the Realm of the Diamond Queen*. In particular, she re-presented Uma Adang, an Indonesian female shaman who helps frame the book and shifts in and out of the reader's perspectives of margins and marginality.

Towards a Biographic Eye

I began my research life with a masters thesis that required archival work with letters, journals and the meticulous book-keeping of mid-western farm women, as well as interviews with women who worked the land. My prose focused on themes and patterns, not individuals. My doctoral dissertation research produced a traditional ethnographic "almost village" study. I lived for a year in a rural Caribbean valley investigating young people and their relationship to the land and the role of education in their lives. My questions focused on agricultural and educational participation. While analyzing my data, I began to wonder why some people fatalistically accepted their lives; others opted to use alcohol, drugs or religion to drop out; and yet others became change agents. What made the difference, I wondered, when all participants had little formal education and low economic status? I wanted to know more about each interviewee's life, but by that point I was no longer "in the field."

Several years ago, during a sabbatical, I moved to a rural community in Costa Rica and became part of a grass-roots environmental group, conducting the research they needed. I also conducted a series of life-story interviews with the group's leaders, following up on my interests in the development and motivation of leaders in contexts where education and credentials were unimportant factors. My interest in leaders continues in a currently evolving project with elderly women active in higher education.

One reason for this increasingly biographical orientation is practical: When conducting thorough interviews with a few, I can take my time, fitting their lives into my own. A major reason is, however, theoretical: I no longer desire disembodied information, but rather realize how much I need to know about the life of one person in order to understand something as complex as leadership. Categorizing may help me manage data, but probing the depths of people's respective stories kindles my imagination.

Life and Lives: Research Encounters

> "It's very interesting," I reply unwittingly. Still laughing, Esperanza exclaims, "My compadre! Everything is interesting, isn't it?"
>
> Ruth Behar (1993, p. 52)

Biographers generally focus on the life of one person, although, in the process, they often become interested in and consider the lives of many. Ethnographers focus on a cultural system, looking for patterns in the lives of individual people within that system. Biographers often talk about the intimate relationships they develop with their subjects, even if those subjects died long before the biographers were born. The biographer is expected to become intimate with his subject because, as Kendall states, "[he] lives another life along with his own. . . . A biography may take a dozen years or more to write. Who would be willing, who would be able to spend that much time with a man for whom he had no feeling?" (1986, p. 40). As ethnographers move away from the "fly on the wall" approach to research, they acknowledge the important roles both friendship and rapport play in their fieldwork. In general, however, the ethnographer's broader focus discourages intimate relationships with all her informants. She may establish close friendships with an interviewee or with someone at the research site but feel uneasy highlighting that intimacy.

Collecting the public events of a life in combination with developing an intimate relationship with that life, the biographer creates the biography through *intuiting* private meanings (Pachter, 1981, pp. 14-15). Immersing herself in the culture of her participants with whom she has rapport, the ethnographer *intuits* the deeper structure of that culture. For Myerhoff, community themes emerged as the glue in the senior citizen center. For Tsing, variations on the theme of marginality created the choruses of meaning. The biographer intuits an individual psychological meaning; the ethnographer, a collective social meaning.

When considering implications of research relationships for biography and ethnography, I think about traditional ethnographic practices of promising confidentiality and how that contrasts with the biographer's focus on someone who is *known*. Using pseudonyms for characters in biography makes no sense. Biographers assume their right to research another's life, but that other is usually a public figure. Public lives, states Pachter (1981),

> are not lived in isolation; they have impact far beyond their immediate circle and therefore invite a response. If certain lives have the power to touch or to transform our own . . . , to exalt or to terrify us, then we . . . have the right to make sense of those lives, of their innermost nature (p. 7).

Biographers may conceal their sources, but they do not disguise their subject, the focus of their work. As a result, readers frequently remember about whom they read, but rarely the author, a point bemoaned by Ascher (1984) in a fictional letter to Simone de Beauvoir, the subject of her biography: "But when I feel deprived and unacknowledged, I resent your righteous success and feel stingy about contributing toward the attention you already receive" (p. 94). In contrast to biographers, ethnographers, with their focus on cultural patterns, generally promise their research participants confidentiality. Subjects receive pseudonyms and the ethnographer enjoys an opportunity to stray from facts (to change names of places and even the ages and genders of participants if it might help protect them). Aspects of a life receive publicity but are separated from the person, like the screen that casts facial features in shadows to conceal the speaker's identity. As a result, readers often remember the author of the text, but know subjects only by their pseudonyms.

Ethnographers may ask research participants to read through their transcribed interviews to validate data, but their subjects, unlike the biographer's, are often less powerful, less educated, of another culture, and without the means to refute and challenge the researcher beyond asserting that some interview sections were not accurately transcribed. Confidentiality, therefore, can protect the researcher as well as the research participants. Some situations call for confidentiality; but when ethnographers re-present lives that exemplify, I believe they should (with permission) connect stories to real names as a biographer would.

Not all biographies *honor* their subjects. Biographers use the term "pathography" for works that dig up the "glamorous dirt" (Wilson, 1991, p. 169). In ethnography, pathography may be more abstruse, although citizens of Vidich and Bensman's (1968) *Small Town in Mass Society* or West's (1945) *Plainville U.S.A.* hardly saw the negative portrayal of their towns as subtle (Johnson, 1982). Harmful interpretations can occur unconsciously as well. William Epstein (1991) observed that biographers "lose their (biographical subjects') lives *figuratively*, in and through the interpretive violence inflicted upon those lives by biographical recognition" (p. 222). Similarly, in a response to discussion concerning interpretations and effects of Whyte's (1955) *Street Corner Society*, Richardson (1996) challenges the traditional ethnographic enterprise by stating that she would avoid conducting a community study like *Street Corner Society*: "I would not want to give voice to real, live people who know each other and could identify each other in my text. For me, it might be text; for them it is life" (p. 228).

At one time, ethnographers were content to follow the research ethic of *doing no wrong*, thinking of wrong as physical or emotional harm to individual participants during data collection or through publication. Biography and ethnography, however, can also help maintain traditional assumptions, myths and power relationships, thereby perpetuating evil or violence upon whole groups of people. Postmodern theorists like Epstein (1991) accuse anthropology, thus ethnography, of ignoring "the radical situatedness of the subject" by applying a lens that, in effect, decontextualizes the subject and "effaces the specificities of race, class, gender" (p. 221). Although biography might be perceived as a way to avoid decontexualization, both biographies and ethnographies are rooted in dominant structures. The genre of American biography defines, in ways, what counts as a "significant life" (Wilson, 1991, p. 169) with emphasis placed upon "honor, shame, loyalty to ideals, the hunger for achievement" (Epstein, 1985, p. 69).

How then, can ethnographers (or biographers) continue their work? Should they consider becoming novelists or animal behaviorists instead? As with the Dayak of Tsing's (1993) *In the Realm of the Diamond Queen*, they occupy a kind of marginal territory, dwelling in a neither-nor land between science and literature. And as the Dayaks exploited the ambiguities of their marginal status, ethnographers and biographers also enjoy access to a kind of freedom in their marginality. They can shift their perspectives as researchers and their writing forms as authors to create their own distinct norms.

Re-presenting Lives: Form and Authority
"We cannot write true nonfiction," stated Kenzaburo Oe, the Japanese recipient of the 1994 Nobel Prize for Literature. "We always write fiction, but through writing fiction, sometimes we are able to arrive at the truth" (as quoted in Vourvoulias, 1996, p. 54). Oe presents the dilemma (and hope) for ethnographers and biographers: They collect facts, unable to invent any of their data, but through selection and interpretation, they create fictions that, ideally, portray truths perhaps never fully perceived by the person or community they study.

Biography is aligned with literature, but writers rarely accept it as true literature because of its association with facts. Ethnography is aligned with social science research, but within the research community, it has occasionally been accused of being insufficiently factual. Biography and ethnography as *process* are similar. As *product* (text), however, they often differ, primarily because of their disciplinary alliances. Biographers generally recognize the art of writing, of telling a story. Ethnographers use the "story" metaphor, but their stories sometimes fail to mesmerize, probably because ethnographers see themselves as researchers first and only then as writers. As Wolcott (1996) says, "Fieldworkers become writers out of necessity" (p. 210). In contrast, biographers align themselves with writers first and only then with researchers. At one time, anthropologists recommended that all fieldworkers undergo analysis. The day may come when budding ethnographers feel compelled to take courses in creative writing.

It is not, of course, the case that all biographies are aesthetic compositions or that all ethnographies are not. Biographers

(Kendall, 1986; Mariani, 1984; Wolff, 1981) describe two basic styles of biography. One form (the Augustan convention) "inclines toward the archival, the archeological" (Wolff, p. 64). All gathered data are sifted together into a tome that often runs to several volumes. Kendall referred to this as the "magpie school of scholarship-as-compilation," which "worships the materials at hand but does not simulate a life" (p. 40). The other style (the Romantic convention) is more artistic and akin to literature in that it aims to get at the essence of the life of the subject, to simulate that life, and yet to stay true to the materials at hand. Although ethnographers may think too little about the Romantic convention, they certainly know of Augustan ethnographies where the researcher resists excluding any data at all. To do justice to the lives of subjects, researchers must sometimes do violence to data from their lives, sorting and grouping, eliminating and emphasizing, recreating with imagination in order to evoke rather than merely document.

A few ethnographers have begun to experiment with form, some drawing from such literary genres as drama and fiction (Benson, 1993; Richardson, 1994; Stewart, 1989), others attempting different textual strategies (Lather, 1995). Biographers also push on the borders of traditional form. Iles (1992) discussed Fay Weldon's biography of Rebecca West in which Weldon included her letters to West with imaginary responses. After noting that Weldon's book is considered "fictional" biography, Iles asked, "Or is it simply another side of the same process?" (p. 5).

The postmodern perspective highlights, in particular, how language inscribes value; how textual representations are, in a sense, fictions; and how the research tale cannot be separated from the teller. Perhaps because ethnographies traditionally included methods sections in which researchers described their fieldwork, it has been relatively easy for (and increasingly expected of) ethnographers to extend subjective reflections or to discuss their roles as authors and researchers. For example, in *Translated Woman* by Behar (1993), readers come to know Esperanza, but they also learn about Behar because she includes descriptions of her life in relation to Esperanza. They come to know Uma Adang in Tsing's (1993) *In the Realm of the Diamond Queen* through Uma Adang's words and through Tsing's interpretation and discussion. Although readers learn less of Tsing's personal life than Behar's, they remain aware that Tsing is the interpretive fieldworker. Biographers appear to have found it more difficult to insert themselves into the text so obviously: "The highest biographical art is the concealment of the biographer" (Kendall, 1986, p. 38); and "the biographer must avoid center stage" (Pachter, 1981, p. 8). Biographers who become visible challenge the accepted form. Portraying Simone de Beauvoir, Ascher (1984) wrote a chapter that described her own thoughts and her problems with Beauvoir. Although one reviewer called the chapter an "interesting interlude," another headlined the review, "de Beauvoir Biography Overshadowed by Its Author." Nonetheless, as more and more ethnographers and biographers experiment with form, they also experiment with their position(s) in the text, taking into account as well how they desire to relate to readers.

Intended audiences shift from academic peers to a variety of social groups as ethnographers shift research purposes from documentation or theory building to communication and applied research. Applied ethnographers desire a readership of research participants, the general public and colleagues because meaningful social change requires their participation. Thus, research must be written in ways that engage these publics. Through the more critical lens, the reader is no longer an empty vessel to be filled with an authoritative account of the life of (say) John Dewey. Rather, the reader becomes an active participant in the meaning making. The writer's task is to involve readers in analysis and guide them toward individual meanings. As Linda Wagner-Martin (1994) notes, although good biography has meant answering questions for the reader, it may be the unanswered questions that involve the reader most fulfillingly.

In addition to analytical involvement, ethnographers are learning from their literary friends that emotional involvement can also be a form of effective communication: "[T]he expression of precise feeling is instantaneously transformative. . . . It is the ultimate change of pace that reintroduces us to what matters and what does not" (Hazo, 1996, p. 31). "Transformative" and "what matters" are abstract terms for an aesthetic product that connects to readers in a way that encourages them to reflect upon their own lives, and to create new visions, new possibilities.

In the End

> One may merely know that no one is alone and hope that a singular story, as every true story is singular, will in the magic way of some things apply, connect, resonate, touch a major chord.
>
> Geoffrey Wolff (1981, p. 72)

Good biography and good ethnography accomplish similar ends. They illustrate both the uniqueness and the universalities of a person or a people (Oates, 1991; Langness and Frank, 1981). The text portrays an individual's or an organization's specialness. At the same time, readers see themselves and their communities in the portrayal: "[W]e read lives because they do teach us something about human and moral conditions which none of us, I suspect, can ever escape or ever afford to dismiss" (Mariani, 1984, p. 31).

As an ethnographer, my perspective is enriched when I use a biographic eye. I am persuaded of the importance of researching deeply into the lives of a few. Rather than a yearbook of snapshots, I would like a few fine portraits situated in socio-cultural landscapes. The biographic perspective reassures my movement with other ethnographers towards intimate, long-term research relationships that include sharing recognition, collaborating in the research process, and scanning the text together for unintended harm. The biographic perspective also has a literary effect. After reading about writing biography, I want to return to reading biography, knowing that now I will be observing, as I read, how authors shape data, what writing techniques they use, and how they join fact with imagination. I now read biographies with an eye toward adapting their aspects to my own ethnographic writing.

To become a biographer, I imagine that I would for a time commit myself to the life of one person, to detailing her or his behaviors and actions, and to understanding the psychological meaning of those actions. I imagine that I would be moved to delve more deeply into my own emotions and ways of being, to explore the autobiographical nature of the biography. I imagine too that I would learn to convey my insights in a way that *spiritually connects* as good music connects with complete strangers. All this I would like, yet I remain rooted in ethnography. I also want to look closely at a person's socio-cultural environment and to portray ways in which that person determines and is determined by his or her context. I want to understand better how we, as a group of people, make sense of the social systems we construct; what informal rules guide our interactions within and beyond our social groupings; and what we, as a whole, value as a *life*. I have much to learn from biography, but I see my exploration as a way to strengthen, not replace, ethnographic eyes.

In an old story, the Coyote lost his eyes by disrespecting a gift. Mouse shared one of her eyes with Coyote, a focused, close-up lens. Coyote remained unhappy. He couldn't see far enough, wide enough. So Buffalo indulged Coyote and gave him one of his eyes, a wide angle lens that pained Coyote with all the light it let in. We need to borrow the eyes of others to enhance our perspectives; at the same time, we should go on valuing our own.

Chapter Three

Revealing Human Agency:
The Uses of Biography in the Study of Educational History

Barbara Finkelstein

Biography is to history what a telescope is to the stars. It reveals the invisible, extracts detail from myriad points of light, uncovers sources of illumination, and helps us disaggregate and reconstruct large heavenly pictures. Through the particularities of its own refractions and observations, biography reveals particular features within large views. In the case of viewing history, biography provides a unique lens through which one can assess the relative power of political, economic, cultural, social and generational processes on the life chances of individuals, and the revelatory power of historical sensemaking.

For education historians, biography as a form of historical inquiry has had its ups and downs. I myself witnessed an assault on its uses by the former president of Smith College, Jill Kerr Conway, an insightful and innovative social historian who, like many other historians in the so-called revisionist tradition, viewed biography as a demagogic form of history writing that concealed power inequities under a rosy veneer of individual accomplishment. Other historians, Michael Katz and Harvey Graff as examples, aimed to recover history from the perspective of the previously invisible—laboring and dependent groups among whom autobiographies, diaries and other forms of qualitative information were difficult to find. Proceeding on an assumption that individuals were more or less powerful legatees of their social positions and class status, and that individual lives were less sensitive guides to social structure than an array of statistically more significant social, political, economic and demographic indicators, historians like Katz and Graff avoided biography and embraced structural analyses instead.

All three of these historians, Conway, Katz and Graff, have, since the 1970s and 1980s, reconstructed their views of biography either by writing their own or constructing others (Conway, 1990, 1992; Graff, 1995). In the process, they have reconnected their work to the traditional preoccupations of historical biographers who, as they have done their work, have joined human agency and social structure in uncommonly evocative ways (Antler, 1986; D. Ross, 1972).

Through the lens of biography, historians have constructed creative windows through which one can glimpse several otherwise undiscoverable realities. Indeed, biography constitutes a unique form of historical study that enables education scholars to explore intersections between human agency and social structure. Biographical studies situate historical storytelling at the margins of social possibility where social change originates, constraint and choice merge, large and small social structures intersect, cultural norms converge, and the relative force of political, economic, social and cultural circumstance becomes clear. Historical biography reveals the relative power of individuals to stabilize or transform the determinacies of cultural tradition, political arrangements, economic forms, social circumstances and educational processes into new social possibilities.

As we shall see, biographical studies constitute four otherwise indispensable entrees into the study of history. First, there is the use of biography as a lens through which to explore the origin of new ideas. Second, biography offers a window on social possibility, revealing, as historical biographies unvaryingly do, an array of social choices and alternative possibilities individuals and groups perceive and construct as they grow up, acquire identities, learn, labor, construct meaning, form communities and otherwise lead their lives. Third, biography provides an aperture through which to view relationships between educational processes and social change. Fourth, biography can be constituted as a form of mythic overhaul—a way to see through the inevitable over-determinacies of historical story-telling—and glimpse the variabilities and complexities of life within a single era or over longer periods.

The following discussion illustrates the possibilities in the craft of biography, focusing on a particular genre of biography: literacy narratives of the nineteenth century. "Literacy narratives" are forms of biography that capture history at the intersections of small and large cultures where oral and written forms of cultural transmission intersect, where neighborhoods and nations come together, where family and political cultures converge, where habits of heart, mind and association are molded, and where individuals acquire the wherewithal and motivation to make sense and non-sense of the world into which they were born and then enter as adults.

Literacy narratives include stories about boys, girls and adult illiterates learning to read and write. They include stories about dreams, aspirations, hopes, fears and ambitions-in-the-making. They include stories of reality-taking, meaning-making, communication and communion. They include stories of people who—as they memorized, recited, declaimed, wrote and read—entered into social spaces where kin, home and neighborhood became inextricably linked to the world outside of them. As incipient readers and writers became literate, they connected the spoken and written word and found tangible power and authority. They entered into a refracted world mediated by teachers, textbook writers and forgers of technology. They communed with great minds and petty ones, tyrannical authorities and benevolent ones. They were thrust willy-nilly into a world only partially theirs to remake. School stories reveal the possibilities and the limitations of education and the possibilities of biography as well.

Biography and the Origin of New Ideas:
The Life of Horace Mann

Among the more engaging features of biographical study is its capacity to reveal the ideological, economic, political, social and cultural crucibles within which a person develops new ways of knowing, thinking, acting and being. Through the revelation of individual lives and circumstances, biographers can probe the sources of creativity, the origin of new sensibilities, the forming of original thoughts. The early life of Horace Mann provides an example.

Horace Mann was born in 1796 in Franklin, Massachusetts, during a decade when manufacturing and urban diversification had begun, sectarian rivalries and political discourse were the stuff of daily conversation, and evangelical children like himself learned to associate literacy, morality, commerce and spirituality closely together. He died in 1869, after a quarter-century of unprecedented creativity in the forming of educational arrangements, practices and goals in the United States. From 1840 to 1865, he led an array of elite middle class and highborn reformers who became acutely conscious of the structures of authority, circles of acquaintance, qualities of intellect and the character of activities their children experienced as they grew up. No detail of children's lives escaped their notice. They discovered mothers as educators and the paternal state as an educational agency. They constructed an array of tutorial complexes to serve the young— public schools to cultivate their minds and civic sensibilities, teacher education institutions to train proper moral and intellectual guardians, kindergartens to ease transitions from home and neighborhood to society and nation. Aware of the power of building arrangements, they re-created school architecture and interior design. Sensitive to the influence of intellectual as well as physical environments, they created pedagogical paraphernalia, rewrote textbooks for schools and families, offered advice to mothers and teachers. They championed the construction of public libraries and then attempted to control the materials which they housed. They attended assiduously to the networks of association in which the young were prepared for life, leaving no authority unchallenged, no domestic detail unexamined, no schoolhouse unreconstructed, no curriculum uncriticized. In short, they wrought a revolution in the quality and character of the child's environment.

How does one explain a social and political effusion of such creative magnitude? What do the literary circumstances of Horace Mann's early life have to tell us? How did his educative consciousness develop? How did he transform the determinacies of daily living into educative vision? How was the force of material or ideological circumstance expressed in the daily rituals of growing up and in the educational fare that informed his consciousness? What do the circumstances of his growing up reveal about the origins of educational transform- ation, the relative effects of intellectual, material or cultural conditions on the emergence of new educational forms in the nineteenth century? Biography can answer these questions (Finkelstein, 1990).

For Horace Mann learning to read and write was multiply nuanced. The process brought him face to face with daunting ministerial authority, loving women, drunken tutors and librarians. His literacy story involves fear, love, commercial enterprise and cultural capital building. His tale describes unremitting intellectual exercise, moral reproach, unqualified affection and agricultural toil in a face-to-face universe of instructive conversation, unremitting oral exchange, prayer, piety, toil, death, obedience, submission and self-effacement. His more compelling memories focused on formal education. Learning to read and write brought him face to face with the terrifying rhetoric, relentless determinacies, hierarchical dis- positions and psychological invasions of the brilliant Calvinist minister, Nathaniel Emmons. From Emmons' lips, the word of God came clear: humans were unregenerate, polluted sinners with a predetermined fate, utterly subject to the will of a fearsome, angry God. Mann took those words literally when he was young. Indeed, he attached the written word firmly to the contemplation of suicide and depression, and the cultiva- tion of fear, trembling and spiritual death.

His imaginative impulses fared little better in schools, which he attended sporadically and reluctantly. In these rural schools, students stood before the teacher to "say their lessons." When they learned in classes and groups, they proceeded in choral form with the teacher acting as a kind of choirmaster. Declaiming pieces, reciting selections from readers, engaging in spelling and speaking contests, students could neither question nor criticize, neither create nor re- create meaning through the study of the written word. As Horace Mann put it, teachers exercised and appealed to only one faculty, "the memory for words. . . . All ideas outside the book were contraband material, which the teacher confiscated or rather flung overboard" (M. Mann, 1891, p. 12). Mann experienced the processes of schooling as assaults on sensibility and intellect. For him, the combined ministrations of the Reverend Emmons and district school teachers revealed links between literacy and the repression of the imagination, and created an intolerable reality which he was able to overcome with the greatest of difficulty.

He broke the hold Emmons and his teachers had on his imagination when, first in the throes of grief over the deaths of his father and then brother, he turned to Emmons for solace. What he got instead, in the church service preceding his brother's burial, were visions of the pit of Hell awaiting his brother who had broken the Sabbath, gone swimming and drowned. As though he had enough of grief and horror, Mann rejected Emmons' teaching, and as he did so, he simultaneously embraced the concept of a loving God and the innocence of children. At fourteen, in the wake of his deconversion, Mann completed a first stage in a quest for personal purification and transformed it into a disposition to purify the world:

> I remember the day, the hour, the place, the circumstances as
> . . . when in an agony of despair, I broke the spell that had
> bound me. From that day, I began to construct the theory of
> Christian ethics and doctrine respecting virtue and vice, rewards
> and penalties, time and eternity, God and his providence, which
> . . . I still retain, and out of which my life has flowed (p. 15).

Like many other children of evangelical parents, Horace Mann identified the kindly and gentle sides of Christianity with his mothers and sisters. Indeed, an association of love and literacy emerged from the practical and more benevolent educational nurture of his mother, sisters and learned female visitors. In his mind, achievement and mother-love became indissolubly joined:

> She deserves my love for her excellences and my gratitude for
> the thousand nameless kindnesses she has . . . bestowed upon
> me. . . . I can truly say that the strongest and most abiding
> incentives to excellence, by which I was ever animated, sprang
> from that look of solicitude and hope, that heavenly expression
> of maternal tenderness, when, without the utterance of a single

word, my mother has looked into my face, and silently told me
that my life was freighted with a twofold being, for it bore her
destiny as well as my own (pp. 22-24).

Among the strongest expressions of maternal concern
were "literacy rituals" where members of the family prayed,
recited, repeated and expounded the *Westminster Assembly
Shorter Catechism* and the *New England Primer* together.
Immersed in the language and logic of the *Catechism* and
Bible, Horace Mann learned to revere books and the power of
the written word. Though his parents neither tutored nor
taught him directly, they managed to endow books and learning with a kind of theological reverence: "I was taught to take
care of the few books we had, as though there was something
sacred about them. I never dog-eared one in my life, nor pro-
fanely scribbled upon title-pages, margin, or fly-leaf" (p. 12).

As a teenager, Mann devoured the contents of the public library digesting old histories and theologies, classic works and
general literature. He emerged from the educational web of
Franklin, Massachusetts, with a vision of human environments
awash in possibility. The daily routines and experiences of his
first dozen years provided a crucible for forging a transforming educative sensibility. In an environment of unrelenting
physical toil, moral and psychological intrusion, and with the
loss of a father and brother, he discovered the vulnerability of
childhood. In an environment of benevolent nurture and
feminine sensibility, he became alert to the small spaces and
human relationships in which moral and intellectual responses
might develop. Nurtured in Orthodox Calvinism and the
doctrines of predestination, he learned nonetheless to become
a devout environmentalist. Through daily acts of piety, prayer
and biblical rote learning, he discovered the power of the word
and the liberating possibilities of literacy and schooling.

Horace Mann transformed the particularities of his lived
experience into new visions of educational possibility. In later
life as a politician, educator and reformer, he worked cease-
lessly to provide a rising generation with the political and educational environments denied him when he was young:

> If there is anything for which I would go back to childhood,
> and live this weary life over again, it is for the burning,
> exalting, transporting thrill and ecstasy with which the young
> faculties hold their earliest communion with knowledge (M.
> Mann, 1867, p. 12).

The educative visions of Horace Mann originated at least
twenty years before the advent of industrialization, immigration and urban blight. Although the factory owner, the
immigrant and the tenement may have quickened its emergence and shaped its institutional forms, the public school was
as much the product of Calvinism, social Feminism and economic opportunity as it was a response to urban disorder and
disarray. At least, that is the story one sees in a biography of
Horace Mann.

Biography and the Discovery of Social Possibilities
If literacy narratives reveal the origin of ideas in history, they
also reflect social possibility and constraint. Indeed, biographical studies of less-privileged groups have provided uncommonly lucid views of life at the margins of social and political
possibility—that is, when they have been told from a learner's
point of view.

Biographies of nineteenth-century African American
slaves—whether created as oral histories by journalists of the
Works Progress Administration (WPA) in the post-Depression
U.S. or in slave narratives from the period—reveal ironic twists
and turns in education. They expose the written word itself as
a complex and contradictory site, a place within which oppression and emancipation were deployed simultaneously, and
where imperial imposition and active resistance proceeded
simultaneously, where the schoolhouse symbolized opposing
hopes and fears.

Acquiring the rudiments was, for enslaved African Americans, an essentially solitary process carried on in secret, in
special places, in between times and spaces, illegally, away
from the communal noise of quarters, from the rigors of work,
from the admonitions of owners. Unlike many other children
living in the United States in the first half of the nineteenth
century, slave children typically found themselves enclosed in

a world where the transmission of culture proceeded almost completely through the spoken word. In the world the slaves created, the consciousness of children formed within a community that maintained integrity, coherence and solidarity by creating what Lawrence W. Levine (1977) called "a sacred world," a richly expressive psychological and moral reality. Slaves transmitted this sacred world in song and talk, through prayer and dance, in cabins and fields, both day and night. The stories of those few who were adventurous, courageous, fearless and deeply religious reveal people skilled in the art of stealing time. Listening at schoolroom doors, talking friends into helping them, attaching themselves to people willing to instruct, helping themselves to books from owners' libraries, attending closely to Bible readings, they learned to read and write by stealth. For Peter Randolph, learning to read involved a shuttle from the church door where he listened to a white preacher read a text, to home, where he labored over a Bible to match spoken sermons and visual symbols. Nettie Henry, a Mississippi slave, also worked her way to literacy, explaining to her own children the proper procedure: "[D]e same words in dis book what's in de Bible . . . larn 'de way de is fixed . . . dem de fir' thing you know when you can read the Bible" (WPA, p. 62).

Slaves stole lessons because they were prohibited from learning to read and write. Encounters with literacy meant courting punishment. "De White folks didn't 'low us even to look at a book. Dey would scol' an' sometimes whup us efen dey caught us and our head in a book!" recalled Josiah Henson, reputedly the role model for Harriet Beecher Stowe's Uncle Tom. "I was thirteen years of age when I nearly lost my life because I made an effort to gain this kind of knowledge." Finding Henson with a spelling book in the apple orchard, his master beat him over the head saying, "I'll teach you to get apples . . . for such a vile purpose. Give me that book" (Finkelstein, 1979, p. 128).

If slave stories describe stealing literacy, they also depict race awareness and encounters with power. Lunsford Lane (1842), who grew up on a North Carolina plantation, described his surprise at unequal treatment: "When I began to work, I discovered the difference between myself and my master's white children. . . . They were learning to read, while I was not permitted to have a book in my hand." James Williams, a Virginia slave learned about his degraded status when his relationship with a white friend was transformed. Of his boyhood friend he recalled, "I was his playmate and constant associate in childhood. I used to go with him to his school, and carry his books for him, and meet him there when school was dismissed. We were very fond of each other. . . . He taught me letters of the alphabet, and I should soon have acquired a knowledge of reading, had not George's mother discovered her son in the act of teaching me" (Finkelstein, 1979, p. 130).

Ironically, perhaps, literacy stories also reveal the uses of reading and writing to expand, enhance, dignify and deepen the spiritual worlds within which the consciousness of many African American enslaved persons dwelled. Harriet Jacobs described the blending of the sacred and daily in her story about an Old Black Man:

> I knew an old Black man whose piety and childlike trust in God were beautiful to witness. . . . He had a most earnest desire to learn to read. He thought he should learn how to serve God better if he could only read the Bible. He came to me, begged me to teach him to read. . . . After asking if he knew that slaves were whipped for teaching each others to read he still wanted to. He thought he would come three times a week. . . . I selected a quiet nook . . . and there I taught his A, B, C. . . . As soon as he could spell in two syllables he wanted to spell out words in the Bible. The happy smile that illuminated his face put joy into my heart. After spelling out a few words, he paused and said, "Honey, it 'pears when I can read dis good book I shall be nearer to God. . . . I only wants to read dis book, dat I may know how to live; den I hab no fear 'bout dyin'" (Finkelstein, 1979, p. 130).

Learning to read enabled slaves to enhance the sacred world of religion, to draw closer to parents, inform communal activity, and otherwise enrich the face-to-face world of the quarters. Literacy stories also document the kindling of a smoldering anger. It is no surprise that many who became literate engaged in a series of efforts to subvert and evade the law, transforming their literary abilities into efforts to control their lives and extend their freedom in a variety of creative ways.

Nurtured in two worlds—one that was hostile to literary effort, the other in which literacy went unutilized by most but remained highly valued—the lonely, secret process of "stealin" an education constituted a courageous act of independence, a strike for identity, an expression of defiance that was without precedent in nineteenth-century America. Learning to read and write constituted a process that signaled at once oppression and possibility, and revealed the power and constraints of nineteenth-century education. Without biography, these voices would be silent, these processes hidden.

Biography and Social Change: Girls and Young Women
Beyond their capacity to reveal the origins of ideas and the existence of social possibilities and alternatives, biographical studies also provide a window through which to observe the nature of social change. A third group of literacy narratives, those of educationally highborn women, demonstrates how biography can reveal the processes by which people transform lived experiences into new human relationships, power hierarchies, status definitions, educational arrangements and civic influences as well as into efforts to reconstruct social, political and economic forms. Studies of women's lives have, in fact, provided unusually sophisticated examples of biographical genres (see, for example, G. J. Clifford, 1975; Antler, 1986; Horowitz, 1994; and Alpern, et al., 1992).

For female progeny of the educationally highborn, biographical stories disclose privilege and restraint, educational riches and political and economic poverties. For these young women, the family defined, organized, managed—indeed constituted—the first community within which they acquired the rudiments of learning and the adornments of language. Learning to read and write commonly involved the children of educationally affluent families in a series of intense emotional relationships with their parents. Mary Austin (1932) for example learned the alphabet in her kitchen, where "the letter 'i' evoked the scene of her mother kneading bread and of her brother doing his alphabet"(p. 67). Family rituals commonly reflected and sustained a love of the culture of books and an affection for the social uses of the mind. Abigail Alcott, Bronson Alcott's unjustly ignored wife and Louisa May's beleaguered highborn mother, carried on a tradition of ritual readings typical of a certain class of families: "[O]ne of our number . . . would read aloud while the mother and the two elder daughters sewed. Thus, we read Scott, Dickens, Cooper, Hawthorne, Shakespeare, and the British poets" (Finkelstein, 1979, p. 125).

Writing was as important as reading in the family cultures of the educationally highborn. To Louisa May on her eighth birthday, Bronson Alcott wrote, "You make [me] very happy every time I look at your smiling face, and make [me] sad everytime I see your face look unpleasant" (Finkelstein, 1994). Writing also nurtured practical social skills as girls prepared invitations, menus and greeting cards.

Beyond reading and writing, discussions of current affairs punctuated life in the households of the educationally highborn. Political discussions revolving around newspaper articles, theological discussions of sermons and portions of scripture, and instructive dialogue organized around novel and poetry readings were standard daily fare. Through daily household rituals, the children of the educationally highborn practiced the arts of criticizing, arguing, persuading and exhorting.

In close proximity to powerful fathers and cultivated mothers, highborn male children learned how to acquire influence and to keep it. Girls in this elite culture learned about status barriers and power realities. Elizabeth Cady Stanton (1898), later a suffragist, recalled two domestic incidents which, for her, defined women's status. When her younger sister was born, the fifth female of six children, many friends remarked "What a pity she's a girl!" Only later did she come to understand that "girls were considered an inferior order of beings." When she was eleven, she recalled yet another transforming experience:

> When I was eleven years old, my only brother, who had just graduated from Union College, came home to die . . . . We were all assembled in the silent chamber of death . . . and my father seated by his side [was] pale and immovable. I climbed

upon his knee . . . we both sat in silence thinking of the
wreck of all his hopes in the loss of a dear son, and I
wondering what could be said or done to fill the void in his
breast. At length he heaved a deep sigh and said, "Oh my
daughter, I wish you were a boy!" (p. 4).

Convinced that she could help her father cope with the
loss of his son, she began to study Greek, Latin and mathematics, and to ride horses: "I taxed every power hoping some
day to hear my father say: 'Well, a girl is as good as a boy
after all'." But he never said it. After she had attended a
boy's academy and won second prize for achievement in
Greek, she hoped her father would be satisfied with her.
Instead "he kissed me on the forehead and exclaimed, with a
sigh, 'Ah you should have been a boy'." Finally, at the time
of her graduation from academy, "I learned of the barrier
that prevented [me] from following in the footsteps of fellow
male students who were admitted to Union College where no
girls were admitted."

Stories like Elizabeth Cady Stanton's abound in the autobiographical literature. Unlike Stanton, who went on to cultivate
new visions of political power and economic ambition, other
intellectually cultivated females tell stories of struggle to
reconcile ambition and piety within a context of domesticity
and high culture. In the depth of struggles to balance ambition and humility, and to escape the confinements of
traditional domestic roles, women like Catharine Beecher,
Mary Lyon, Lydia Marie Child contrived to create new
possibilities for educated women—institutions that would
enrich their intellectual lives, and a teaching profession that
could both serve and join their political and economic
ambitions. As adult women, they advised mothers, explored
child development, and filtered child-rearing ideals through
textbooks, mass circulation magazines and moral treatises.
They also created new spheres of authority for themselves and
formed new alliances with physicians and ministers.

From a web of contradictory messages, women forged
option-creating institutions that nurtured both bold and
conservative leadership. Learning to read, write and pursue
knowledge expanded their intellectual range and social

imaginations. At the same time, acquiring the rudiments limited and directed their expression. As Mary Lyon, the founder of Mt. Holyoke put it, "[Y]oung ladies scarcely out of their teens, whose souls are burning for some channel into which they can pour their benevolence, and who will teach two, three or four years . . . [can become] firm pillars to hold up their successors" (Finkelstein, 1989, p. 687).

By the very nature of their involvement in the founding and conduct of teacher education institutions, women crafted previously unimagined options for themselves. Emerging from these alternative institutions, many proceeded to become politically active, independent and adventurous. Others did not. Biographical studies have been unique in their ability to present both possibilities.

Biography as Mythic Overhaul:
A Form of Critical Historical Study

Biography can play one more important role in the study of educational history: the idea of mythic overhaul, or "intellectual spoiling." Biographical studies have the power to correct a persistent fallacy in historical reasoning: the tendency to promulgate interpretive schemes or sense-making myths that reveal historical developments and processes of social change with uncommon elegance while muting, distorting, oversimplifying and obscuring both human agency and historical processes. Indeed, some of the most creative sense-making myths of educational history have also served as the greatest nonsense makers, cultivating stereotypes; overstating the force of economic, political, psychological, and cultural circumstance; and detaching historical processes from human doing. One thinks of those traditional interpretations that revealed educational history strictly in its relationship to the expansion of democracy, the triumph of democratic politics, and visions of schools as opportunity structures. Or, one thinks of the mirror-image sense-making myth that linked educational evolution to market forces and status-seeking elites, and transformed the history of education into a history of regulatory processes through which successive generations of economic elites managed the socialization of working-class children, sustained their own social position, assured a docile laboring force, and imposed upon others an array of imperial impulses (Finkelstein, 1992). Or, think of the grand interpretive schemes of those historians of children and youth who conceptualized polar opposite interpretations of the historical role of schools as regulatory or liberating, protected or unprotected, love-filled or hate-suffused, happy or sad, dangerous or safe, dependent or autonomous, standardizing or choice-revealing, harmonious or conflict-laden institutions (Graff, 1995).

No matter how grand or elegant or how evocative or compelling their schemes, grand historical interpretations never become complex enough to integrate the whole of history. But biographical studies, life histories and historical memoirs provide documentary reminders that historical processes are inevitably more complex than our capacity to define and understand them.

Conclusion

Biographical studies are more than simply individual chronicles—ornamental, illustrative or exemplary of larger processes. Taken together, biographical treatments of diverse persons like Horace Mann, enslaved African Americans and educationally highborn women reveal the origins of ideas, the evolution of alternative social possibilities and the roles of individuals in history making. They provide a documentary context within which to judge the relative power of material and ideological circumstances, the meaning of education policy, the utility of schooling, the definition of literacy and the relationship between teaching and learning and policy and practice. Biographies and individual narratives provide both the stuff and substance of history and its more elegant and evocative examples.

Chapter Four

Construction Scars:
Autobiographical Voice in Biography

William F. Pinar and Anne E. Pautz

> The closeness and distance between a biographer and her sub-
> ject is given . . . perspective by Liz Stanley when she asks
> "how close are the links between the experience or lives of
> autobiographers and . . . written biographies . . . ?" This sug-
> gests an experiential link between the life of the writer and the
> way she expresses her understanding of the life of her subject.
>
> Teresa Iles (1992, p. 2)

The concept of voice has been evocative in several contemporary curriculum discourses. Dwayne E. Huebner (1995) spoke
of "being called" to teach, reminding his readers that teaching is a vocation and a vocation is a call. The vocation of
teaching, he explained, involves three aspects:

> Three voices call, or three demands are made on the teacher.
> Hence the life that is teaching is inherently a conflicted way of
> living. The teacher is called by the students, by the content,
> and by the institution within which the teacher lives (p. 27).

In the contemporary field of curriculum theory, which
Huebner's own work helped bring into being, voice has
become crucial in portraying these calls to speak and teach. In
the efforts to understand curriculum as political, racial, gender,
phenomenological and autobiographical text, voice has been
embroidered and employed extensively. The contemporary
interest in voice has, of course, a history.

Autobiographical Voice
Janet L. Miller (1982) employed voice in her ground-
breaking exploration of the relationships among identity, the
self and others. In "The Sound of Silence Breaking," she
wrote, "The dream is recurring: the quiet is everywhere. It
surrounds my classroom, penetrates the halls of the building
in which I teach. I wait with my students for the voices,
horrified that they might scream in rage, trembling that they
may never whisper" (p. 5). This is the silence of women's
experience and voices, the separation of women's lived worlds
from the public discourse of education. In this situation,
Miller asked how much it takes to break silence. She
suggested that "breaking silence with my students creates a
way for me to ground my fears of the unnatural silences and
to focus my voice, my energies upon the articulation of our
work together" (p. 10). In *Creating Space and Finding
Voices* (1990), she proceeded to document in a lyrical,
autobiographical voice her collaboration with several teachers:

> This narrative, then, attempts to bring teachers' voices to the
> center of the dialogue and debate surrounding current educa-
> tional reform, teacher education restructuring efforts, and
> research on teachers' knowledge. Our group's explorations of
> the possibilities of collaborative and interactive research as one
> way in which we might "recover our own possibilities" are at
> the heart of this chronicle (p. 10).

While making one of the most important statements in this
area, Janet Miller was not the only theorist working with the
experience of voice. As Jo Anne Pagano (1990) asserted,
"The task I see for feminist theory in education just now is
one of making conversation with our professions and with our
history within them. We can theorize our vulnerability as
practitioners of our disciplines and as teachers, speak our exile
and, in doing so, resettle our disciplinary communities" (p.
14). Far from oppressing and silencing that superiority
characteristic of patriarchy in such resettlings, women seek
only the power to speak their voices and experience: "If we
women are to find our voices," Pagano continued, "we must
insist on describing and claiming the difference produced in
experience and on naming and claiming the original connec-

tion denied and forbidden in patriarchal discourse" (pp. 14-15). That connection and difference creates space for moral imagination and humane practice. In that practice, women resist patriarchal structures and languages. Petra Munro (1992) noted that "When curricular practice is seen and remembered as fluid and embedded in lived experience, these women [those she studied] not only subvert traditional forms, but also deflect the standardization of curriculum that has traditionally functioned as a form of control" (p. 15). In these phases of understanding curriculum as gender and auto-biographical text, the concept of voice allowed curricularists to speak their silence, and in so doing, resist patriarchal structures.

In breaking the silence, scholars worked to report and honor the voices of the formerly marginalized in curriculum research. Paula Salvio (1990) reported undergraduate voices, William Ayers (1990) children's voices, and Bonnie Meath-Lang (1990) deaf students' voices via dialogue journals. Magda Lewis (1990) elaborated upon the gendered, and Lisa Delpit (1988) analyzed race vis-à-vis complexities of power, pedagogy and voice. Donald Blumenfeld-Jones attended to the voices of young women dance students while collaborating with Susan Stinson and J. Van Dyke (1990). Voice surfaces in certain strands of phenomenological scholarship (see, for example, Pinar and Reynolds, 1992). Feminist scholars concentrate on reporting the voices of women (Miller, 1990; Grumet, 1988, 1990; Munro, 1992, 1993, 1996; Ellsworth, 1993; Pagano, 1990; M. Doll, 1995). All this reporting explores fundamental questions regarding politics, community and relationality. As Deborah Britzman (in Connelly and Clandinin, 1990) explained,

> Voice is meaning that resides in the individual and enables that individual to participate in a community. . . . The struggle for voice begins when a person attempts to communicate meaning to someone else. Finding the words, speaking for oneself, and feeling heard by others are all a part of this process. . . . Voice suggests relationships: the individual's relationship to the meaning of her/his experience and hence, to language, and the individual's relationship to the other, since understanding is a social process. (p. 4)

Embedded in the social and political field, voice emerges as a relational concept. Along with Britzman, other scholars have observed, for instance, that teachers' and students' voices have been silenced as conservatives attempt to impose curriculum dissemination without "distortions," a version of the so-called "teacher-proof" curricula. For Henry Giroux and Peter McLaren (1986), the so-called critical pedagogy is expressed, in part, through voice, through the stories that teachers and students tell each other. Voice becomes a key element in critical pedagogy as, in McLaren's (1989) words, "it alerts teachers to the fact that all discourse is situated historically and mediated culturally" (p. 229). Teachers and students understand experience through voice as "cultural grammar" and "background knowledge," critical pedagogues distinguished between teacher and student voice:

> A student's voice is not a reflection of the work as much as it is a constitutive force that both mediates and shapes reality within historically constructed practices and relationships of power. . . . Teacher voice reflects the values, ideologies, and structuring principles that teachers use to understand and mediate the histories, cultures, and subjectivities of their students (p. 230).

Additionally, critical "educators must find a way of making female voices heard in classrooms" (McLaren & Hammer, 1989, p. 46). But one important theorist has viewed this apparent solidarity with skepticism.

In her widely-read essay, "Why Doesn't This Feel Empowering? Working Through the Repressive Myths of Critical Pedagogy," Elizabeth Ellsworth (1989) pointed out that critical pedagogy should not be confused with feminist pedagogy, which "constitutes a separate body of literature with its goals and assumptions" (p. 298). The key terms of critical pedagogy—empowerment, student voice and dialogue —represent code words and a "posture of invisibility." Relying upon a decontextualized and universalistic conception of reason, Ellsworth saw critical pedagogy leading to "repressive myths that perpetuate relations of domination." She continued to criticize the concept of "student voice," as discussed in the critical pedagogy literature, relying on her experience in a course she taught at the University of Wisconsin-Madison to suggest its flaws. From a gender perspective, for instance, she noted "the desire by the mostly white, middle-class men who write the literature on critical pedagogy to elicit 'full expression' of student voices . . . becomes voyeuristic when the voice of the pedagogue himself goes unexamined" (p. 312).

Ellsworth concluded that as long as critical pedagogy failed to understand issues of trust, risk, fear and desire, especially as these gain expression through issues of identity and politics in the classroom, its "rationalistic tools will continue to fail to loosen deep-seated, self-interested investments in unjust relations of, for example, gender, ethnicity, and sexual orientation" (pp. 313-314). After critiquing critical pedagogy's ahistorical use of "dialogue" and "democracy," Ellsworth suggested a "pedagogy of the unknowable," in which knowledge was understood as "contradictory, partial and irreducible" (p. 321).

Other reservations regarding the use of voice have appeared. Madeleine R. Grumet (1990) acknowledged that she is less than comfortable "with voice as a metaphor for feminist theory and pedagogy" (p. 277). In the 1970s the notion of "voice" enabled Grumet to distinguish her work from male work and to differentiate her text from male text. Grumet observed that voice is gendered: "Drawn from the body and associated with gender, voice splinters the fiction of an androgynous speaker as we hear rhythms, relations, sounds, stories, and style that we identify as male or female" (p. 278).

Voice may express more than just the self-affirmative, self-differentiating complexity that is a woman's voice. Indeed, in the gaze of an objectifying, voyeuristic heterosexual male, Grumet observed, voice may be defensive:

> If the voice is the medium for the projection of meaning, then woman as a meaning maker is undermined by the visual emphasis on her body as an object of display and desire. . . . If he projected the gaze as accuser or interrogator, she receives it, and I suspect, uses speech to deflect it. Teacher talk is then a defensive move deployed to assert her subjectivity in the face of the objectifying gaze (p. 279).

Grumet located this defensiveness in the fantasy of objectification, deflected and reorganized as a projection of maternity.
Voice may represent a male narrowing of female possibility, a
reduction of freedom to social role. She worried that
"burdened by nostalgia, the maternal voice in educational
discourse is prey to sentimentality and to an audience that
consigns its melodies to fantasy, no matter how compelling"
(p. 281). Can women escape the objectifying gaze of male
subjectivity? Grumet suggested that a route out may be found
in the very same location, the "voice," although understood
multivocally: "One escape is found in the chorus that is our
own voice. . . . We need not dissolve identity in order to
acknowledge that identity is a choral and not a solo performance" (p. 281).

To elaborate upon this already complex construction of
voice, Grumet identified three elements of educational voice—
situation, narrative and interpretation:

> The first, situation, acknowledges that we tell our story as a
> speech event that involves the social, cultural, and political
> relations in and to which we speak. Narrative, or narratives as I
> prefer, invites all the specificity, presence, and power that the
> symbolic and semiotic registers of our speaking can provide.
> And interpretation provides another voice, a reflexive and more
> distant one (pp. 281-282).

Janet Miller (1990) also saw voice as a problem. She
rejected a fixed notion that implies that, once finding a voice
one can always articulate oneself, pronounce one's identity,
and be heard:

> However, in openly grappling with the possibility of
> imposition and in presenting the many voices, the multiple
> positions and changing perspectives from which each of us
> speaks, I have tried to point to the ways in which each of us
> shared in the formation and constant reformation of our
> collaborative processes. . . . We have begun to hear our mul-
> tiple voices within the contexts of our sustained collaboration,
> and thus recognized that "finding voices" is not a definitive
> event but rather a continuous and relational process (pp. x-xi).

Grumet's and Miller's elucidations of voice are heuristically rich. Understanding the autobiographical voice as the site for society, culture and politics—a "site" that one can reflexively reconfigure by interpreting of multiple subject positions—hints at both political programs and pedagogical processes. Ellsworth's concern is also key: Can rationalistic tools associated with modernism possibly reconfigure the politics of voice? How can we speak our minds without losing our bodies to the gaze of the other, becoming categories in the great (white male) chain of being? Can our voices disclose the continuous and relational process of which Miller speaks? These questions become pertinent for the student of biography.

Construction Scars

Grumet's insight that voice is a choral sound and Miller's elaboration of the collaborative process speak to the intersections between autobiography and biography. Biography is far from an objective reporting of another's life. The biographer's autobiographic voice sounds in the biographical subject; indeed it may overwhelm or distort that subject, through the decisions of inclusion and exclusion, emphases and de-emphases. In turn, as Carolyn Heilbrun (1988) observed, the voice of the biographical subject resonates in the biographer's own life. Biographers unmindful of their own autobiographical investment in their subject may ignore this reciprocal and complex relationship. Ann Game noted in this regard, "What frequently [goes] unacknowledged [is] the position of the researcher, the fantasies and projections involved, the ways in which interviews are produced by the interviewer" (as quoted in Iles, 1992, p. 6).

Merely quoting the biographical subject is far from a transparent process leading to an authentic representation or voice. Teresa Iles (1992) discussed this phenomenon, revealing "how thoroughly the writer is the subject of interpretations she produces" (p. 6). It is just these strands and threads of others represented in the self that Grumet insists be acknowledged. Just as the autobiographical voice is choral, so the biographical voice must be heard with an ear attuned to its different strands. And so biography intertwines with the life history of the writer to reveal aspects of both the writer and the subject—different people whose merged and separated voices collaborate to form a complex text: biography.

One can hear an echo of many feminists' and curricularists' interests in collaboration (Miller, 1990; Schubert and Ayers, 1992) in Adrienne Rich's description of her wish to connect with others as a "dream of a common language" (1978, p. 7), a dream that can speak to both autobiography and biography. These forms each tell a story in a voice that simultaneously creates distance and intimacy between a reader and the subject of the story, even when the subject is oneself. Both the autobiographer and biographer construct a narrative through a creative process of composing and editing. Each requires extensive life-history research, albeit different techniques. Both can provide insight into the subject's historical, political and social situation. Traditionally seen as "realistic" representations of a person, autobiography and biography each serves in fact as a constructed cultural account, as Miller, Pagano and Grumet have all shown. What Clifford Geertz (1988) said of ethnography is true for autobiography and biography: "The devices, the construction scars, the brush marks are all more or less invisible, at least to the unwary eye" (p. 29). The autobiographical and biographical voice calls us to listen to our lived experience, acknowledge the "construction scars" and, in so doing, understand the complexities of our lives and the lives of others.

As feminist and political theorists have shown, autobiography and biography can present social problems vividly and concretely. The task for contemporary autobiographers and biographers is to disclose the "construction scars" to avoid the illusion of "realism." They can achieve this disclosure when they make the process of constructing autobiographical or biographical text explicit, and when they leave the layers of autobiographical identification with the biographical subject visible. The instability of text and the illusory nature of the "author" must become visible (W. Doll, 1993; Pinar and Reynolds, 1992).

As Miller, Grumet, Britzman, and others have shown, autobiography can also give voice to those marginalized cultural groups and individuals whose voices can break the illusion of cultural homogeneity (Andrews, 1993; Castenell and Pinar, 1993; McCarthy, 1997). They provide a sharp focus, bringing about change in the culture, bringing to bear, as Langness and Frank (1981) noted,

> autobiography's transformative power . . . through which people . . . on the margins of mainstream America and its values have shaped self-images of their own design. Among these, Blacks, pacifists, women, expatriates, homosexuals . . . and others have described their own feelings, actions, ideas, desires, relationships, aspirations, and efforts to survive—in their own words (p. 93).

This political potential of autobiography and biography may be their most exciting aspect. Autobiographers and biographers can create spaces in which to exist, spaces that function as self-affirmative zones within the larger, often hostile society. The particularities of individual lives subvert the objectification and commodification of a bureaucratized state. These zones allow the marginalized to understand and distance themselves from vicious criticism and that ostracism that defines them as irrelevant or dangerous. Writing these self-defining texts can be revolutionary for marginalized individuals and groups. While the autobiographies and biographies of women and such other marginalized persons as lesbians have traditionally been ignored or even reclassified as fiction (Gilmore, 1994), these texts carry a potential influence on the society and add richness, depth and discernment to the public discourse. Honoring the autobiographical voice of both the writer and the subject of biography—especially when that voice has been marginalized or ignored—functions to destabilize monolithic, abstract and thereby distorted portraits of time and place.

Merging Genres and Conflicted Voices

One can often hear the autobiographical voice in biographical narratives. In fact, the genre often requires its explicit use. Obtaining material for biographical writing can be difficult when previous generations of publishers and historians have considered certain lives culturally insignificant. The writer must connect fragments of records—often an intuitive process which draws as much from the writer as the subject—to create an understandable image. Discussing this lack of access to the interior lives of slaves, Toni Morrison (1987) described the process this way: "It's a kind of literary archeology: on the basis of some information and a little bit of guesswork you journey to a site to see what remains were left behind and to reconstruct the world that those remains imply" (p. 112). Like archaeologists, the biographers of the marginalized must treat what they discover as a sleuth treats clues at a crime scene to re-create the obscured event.

Just as educators developed autobiographic theories to express teachers' and students' voices, so too autobiographic and biographic exploration reveals the occasionally conflicted character of those voices. Because they serve in roles ideologically linked with motherhood, teachers occupy contradictory positions; they sometimes, for example, represent both femininity and the power of the patriarchy. When advocating change in social definitions of femininity and motherhood, women often confront contradictory (and arbitrary) definitions of feminine and unfeminine behavior, especially in regards to using power and expressing anger. The nostalgia traditionally associated with the teaching profession restricts teachers' voices, a point Carolyn Heilbrun (1988) underscored: "[N]ostalgia that has for so many years imprisoned women . . . is likely to be a mask for unrecognized anger. If one is not permitted to express anger or even to recognize it within oneself, one is, by simple extension, refused both power and control" (p. 15).

Teachers might confront these issues, working to resolve for themselves what it means to be a woman in school. Women might learn those political skills that allow them to remain "woman-identified" in order to obtain power without succumbing to those patriarchal expectations that undermine their feminist allegiances. As Heilbrun explained: "Women of accomplishment . . . have had to confront power and control. Because this has been declared unwomanly . . . women have been deprived of the narratives, or the texts, plots, or examples, by which they might assume power over—take control of— their own lives" (p. 17). As we know, the contradictions between the desire for control of one's life and the desire to be viewed as a woman can often be difficult to negotiate. Such autobiographic and biographic research helps support teachers' voices and to keep those teachers from being caught in the male gaze. The same complication can accompany the writing of women's biographies. Biographers negotiate a balance between presenting their subjects as woman-identified and as successful in the masculine pursuits of success and power. Biographies of women can provide a locale in the curriculum to examine what constitutes knowledge and who defines and legitimates it. Biographies can critique the oppression of women and can themselves become occasions for analysis and further critique by others. The merging of genres can provide avenues for exploring previously uncontested views. By challenging the hegemony of particular constructions of knowledge, women can also, through autobiography and biography, challenge their silence in the patriarchal state. This challenge can encourage the representation of women and other marginalized groups so that women can speak in voices that are, perhaps, neither masculine nor feminine, but are, to recall Madeleine Grumet's metaphor, a chorus fully and uniquely their own.

Conclusion

Several implications for biography inhere in the concept of autobiographical voice. For example, the biographer might make explicit his or her autobiographical interest in the biographical subject. In biography, one honors one's autobiographical voice indirectly, through the voice of others. For women, African Americans, and others deprived of full and free voices, such articulation functions politically, insisting on a more complex view of history, culture and politics. Further, by avoiding the abstraction of theory—for example, Marxist theory—we can hear vividly the immediacy of a concretely existing individual. We must be watchful of such subterranean motives as the gendered gaze Ellsworth observed in the critical theorist's use of voice. We cannot patronizingly invite others to speak if their voices are the objects of our desires, our fantasies of our own power and pedagogy. Rather, we might act the way midwives act, providing support for other voices.

This may mean, of course, remaining silent while the other speaks. As biographers, we might make intelligible the ground—what Grumet terms "the situation"—on which the other's voice speaks. We quote the other, providing opportunities for the others' voices, for what is termed narrative. As Grumet reminds us, we must not relinquish our obligation to interpret the others' voices, but in doing so we must not "dub" the actions of others with our own motives and voices. Grumet's delineation among situation, narrative and interpretation makes explicit the "construction scars" Geertz discussed, by separating the various sounds that constitute the "chorus" of voice. In making explicit our autobiographical relationship to our subject, we make biography vivid and immediate.

Curriculum theorists now depend upon autobiography to provide new understandings in the curriculum, emphasizing the lived experience of teachers and students. In like fashion, biography can illuminate the complex layers of society, culture and politics by explicating the lives of others. By listening to the multiple voices in biography and life-history research, one can reconstruct the "remains" of the lost, silenced lives of others. Attending to the details of particular lives provides occasions to question and even escape the myths of schooling. The resonance between biography and autobiography can spur an articulation of lives that contest social norms and provide narratives that help teachers and students redefine their educational experiences on their own terms and in their own voices.

In learning to recognize, express and heed our own voices and the voices of our students, through reflection and interpretation, we are better able to heed the multi-voiced call to teach. The response makes conflicting demands on our lives, as Huebner (1995) noted. Yet we can resolve these conflicting calls: "That part of the teaching life which is a response to the call of the student results in the work of love; to the call of content, the work of truth; to the call of the institution, the work of justice" (p. 28). Drawing on the multiplicity of voices that autobiography and biography provide, perhaps we can find our way to negotiate and fulfill these calls to teach.

PART TWO

Methodological Issues and Biographical Research

Introduction

Methodological issues encompass all aspects of biographical inquiry, but discussions in recent decades have often been concerned with documentation and interpretation. How does one cope with archival gaps? What are the motives of the subject? the ethics of documentation? the "figure under the carpet" (Edel, 1981)? Currently, however, issues of method include not only these traditional but many postmodern concerns as well: How does one justify the selection of a subject? Can one overcome the "futility" of biographic portrayal? Can one accurately portray a subject in a chronologically linear narrative? Why do certain biographers write as if the subject had a unified or "essential self"? Does the act of biographical writing actually "skew reality so that the light may fall more brightly on one figure"? (Peters, 1995, p. 46). The complexities of biographical method—traditional, postmodern, and "new biography"—abound. Yet, in spite of all the problems, biographers continue to write their biographies, and even with the overwhelming complexity of methodological issues, they continue to find ways to portray lives. As Linda Wagner-Martin (1994) asserts, "[I]n this age of fluid moral positioning, when a subject can be praised by one group of readers and reviled by another, it is finally the biographer's conviction that directs the narrative" (p. 10). Thus, in this section I decided to present issues of biographical method within the context of the biographer's relation to the subject. Blanche Wiesen Cook addresses the topic specifically in the first essay, and it receives consideration in relation to the constructs of "gender," "race" and "trust" in the remaining three essays. The first two essays come from outside the field of education, the second two from foundations of education professors.

Blanche Wiesen Cook reports that a basic ingredient in her research is a personal identification with the views and beliefs of her subjects. In effect, for Cook, who is completing the second volume of her biography of Eleanor Roosevelt, personal involvement is central, and "the most compelling biographies are those, written with passion and intensity, that seek to redress the wrongs, reconstitute the spirit and restore the subject." Implications for the aspiring educational biographer appear significant since these researchers often wonder what subject they should select. Seemingly, a biographer does not "just select a subject" but, as Cook suggests, a biographer and subject select one another.

Linda Wagner-Martin's numerous biographies and her theoretical work, *Telling Women's Lives*, have added greatly to our understanding of gender issues in biographical research. In this essay she examines issues of gender within the realm of theory as well as the "day-to-day" difficulties in finding information. She recognizes that "Traditional biography normally concentrates on the subject's accomplishments, and given that, until recently, women's lives were seldom shaped in direct response to history, such a focus in the writing of women's lives would be inappropriate. One of the central questions in writing biographies of women, then, becomes, What *are* the accomplishments in a woman's life?" As Wagner-Martin discusses women's "new biography" and biographer-subject concerns, she concludes by underscoring the relation between writer and reader: "[T]he practice of biography is 'life-writing' in a number of senses, and one of the most important of these is the sharing of a moral perspective that, through the art of the biography, may prove as convincing for the reader as it has been for the writer."

Wayne Urban discusses the influences that led him to write a biography of the African American educator-administrator-historian, Horace Mann Bond. Personal involvement guided Urban's research as he explored a life that included certain similarities to his own—historian of Southern education, administrator, scholar. With these similarities, however, came one overriding difference—race. Urban discusses this dimension in relation to Afrocentrism and postmodernism and reflects upon the issue of biographical interpretation as it relates to racial differences of subject and researcher. Alan Wieder concludes this section by discussing issues raised by oral history. Interviews are a crucial component of biographical inquiry, not merely as a research tool but also as a dimension of the interviewer-interviewee relationship. Wieder asks, "How do people select their memories? What cultural process do they follow? . . . What happens to experience on the way to becoming memory?" Trust and its impact upon memory becomes, as Wieder displays, a response to these issues. Moreover, trust as an aspect of the interviewer-interviewee interaction affects the "thoroughness" of the research.

All four essays escort a biographer into the realm of research methodology where, as we see, the relationship of biographer to subject arises out of the narrative. Such questions of method, then, are addressed not hypothetically but, instead, as these essays have depicted, within the context of actual biographical inquiry. While a reader may be disappointed that the contributors failed to resolve all the methodological problems, a compilation of solutions would be impossible. We can only hope that the emphasis remains on the examination and self-examination of biographical method. Wagner-Martin calls for this examination of method now that more than ever: "as postmodern readers reject oversimplification—preferring an unfinished narrative or one with gaps in its construction to the deceit of the contrived finish— the form of biography must become more open to inquiry."

Note

Blanche Wiesen Cook's essay extends work first published in 1984 in *Between Women* (pp. 387-411). Her original chapter was entitled "Biographer and Subject: A Critical Connection." The contribution by Linda Wagner-Martin emerged from correspondence for the Museum of Education's Contemporary Biographers Acquisitions Project. Wayne J. Urban delivered a presentation version of his essay at the 1993 Witten Award for Distinguished Work in Biography Lecture at the

Museum of Education, University of South Carolina. Alan
Wieder delivered a presentation version of his essay at the
1994 keynote session of the Explorations in Biographical
Method Conference at the Museum of Education, University
of South Carolina.

Chapter Five

The Issue of Subject: A Critical Connection

Blanche Wiesen Cook

Who do we choose to write about? What moves us? What do we care about? What can we learn by writing a life? For biographers, I think, all choices are autobiographical. Biographers traffic in individual sensibilities. We seek to understand change and process through individual lives and how they are lived. We believe in the influence and impact of the individual on the political, economic and social forces of society. We feel profound chemical and emotional connections to our chosen subject. We may not always like everything our subject does or agree with every decision, but there is no reason for selection unless there is a quest for real understanding.

As a journalist and historian, I have been attracted to biographical subjects whose ideas and politics seemed to me not merely influential but unusual and imaginative. As an historian I am concerned with the process of social change. My own commitment to peace research, economic justice and human rights always influences my choice of focus. My subjects reflect my interests. I am moved deeply by what moved them. The initial contact is strengthened when I notice that a subject stands apart, assesses circumstances critically, imaginatively, and well (from my point of view), and offers new bases upon which to build alternative visions. A relationship develops as I seek to investigate and analyze why my subject made the decisions he or she did and came to follow the path he or she followed.

I studied Crystal Eastman (1881-1928) at first because she was an antimilitarist during a period of violent international tension. During the early years of the war in Indochina (1962-1964), my professional interests turned from foreign economic policy to peace research, and Crystal Eastman emerged as significant. That she had also been a feminist and a socialist in the World War I era concerned me only later, when my own vision and priorities changed and developed as a result of the contemporary feminist movement.

Similarly, Dwight David Eisenhower appealed to me as the war throughout Indochina continued to rage, because he had set limits. Of all post-World War II presidents, only Eisenhower insisted that there were real fiscal and political dangers to America's imperial commitments, actual limits beyond which the United States could not afford to go. His warning against the growing influence of the military-industrial complex was not the coda of his career but a theme that ran through it. I was fascinated also by his innovative use of power, both strategic and covert. My current work on Eleanor Roosevelt enables me for the first time to combine my interests—the role of women in society, the importance of and potentials for women's support networks, human rights, international relations and the various forms of power.

Although there are many reasons to select a subject for study, including the need to understand the craven and violent as well as the virtuous and noble, most biographers choose to write about people they care about and can identify with. I find the most compelling biographies are those, written with passion and intensity, that seek to redress the wrongs, reconstitute the spirit and restore the subject.

For me the process of writing is itself a time of joy. During the course of research I develop very personal, intimate relations with my subjects. They grow and change and are generally full of surprises. I dream about the people I write about. They enter my conversations, intrude on the privacy of my bath, join me in the ocean and the garden. They tell me stories, offer me responses, disagree, suggest new sources. I listen very carefully. Frequently a great flirtation emerges. In the process of writing about several radical women, two presidents and Eleanor Roosevelt, I became aware of vastly different relations with each. Except for Woodrow Wilson, who bored me (although he was the subject of my dissertation), all the women and men I have written about interest me personally and politically. And I have had personal and political relations with them. My identification with the views and style of Crystal Eastman became key to my ongoing work. Personal involvement is central for me. If it fails to emerge in the course of research, I change subjects. My writings on the progressive activist women have focused more on Lillian Wald, Emma Goldman and Crystal Eastman than on Jane Addams. When I consider future projects, I never consider Jane Addams. Objectively, that is too bad, since no full biography of Jane Addams exists to date. On the other hand, I have never felt sufficiently engaged by Jane Addams to flirt with her. I flirt regularly with Lillian Wald, a champion flirt. More precisely, I fancy that she flirts with me—as is only appropriate given her daring and prowess. She excites my imagination. She is bold. Her letters are forthright. Her presence in any group is stirring. I can easily imagine the scene of a conference or an argument between Wald and Eastman. They are alive for me, and I identify with them both. But my imagination tucks in when I try to imagine Addams in the room. A brooding, quiet presence emerges, and I know I will never write deeply about her. I may write accurately, but not deeply. Her failure, in the words of Virginia Woolf, to "stir my imagination" renders it impossible to write with the kind of intense and caring understanding required. I am mindful of a range of connection. Emma Goldman, for example, does excite my imagination. Her presence is always vivid. I like to quote her. It is always thrilling when she enters the page. But I do not identify with Emma Goldman. Although I often admire her, her ways are not my ways, even when her choices might be mine. Then, all too often her choices are not mine. She is mendacious, cruel, self-absorbed. Occasionally delightful and flamboyant, she is ultimately narrow-minded and vicious to both enemies and allies. As a result, I will never commit myself to the time needed for a serious study of her life.

On the other hand, I have been deeply involved with Crystal Eastman since I first read her antimilitarist correspondence twenty years ago. On occasion, the identification became total. While I was writing the biographical essay for *Crystal Eastman: On Women and Revolution* (Cook, 1978), I drank too much, as she did, became red-faced with rage, wrote vigorous letters to editors, and thought that, like Crystal Eastman, I was dying of nephritis. I had kidney pains until I turned in my manuscript—months before it was due because I thought myself in a race with death. Some aspects of identification proved more difficult to achieve. I never grew taller, for example, and Crystal Eastman was, after all, over six feet.

"Life is a big battle for the complete feminist," Crystal Eastman wrote in 1918, entirely convinced that the complete feminist would one day achieve total victory. In 1923, as one of the founders of Alice Paul's Congressional Union and National Women's Party, which introduced the ERA, Crystal Eastman wrote that the battle was worth fighting even if it took ten years. Although her timetable was off, her legacy continues. She was in the vanguard of every major movement for social change. From her student days at Vassar (1903) and New York University Law School (1907) until her death, she remained a radical feminist and suffragist.

Suffrage represented for Crystal Eastman only a part of the power that women were denied and needed to reclaim. Tall, athletic, robust, she sought to extend the contours of women's strength and women's sphere far beyond the vote. In 1909, she and Annette Kellerman, a champion swimmer and diver from Australia, then in New York to dive before Broadway audiences, attempted to work out a program for the physical regeneration of the female sex. At that time, Crystal spoke before large audiences on "women's right to physical equality with men." Freda Kirchwey, long-time editor of *The Nation,* recalled that Crystal pictured a utopia of athletes, with women "unhampered by preconceived ideas of what was fit or proper or possible for their sex to achieve." Crystal believed that "when women were expected to be agile, they became agile; when they were expected to be brave, they developed courage; when they had to endure, their endurance broke all records."

From adolescence on, Crystal recognized that fashion served to confine and limit women's ability to move freely. In matters of style—from short hair and short skirts to bathing suits without the customary stockings and skirts—her guiding principle was the achievement of greater and easier activity. Freedom involved discarding antique and unnecessary encumbrances. She never rode sidesaddle but careened about her home town "on a man's saddle in fluttering vast brown bloomers" that shocked polite society. When her neighbors complained to her father about her swimming clothes, she received her family's support. Although her father never once reprimanded her, Crystal believed him to be "startled and embarrassed to see his only daughter in a man's bathing suit with bare brown legs for all the world to see."

She was a pioneer in the field of labor legislation and industrial safety. Her book *Work Accidents and the Law,* published as part of the massive Pittsburgh Survey, became an international classic. Arno reprinted it in 1970, when occupational safety and health returned once again to the American agenda. In 1911, she drafted New York State's first workers' compensation law, a model law used by many states thereafter. Before World War I she was appointed to state and federal commissions of labor. During the war she committed her vast energies to the international peace movement. She founded the Woman's Peace Party, which became the Women's International League for Peace and Freedom, and served as executive director of the American Union Against Militarism, which parented the American Civil Liberties Union.

After the war Crystal Eastman and her brother Max co-published and co-edited *The Liberator,* the only American journal to print information about the new Communist governments and parties of Russia and Europe. In March of 1919, she was the first U.S. journalist to visit and report from Communist Hungary. In 1922, she moved to England to live with her second husband, Walter Fuller, and their two children, Annis and Geoffrey. She remained identified with radical equal-rights feminism and wrote regular columns for Lady Rhondda's *Time and Tide.*

The writings of Crystal Eastman's later years relate to issues and visions that concern all who seek a better, more humane environment. They relate to visions of socialism that would end poverty, racism and privilege; visions of feminism that would end dependence and subservience; visions of internationalism that would end imperialism and devastating warfare.

"Freedom is a large word," she wrote in 1920. It demanded a large struggle, a long battle. Personally, Crystal Eastman was dedicated to freedom. She loved life and was surrounded by family and friends. Protected and fortified by the support of women and men who shared her ideals and battled beside her, she was free and bold. Her close friend Jeannette Lowe once said, "You wouldn't believe how free she was." Her brother wrote that she "poured magnetic streams of generous love around her all the time" and boldly plunged into new experiences. She was impulsive and passionate and, evidently, consulted Dr. A. A. Brill, the first psychoanalyst to practice in America, to bring her intense "libido down."

Crystal Eastman appeals to me both as historical figure and private personality. I consider the challenge of her legacy my current work: work for women, civil liberties and international peace; and the quest for individual freedom and public control over a self-aggrandizing state. Her visions remain brave and distant. She demanded radical change and committed herself to the long struggle on many fronts required for its achievement. The dynamism of her feminist, socialist and antimilitarist visions still inspire further explorations.

As I considered new projects, I longed above all to obtain Crystal Eastman's papers to complete a full biography. The long-denied status of Crystal Eastman's papers results, in part, from my own belated feminist awareness. My relationship to Crystal Eastman, it must be noted, began very slowly. In 1966, when I visited Max Eastman, I was writing "hard history" about Woodrow Wilson and World War I. When Max Eastman suggested that I might want to write about Crystal Eastman and showed me the enormous collection of letters she wrote to her mother, to him and to their closest friends, as well as the manuscripts of her feminist writings, I politely refused his offer. Reflecting my culture and socialization, I did not fully realize Crystal Eastman's importance until the women's movement altered my own consciousness and I began to think about all the women—activists and writers—who came before and whom we were until recently programmed to deny.

That programming not only caused us to lose contact with our political foremothers but also contributed to our loss of control over the very sources of our history. Currently, access to sources, the documents of our heritage, has now become a major battlefield upon which knowledge—or truth—frequently lies, a bloodied corpse. I worked for years to get Eisenhower's most significant international relations documents declassified. After some successes during the halcyon Freedom of Information Act (FOIA) days under Nixon, Ford and Carter, all Iranian and Guatemalan records were reclassified under Ronald Reagan. The battle for sources has much to do with silence and secrecy under the rationales of property law and copyright law. But much more than who owns which words is involved. Issues of censorship and sensibility dominate the situation.

For the biographer, the fight over access to documents is just the beginning. Then comes selection, understanding and impact. Crystal Eastman and Eleanor Roosevelt have both exerted an impact on my life. My ongoing work, whether related to international relations or feminist issues, reflects their influence. I feel a connection between Eastman's life of relative freedom, Eleanor Roosevelt's struggle for fulfillment and identity, and my own effort to understand them both.

As a student activist and a vice-president of the National Student Association (NSA), I met and worked with Eleanor Roosevelt between 1959 and 1962. In those years her vision stood in marked contrast to the prevailing "better dead than red" winds that froze student politics in Cold War America. She encouraged student leaders to think boldly about the future, about a world in which competing economic systems would in fact "coexist." Her support for human rights and civil rights was passionate and absolute, at a time when NSA, the voice of America's student leadership, endorsed segregation. I was suspended by the southern president of my college for "misappropriating" the student funds that underwrote our bus to the North Carolina sit-ins. The college president spoke of "breaking the law"; but Eleanor Roosevelt spoke of natural law, the laws of justice and humanity. There was in my mind no contest—just the ongoing struggle between good and evil. At graduation, I received the Roosevelt Memorial Scholarship for academic excellence and service. Upon shaking my hand and presenting the awards, the president hissed between clenched teeth, "You know how this hurts me." But whenever Eleanor Roosevelt shook my hand, she smiled. I was very proud. I saw her in those years as warm and gracious but also firm and uncompromising. Her manner and her vision were inspiring. Now, after reading through her correspondence, I am also amazed by her incredibly complex days of political work and social whirl, but above all by her enduring political integrity and her abiding ability to change over time.

Most of the information available about Eleanor Roosevelt derives from her own words: her remarkably frank memoirs *This Is My Story* (1937), *This I Remember* (1949), and *Autobiography* (1961), her frequent columns and essays, and, more recently, her letters. Her own words remain the best source for the details of her lonely, soon-orphaned childhood, her years at Allenswood (the famed school near Wimbledon Common for the daughters of the *fin de siècle* smart set), and the early years of a marriage we now know to have been a bruising disappointment. According to Eleanor Roosevelt, the early phase of her life was highlighted by her experiences at Allenswood and her association with its cultured and cosmopolitan headmistress, Marie Souvestre, about whom she wrote, "Whatever I have become since had its seed in those three years of contact with a liberal mind and a strong personality."

But Eleanor Roosevelt's journey toward personal independence and fulfillment evolved slowly, as did her political vision. Her sense of social responsibility and consideration for political activism were only partially awakened during her school years at Allenswood. Similarly, she did not become the kind of independent spirit that Marie Souvestre had encouraged her to become until the last half of her life. Not until Eleanor Roosevelt was nearly 50 did she recast and define fully the contours of her life and creativity.

One is stunned, for example, to read that the woman who stands above all others in her generous support for Jews during and after the Holocaust wrote an anti-Semitic letter to an Allenswood classmate in Germany as late as 1939. Also, during the 1930s ER identified with the women of the South as portrayed in *Gone with the Wind*. She called Black adults "darkies" and children "pickaninnies," until she received a letter of protest from a Black woman who was stunned because Mrs. Roosevelt had spoken so sincerely on behalf of civil rights. Eleanor Roosevelt explained that her Georgia family had always used those words as terms of affection. "What do you prefer?" she asked her correspondent. Yet at the same time, ER struggled as early as 1934 to change United States racial policy. From her early refusal even to walk with her suffragist cousins for women's votes to her celebrated demand for all-women press conferences and her general call for power for women in public life, Eleanor Roosevelt's personal and political journey reflects the full range of the contradictory tides of the twentieth century.

In vision, purpose, strength and ability to change, she is remarkable. I admire her physical stamina and her intensity. And when I cringe at her choices or disagree with her decisions or wonder at her activities, she sits down beside me and tries to explain her evolving sensibilities. Unlike Crystal Eastman's, her life was less than joyful. She was not surrounded by loving, trusting relatives and friends who from childhood supported her visions and her life. Given her tragic childhood and her abusive and alcoholic relatives, the intensity of her warmth is extraordinary. I feel very close to her, even when I disagree with her. Her ways occasionally intrude upon my ways. She made lists—lists of things to do, to read, to inquire about. I now compile lists as never before. Not that I consider myself a chameleon or a dutiful daughter, although I may in fact be both. But I aim to understand, to feel profoundly, to absorb the flavors as far as possible and to learn from my subjects.

This commitment can of course be dangerous, and tiring. Both Crystal Eastman and Eleanor Roosevelt regularly worked from twelve to eighteen hours a day. All the women who interest me did. And some, like Eastman, worked themselves into a needlessly early grave. I am beginning to get self-protective. But most of the joy of discovering is in feeling and experiencing, in knowing the essence of the subject's life as deeply as possible. Twenty years ago it was fashionable to warn students, would-be historians, and biographers to be "objective." I once had a professor who barked, "An intellectual thinks! Think, don't feel!" But she wrote about Cotton Mather, and she was wrong. I would advise, "Think and feel—in order to know fully—with emotion and caring."

Chapter Six

The Issue of Gender:
Continuing Problems in Biography

Linda C. Wagner-Martin

Times occur in any field of study when it is hard to see the line where theory and pragmatic considerations divide. Writing biographies of women writers like Ellen Glasgow, Sylvia Plath and Gertrude Stein, I sometimes find the practical day-to-day stumbling blocks leading to observations one might call theoretical. And because most of my biographies focus on women subjects, some of those pragmatic experiences have led to theories about gender differences.

Biography writing begins with a period of intensive research, of simply finding information. Among the kinds of information biographers must secure is the personal, and if a biographer is lucky, he or she will be writing about a subject who still has living friends or relatives or acquaintances. With regard to this early stage of research, I find some special difficulties when I work on women subjects or try to locate the women friends of male subjects.

What I discovered in the period of early research on my Sylvia Plath biography (Wagner-Martin, 1987, 1988) during the mid-1980s, for instance, was that most women's colleges had policies about providing current addresses to inquirers that differed from those in men's universities. In short, women's colleges were reluctant to provide alumnae addresses and phone numbers. The procedure for many women's college campuses was that I address a letter to the alumna I wanted to find and send the letter to the alumnae office. Then

the staff would address the letter and send it on. Unless the
alumna replied, I had no convenient way to locate her.

What made this procedure so surprising was that I had
already discovered the difficulty of tracing women through
professional directories (comparatively few women belong to
professional groups), or through city phone directories (most
women do not use their given names in such listings but
appear as part of the household under a husband's name).
Beyond that dilemma—that women could easily remain invisible because of these listing procedures—the dilemma of
what happens to women's surnames through their lifetimes
had already complicated research procedures. When I was
trying to find a college friend of Sylvia Plath's, whose name
during their college days had been Marcia Standard, I might
learn from a peer that Marcia Standard was now Marcia
Stemple, having taken the name of the man she married in the
1950s. Unfortunately, a great many women of Plath's generation had married not once but twice, so the trick became to
discover the name of Marcia Standard Stemple's *second*
husband. If I were lucky, and ran into the right friend, I might
discover that Marcia Stemple had, sometime in the 1970s,
become Marcia Winocur. Unless her college alumnae office
was thorough, they would not have the current name on file.
Or if they had the current name on file, I might not know what
current name to use in my inquiry.

Tracing elusive friends was complicated not only by
college policy about releasing current information but also by
the failure of many alumnae to keep in touch with their
colleges. One of the ways educational institutions have of
tracking their graduates is through fund-raising, and it seems
that married women seldom give. The more likely pattern is
that the male wage-earning alumnus gives to *his* college. Once
I realized this, I was able to find a few of Sylvia Plath's college
friends by corresponding with their husband's colleges and
locating a spouse inclined to be helpful.

With inventive procedures, and with the good will of the
women I sought, I managed to talk with, or at least correspond
with, a generous number of Sylvia Plath's college friends, and
particularly with the nineteen other women who with Plath had
comprised the *Mademoiselle* magazine College Board in the

summer of 1953. Many of these latter women had become
professional writers, and locating them and securing their help
in reconstructing that period of Plath's life was comparatively
easy because they had kept in touch with their colleges,
attained some visibility, followed the narrative of Plath's life,
formed opinions about it. Like Plath, they were exceptional,
career-minded women who had refused to accept a position
subordinate to a spouse. They had not just disappeared into a
telephone directory.

I realize this kind of "difficulty" is not the kind of crucial roadblock one thinks of when discussing the difficulties
of writing biography. But given the amount of time and
frustration occasioned by the simple unavailability of women
subjects' names and addresses, it can take its toll on the eager
biographer. Despite our current understanding of some of the
problems of working with female subjects, I doubt that these
tiresome frustrations have ever been chronicled. Many more—
and more significant—differences exist between writing
biography of male subjects and female subjects. But one can
glimpse an index of the difficulty in the semi-comic situation
that sometimes an earnest biographer cannot even *find* a
female subject.

The primary difficulty of writing about female subjects is
that our traditional pattern of biography as we know it from
Samuel Johnson through Lytton Strachey is the narrative of a
male life. Men's lives, in biography and in actuality, often
focus outward, so that many of the important "facts" of their
existence are external and, therefore, public. For example,
early biographies of American historian and writer Henry
Adams scarcely mentioned the suicide of his beloved wife
Marian (Clover) Hooper. In this silence, the biographies
follow the lead of Adams himself in *The Education of Henry
Adams*. Descriptions of his life were so linked with public
events that college education and his travels in Europe (and to
World War I, as an external event of note) receive more space
than his many years of grieving for his lost wife.

Part of the explanation for the general omission of Clover
Adams' death is that biographies tell success stories. Their
narratives build through dramatic action which recounts
accomplishments; then a subject's old age is filled with

accolades and public testaments to those accomplishments.
What place would Adams' lament for his wife, and the deep
unhappiness that wife felt in her marriage to him, have in such
a positive account?

This kind of high selectivity—a polite falsification of the
life, if you will—is justified because traditional biography
attempts to inscribe moral norms. From stories of Thomas
Jefferson and Patrick Henry to Thomas Wolfe and Harry
Truman, readers can see the way observable history is intertwined with men's lives, and then, ideally, associate the
subjects' correct behavior with the contemporary issues. Complex issues that might interfere with the reader's absorption of
the stark moral narrative may well be left out.

Traditional biography normally concentrates on the subject's accomplishments, and given that, until recently,
women's lives were seldom shaped in direct response to
history, such a focus in the writing of women's lives would be
inappropriate. One of the central questions in writing biographies of women, then, becomes, What *are* the accomplishments
in a woman's life? Or, more basically, where *does* the narrative
of a woman's life lie? Which *are* the events that must be
selected to show the essential composition of that life?

Biographers of women face the dichotomy of the public
versus the private at every turn. The issue becomes not so
much one of choice—does the bombing of Hiroshima have as
natural a place in a narrative about Sylvia Plath as it does in
the narrative about Harry S. Truman?—as one of limitation. If
Plath's writings and conversations revealed that she was more
than normally affected by the bombing, there might be a way
to incorporate the event. For Truman, of course, much of his
biography hinges on the moral judgments he made throughout his life leading up to his decision to use the bomb to end
World War II. The uses of what we think of as "history" are,
in these cases, quite dissimilar.

Definitions of "dramatic narrative" also vary. Creating
reader interest when one writes about a woman subject who
has been at home much of her life living the true "domestic
plot" is difficult. For all our supposed interest in the way
people develop, in the psychological evolution of strength and
competence, the subject of a best-selling biography today is

not ordinary life but *exceptional* life. People read biographies in the 1990s for the same reason they read them fifty or a hundred years ago, to learn about someone other than themselves. The success of a biography depicting lives of great success, great acclaim, or great personal satisfaction depends on reader expectations, and on contemporary culture's definitions of "success," "acclaim" and "satisfaction."

Even today, few women have had the kind of visibility or success that attracts public notice. Women's biography is more often based on private events because few women—including even women like Eleanor Roosevelt or Hillary Rodham Clinton—live public lives. A subject may keep private episodes purposely secret (for example, her dislike for her parents, her emotional or sexual abuse, or other unfortunate but formative childhood or adolescent incidents), or—those that become public society may regard as insignificant. When a woman spends much of her life doing housework, driven by economic need as well as societal expectation, does the biographer simply discount those hours or days or years because the activity itself is boring? Even in the hands of a skilled biographer, how dramatic can shopping and taking children to dance lessons become?

In the 1990s, we know that biographies often attempt to explain a subject's acts. Biography presents the ultimate opportunity to apply psychoanalytic knowledge; it takes insights about the figure's behavior and shapes a life story from those fragments. Traditional biography completes the narrative of the subject's life. Yet, as postmodern readers reject oversimplification—preferring an unfinished narrative or one with gaps in its construction to the deceit of the contrived finish—the form of biography must become more open to inquiry. What we have always considered good biography leaves few questions in the reader's mind. Yet those unanswered questions may bring a reader to some fulfilling involvement in the story. In the case of a subject who committed suicide, for example (Plath, John Berryman, Virginia Woolf, Vachel Lindsay, Anne Sexton, Sara Teasdale, Ernest Hemingway, Hart Crane), a biography that declines to answer every question can still provide explanations that both satisfy readers and lead them past the death to the writer's legacy.

For the subjects of most biographies, the life curve is less mysterious and less abrupt. The subject develops, accomplishes and ages into death. Sometimes biographers rearrange chronology in their telling, as Justin Kaplan did in his biography of Walt Whitman. Kaplan (1980) found the period of Whitman's old age and dying comparatively uninteresting, so he began his biography with those years. Like fiction, biography tries to avoid the completely predictable, even though by definition a life must have a logical, and literal, end. Because biography has this factual scaffolding for whatever its narrative may be, the biographer's choices about the writing come largely in the process of determining style. Finding the ideal shape, texture and pace for the story is the way biographers put their mark on the work. Formal, balanced sentences and page-long paragraphs may be appropriate for a biography of Mahatma Gandhi, but a biography of a child dying of leukemia might better be told without pretension, perhaps more poetically. *The Autobiography of a Face* (Grealy, 1994) is a striking example of the effective use of an elliptical, suggestive style. In choosing to describe only a few of the thirty operations she underwent in the reconstruction of her face after she lost most of her jaw to cancer, Lucy Grealy turned what might have been a heavily scientific and repetitious narrative into a hymn to the human spirit.

The most difficult problems in writing biography, however, extend beyond those of organization, sentence variety or language choice. They are the problems of conceptualization. Biography forces a writer to put real-life problems into place, which means inviting the reader to understand complexity rather than forcing the subject's experiences into a convenient but perhaps distorted pattern. Few life events and their motivations are simple. Just as the human subject orchestrates actions to construct the appearance of a unified or consistent identity, so must that person's biography present that self with integrity. In this regard, biography is the enactment of cultural, or social, performance.

If we define a life as one kind of performance and the way a subject views his or her life as another kind, the biographer must form a matrix of both performances. The biographer is, in fact, forced by the results of factual research to accept, to reject or to modify the subject's self-definition. My need to find Sylvia Plath's classmates and friends arose, in part, because of the temptation to use her letters to her family as a guide to her life experiences. In Plath's case, perhaps more dramatically than in many others, the self she created in her letters to her mother differed from the self she presented to her friends. The difference was so great that reading her mother's collection of that correspondence, *Letters Home* (Plath, 1975), is almost physically painful.

The performative self is often the external self, and describing it may be the easiest phase in preparing the biography. While biography draws on material about that self, the best biography also attempts to unearth the hidden, more interior and perhaps more disguised self. In so doing, it may create quite a different narrative. The story a biography tells is, in some respects, as much a fiction as the narrative the fiction writer creates: though biography is based on the subject's external and internal characteristics, it is also based on the experience of the biographer. When a biographer emphasizes the death of a subject's parent, for example, one might assume that the biographer has either experienced that loss or has intimately known someone who has. For another biographer, one whose parents are both alive, the issue of a parent's death might seem less significant.

Yet despite today's greater cultural awareness of how complicated the shaping of identity can be, we still think of biography as an art dependent on fact. The assumption is that if enough letters and manuscript materials are available, if enough photographs are scrutinized, if enough people are interviewed, somehow objective truth will surface. As Virginia Woolf (1967) wrote, "The art of biography is the most restricted of all the arts." She chose as an example Lytton Strachey, who—no matter what his genius—could not "invent" his subject. "He used to the full the biographer's power of selection and relation," but his boundary throughout remained *fact* (p. 224). While in recent years this definition of biography has been questioned, the reading public still prefers to think of biography as based on those facts characteristically missing in fiction. The market for biography continues, while the market for fiction—at least fiction by

unknown and unproven writers—diminishes. Just how close
the two forms are is a secret all biographers keep.

Finding facts and unearthing information may, in fact, be
the easiest part of writing biography. As I have suggested, the
real art of the form comes with selection: the biographer must
determine which events have been most important to the
subject. Even if the subject has not written or spoken about an
experience, the biographer has the authority to place that
event within the narrative, refashioning and revising that narrative and bringing to it more background and more insight
than even the subject may have had.

Sorting through the events of the subject's life and
creating explanations for the subject's choices, the biographer,
then, also becomes a cultural historian. Part of the writing of
any biography involves letting readers decide whether or not
the subject's choices made sense, given the cultural norms of
the times. A woman's defiance in the nineteenth century need
not have involved the murder of a lover, a minister or a parent;
it might well have been her decision not to marry or to remove
herself from the community, as with Emily Dickinson, who
chose seclusion in her father's home rather than the life of
community service thought appropriate for most unmarried
women in the latter half of the nineteenth century. It took
Adrienne Rich's empathetic essay on Dickinson—speculating
that her choice to withdraw from communal life was a
reasonable means of giving herself permission and time and
space to become the poet she was—to adjust the public's
opinion of the "strange" woman poet. Once Dickinson could
be seen as a hard-working, ambitious writer, as serious about
her art as her peer Walt Whitman was or her followers in the
twentieth century were, the factual biography of her life
became more understandable.

One obvious problem with writing the stories of women's
lives is that a great many of their normal life events have been
called unsuitable or inappropriate for literary treatment. If a
reader expects a dominant focus on external events—on the
Civil War, or stock market crashes, or the deepest snow of the
1970s—then to find a narrative attending at length to such
female biological processes as menstruation, pregnancies and
childbirths, miscarriages and menopause, as well as general

sexual experience, may cause some readers and biographers to wonder, Does this material belong in a biography? Yet for women subjects, whose lives nearly always bridge the public and the private, a biography that simplifies or ignores the complex would be inaccurate.

Life processes can be both unliterary and embarrassing, but they may be necessary to an understanding of the subject's development. Sylvia Plath's description of a woman's vaginal tear in *The Bell Jar* (1971) replicated her own frightening first sexual experience, yet such details as the extensive bleeding—the blood pooling in Esther Greenwood's shoes and through layers of folded towels—struck some readers as being in poor taste. Similarly, Plath's insistence that she breastfeed her children (in the early 1960s) was atypical for that generation of mothers, and becomes important in showing how intensely concerned she was about her children. If what a woman does in her household, in her family life, on a daily basis, is considered valueless to her biography, the representation of women's lives will be badly skewed.

Portraying women's lives adds the complexity of addressing negative impressions of the reading public. (While men's lives present the same problem, social censure of their behavior seems muted in comparison with reactions to women's histories.) If a woman is promiscuous, what kind of response will readers have to this aspect of her existence? If Isak Dinesen, for instance, had contracted her syphilis of the spine—which brought her decades of physical agony and debilitation—from intercourse not with her husband but with a casual lover, the now-universal sympathy for her might instead be denigration. Reactions to women's choices tend to be as complex as the choices themselves. To acknowledge that Gertrude Stein and Alice Toklas had a lesbian "marriage" for nearly forty years is to satisfy some readers and alienate others. Like most forms of art, biography can be double-edged; portraying a woman's life faithfully and explicitly is sometimes dangerous for as many reasons as there are readers of biography.

The psychological development of creative or otherwise achieving women who are candidates for biographies is another problematic focus. Louise DeSalvo's (1989) *Virginia*

Woolf: The Impact of Childhood Sexual Abuse on Her Life and Work emphasized Woolf's sexual victimization by her stepbrothers. The book received a range of impassioned responses. Even though DeSalvo showed carefully, and with astute readings of Woolf's fiction, how the writer used disguising strategies in her work (one hallmark of the psyche struggling to hide past experience, or perhaps failing to acknowledge that experience at all), the biographer's attention to sexual matters was often criticized. Similarly, in the first volume of her biography *Willa Cather: The Emerging Voice*, Sharon O'Brien (1987) described Cather as a lesbian, in the sense of the word as she used it, disapproval was once again the response. Unfortunately, many of the tragedies that mark people's lives—rape, incest and emotional and physical victimization—fall today into the category of "women's issues." Although the male subject who has been victimized by these same traumas—as well as by such more socially acceptable traumas as war fears and wounds—has been written about for years, somehow naming the trauma in women's lives becomes controversial. In fact, when a biographer names a female subject's injuries, he or she may be accused of being political or of sensationalizing the story. Disclosing certain kinds of details about a woman's life is sometimes seen as an arbitrary choice rather than a search for the truth. The long-standing suspicion in literary circles of matters psychoanalytic also colors readers' reactions to the inclusion of such material.

It can be hard to judge just where public opinion will fall on each controversial matter. After I had completed a biographical study of Southern writer Ellen Glasgow's fiction, I alluded in an appendix to her lengthy affair with a married man (Wagner-Martin, 1982). Early in her career, this experience (it ended painfully) influenced the romanticism of many of her early novels; therefore, it seemed completely valid that the book mention it. Unfortunately, at that time in critical circles, Glasgow enjoyed a reputation as an almost-genderless chronicler of Southern history. To give her a personal life (and particularly an objectionable one) and to insist that her gender was crucial to her work was so dangerous that for the first time in my career, I had difficulty placing the manuscript. For every university press that sent the book to two outside readers, at least one reading came back negative—largely because of my emphasis on "Miss Ellen's" personal life. Finally, the modest book was published, and to universally good reviews. But its use of the then-objectionable biographical material had nearly prevented its appearance.

Another kind of dismissal of information about women's lives may occur when an event seems liable to attract a "sentimental" reaction. Negatively charged from years of condemnation in literary history, the word "sentimental" suggests a melodramatic evocation of feeling, a tactic contrived to arouse a stock response. The negative connotations of the word, and the fact that we often find it applied to women's lives or writings, should be balanced with the reminder that not everything that evokes emotion is false or excessive. In writing the story of Gertrude Stein's life, my handling of two "sentimental" situations during her adolescence—the deaths of her parents—became a source of disagreement with my first editor. I refuse to believe that the long confinement of Stein's mother before her death from abdominal cancer, from the time Gertrude was eleven until she was fourteen, had no effect on her choices in life—particularly her choice to specialize in women's medicine when she studied at Johns Hopkins Medical School, the choice that led to such differences of opinion with her professors that she never completed her degree. In the case of the death of her father, which was sudden and somewhat macabre, the effect on both Gertrude and Leo was traumatic in a strangely positive way.

While my emphasis on the death of the Stein parents has not been criticized in reviews of *"Favored Strangers": Gertrude Stein and Her Family* (Wagner-Martin, 1995), another recent biography that involves death—in this case the death of an adult daughter—and its author have received stern criticism. Novelist Isabel Allende's *Paula* (1994) presents a moving account of her daughter's affliction with porphyria just a year after her marriage. Paula fell quickly into a coma which led, a year later, to her death. The criticism centers on the fact that Allende took the opportunity of this death, a tragedy marked by the almost desperate sadness of both mother and husband, to tell a number of family stories. Rather than biography in the traditional sense of the word, *Paula* is,

the critics contend, just another piece of Allende's commer-
cially successful writing.

There is, however, no question *whose* story this is, and the
author makes doubly sure the reader understands her motivation for writing the book in her dramatic opening. She
disguises the narrative she writes as a story she is telling to her
unconscious child. In fact, the book begins, "Listen, Paula. I
am going to tell you a story, so that when you wake up you
will not feel so lost." Notice that in her traditional role as
comforter, the mother avoids a fairy tale made to distract the
child; rather, she tells the story of their family, mother's
family and daughter's, and such an exploration of family
history is apt because Paula's illness is hereditary. She has
learned several years before that she has porphyria, an illness
so rare that physicians decline to specialize in it. Thus, "the
legend of our family begins at the end of the last century,
when a robust Basque sailor disembarked on the coast of Chile
with his mother's reliquary strung around his neck" (p. 3).

Biography as love letter, Allende's account stresses the ad-
hesion of family members. We come to realize that mothers'
gifts tie even adventurous men to life. Narrative as interactive
dialogue is the format of the early section of the book.
Allende says, "Where are you wandering, Paula? How will you
be when you wake up? Will you be the same woman, or will
we be like strangers and have to learn to know one another all
over again? Will you have your memory or will I need to sit
patiently and relate the entire story of your twenty-eight years
and my forty-nine?" (p. 7). The dialogue of the biography
insists that this family bond, this mother-daughter nexus, is
permanent, no matter the condition of the child. "When you
wake up we will have months, maybe years, to piece together
the broken fragments of your past" (p. 8). Their lives, like the
book, will form a joint account; it is going to exist despite the
fragility of human memory and human life.

The form of the biography, too, demands that the reader
realize it is Paula's story. *Paula* is divided into two parts. The
first describes the illness and Paula's care in a Madrid hospital
from December of 1991 through May of 1992. The second
part, from May through December 1992, charts Paula's
removal to the Allende's California home, and being cared for

there until her death. During the second section, as Paula continues to lie in a coma, Allende brings the control of her life story into her own hands. Late in her illness her husband tells Isabel that during their honeymoon, Paula had awakened from a terrible nightmare and had immediately written a letter, which she sealed and marked, "To be opened after I die." Paula's prescient words, then, haunt the narrative. The actual opening of the letter occurs after months of watching Paula go further and further into what physicians term the brain-dead condition, and it occurs just a few pages from the end of the story. Paula's letter speaks directly and emphatically to the issue of keeping her body alive: "I do not want to remain trapped in my body" (p. 321). Freed from what Allende has assumed throughout to be an obligation to keep her daughter alive, she accepts the death that comes, finally, on December 6.

Through the placement of her letter, Paula regains control of her life. What she has written determines the acts that allow her to die. She is thus much more than a character in her mother's writing; she is a person with voice, volition and a harrowing understanding of what her life is to become. Throughout the biography, Allende honors that sense of Paula as sentient and powerful. She has carefully drawn her as much more than her daughter; she is also the beloved grand-daughter, her father's daughter, her brother's sister and, most tragically, her husband's beloved wife. Through her craft, Isabel Allende allowed the speaking subject, her daughter, to regain control of a narrative that factually had to be focused on the child's loss of volition and eventual death: an unbearable fact that the life and the narrative had to tell.

Literarily, of course, the issue is that bereaved mothers do not write biographies of their dying children. "Sentimental," readers say; "too obvious, a play for sympathy." Whether abolitionists using the dispersal of the slave family to create anti-slavery opinion, or women writers trying to express the ends to parts of their lives, such narratives are literarily disdained. As Joan Hedrick (1994) observed in her recent biography of Harriet Beecher Stowe, much of the power of *Uncle Tom's Cabin* accrued from Stowe's own devastating pain over the loss of her child. And her attention to Little Eva's death scene, so filled with assurances of the happy life in heaven, was hardly more palliative than Allende's moving account of herself as mother doing everything possible to bring Paula as daughter back into what we know as real life.

From the literary perspective, Allende anticipated the problems her book might face. I would say that mothers writing about daughters (and more commonly, daughters writing about mothers) is a more vexing situation than fathers writing about sons, or sons about fathers. Again, gender becomes a consideration in the assessment of how much sentiment is too much, or, by implication, what good biography is. But Allende's conviction, like that of any biographer who felt compelled to write a specific biography, was that describing the life and death of Paula was significant. She undertook, primarily, to honor her subject. But she also informed her readers of the kinds of value achieved by this one particular life. For the practice of biography is "life-writing" in a number of senses, and one of the most important of these is the sharing of a moral perspective that, through the art of the biography, may prove as convincing for the reader as it has been for the writer.

Chapter Seven

Black Subject, White Biographer

Wayne J. Urban

My first book, *Why Teachers Organized* (1982), presents a straightforward history of the early teacher organizations in the United States. Beginning with a study of the teachers in the city of Atlanta, I argued a thesis about the dynamic of these organizations, namely, that early teacher organizations were conservative, devoted mainly to bread-and-butter concerns, and defensive about attacks from administrators and outsiders. I applied and slightly modified that thesis in an examination of teacher groups in Chicago and New York and in the two national organizations of the era: the National Education Association (NEA) and the American Federation of Teachers (AFT).

Upon reflection and prodded by the insights of some of my reviewers (Lazerson, 1984), I became convinced that a major weakness in my research lay in how I fit the evidence to the argument. I had neither altered nor consciously distorted the evidence. Rather, in pursuit of establishing and pursuing a thesis, I tended to shape and to pick and choose that evidence regarding the non-Atlanta organizations which supported the argument I had developed in my case study.

Further, the difficulty with my Atlanta research related to a tendency among many of us historians to look for an over-arching thesis that will encompass all of the myriad shards of reality under study. This search for generalization I attributed in particular to those historians who stress the social scientific aspect of their work. They want to study reality in ways akin

to the practice of those social scientists who value generalization and prediction over particularity and idiosyncrasy.

Thus, I based the decision to write a biography for my
next major project after my teacher union book on a desire to
conduct research distinctly different from that in which I had
just engaged. By concentrating on a single life, I might miti-
gate the various earlier problems. A biography, I thought,
would free me from the methodological straightjacket that had
bound me in my earlier work. Rather than labor to organize a
diversity of data according to an overarching theme, I thought,
a biography—a life study—would probably organize itself.
People are born, mature, marry (or decline to marry), raise a
family, pursue a mature work life alongside of and in some
relationship to their family life, and eventually retire and die.
In concentrating on one individual, I could concern myself
more with the qualitative and literary aspects of the historical
enterprise than with the evidentiary and logical problems of
how one explanation applies to several parts of reality.

My next book, *Black Scholar: Horace Mann Bond, 1904-
1972* (1992), was the result of this biographical foray. Yet, I
decided to do more than just a biography: I wished to write
the biography of an historian of education. I made this decision because I wanted to study a life that was in some ways
similar to my own. I assumed my personal experience would
provide a clear window and an interesting perspective on someone whose life work resembled mine. I narrowed the universe
of educational historians to those who practiced their craft
either in, or on, the American South, the region where I had
spent most of my time as a mature scholar and to which I had
paid the closest attention in my work. By the time I decided to
write a biography, the universe of prospective subjects had
dwindled to two. I would study either Edgar Wallace Knight or
Horace Mann Bond and, since another educational historian
had recently published an article on Knight, I leaned toward
Bond. (Also, I knew Bond's widow was still living in Atlanta
and was positively inclined toward the project, and that the
Bond papers were catalogued at the University of Massachusetts Library in Amherst.)

All of these decisions reflected a desire on my part to
move toward the humanistic, individualistic and interpretive

aspects of historical study and away from the generalizing, social science side of historical endeavor. The process and priorities that drove me to the Bond biography only indirectly related to the racial aspect of the study. Yet that aspect became the one of primary interest to most of my reviewers and, I suspect, to many of my readers. The dynamics of a White biographer and a Black subject still prove interesting, particularly as I now attempt to understand and explore postmodernism, race-relations in scholarship, and the relationship of a scholar of a majority race writing a biography of a subject from the most visible and important minority race. (I use the term "race" here only in a vernacular or popular vein. In no sense do I use the term to impart any absolute quality.)

Any White American writing about an African American in the late twentieth century must do so with some trepidation. It is a time when African Americans are reclaiming themselves in a variety of ways from the shackles of their White oppressors. One of the sites of this reclamation project is the scholarly arena where Whites who study Blacks run an increased risk of alienating Black audiences by misunderstanding and misrepresenting their subjects. The potential for misunderstanding comes from the fact that White people are not Black people, have not experienced much of what Black people have experienced, and are thus handicapped when interpreting the Black experience. Of course, both the "White experience" and the "Black experience" are general concepts hiding as much as they reveal. The many individual experiences of Blacks and Whites call into some question the aptness of the two general categories. Yet, it is difficult to argue against some reality in those general categories, even if the experiences of individuals within them differ dramatically.

Given some of the realities of the Black experience in the United States of America—slavery, then emancipation accompanied and followed by vile discrimination and racism—one can easily understand the suspicions of many Black activists and scholars about the motives of White scholars who study Black subjects. Conversely, the reluctance of White scholars to study Black subjects and to present the results of their studies to Black audiences is also understandable. Having said all this, however, I must note that much of what we know about Black history today results from the efforts of White scholars who have labored productively in this field for much of the twentieth century (Meier and Rudwick, 1986).

One event in the pre-publication history of my Bond manuscript highlighted the tension embedded in my work. Its "Preface" contains the following paragraph:

> Something that helped me to understand Bond was the parallel between his circumstances and those of my father. Members of the same generation, born within four years of each other, they shared the fire to achieve that motivated many Americans, whether they were descended, as was my father, from immigrants, or they were descended, as was Bond, from slaves. Although I was only ten years old when my father died, I have strong memories of his putting in exceedingly long hours in his medical practice in order to achieve his version of the American dream. Bond also worked fervently to achieve his image of that dream. Readers of this book will have to judge if I have adequately portrayed his pursuit of that dream (p. xi).

One of the scholars who reviewed the manuscript for the University of Georgia Press strongly urged the excision of that paragraph. The reviewer's reasoning seemed a bit murky but one can speculate that he or she resisted analogies between a White immigrant experience and the Black experience drawn so glibly without qualification. But I chose to keep the paragraph. I reasoned that whatever the consequences, it was an honest statement of one of the ways in which I came to see a link between Bond's personal motivations and of those close to me; thus, I hoped to understand Bond.

Still, I would be wrong to believe that I came completely or even partially to understand Horace Bond. That judgment is for readers to make; Black readers and White readers may reach different conclusions on that issue or at least be inclined differently in their judgment of the aptness of my portrayal of Bond.

One reason for this potential difference in judgment is that the Black experience in American history embodies a dual quality uncharacteristic of most if not all versions of the White American experience. I am referring here to a quality first pointed out in print by W. E. B. DuBois early in the twentieth century. The African American, DuBois observed, "ever feels his twoness—an American, a Negro; two souls, two thoughts, two unreconciled strivings" (D. L. Lewis, 1993, p. 281). The irreconcilability of the strivings is what White Americans have difficulty understanding. Few White Americans have known such irreconcilability in their own experiences, and this undoubtedly is what undergirds the suspicions that many Black scholars and intellectuals bring to any consideration of a White scholar's interpretations of Black subjects. If Whites cannot "feel" the twoness, how can it inform their work?

Still this realization fails to negate completely the insights of White scholars into Black subjects; it is only to say that they can glimpse just part of the Black experience. Such White scholars as August Meier (1963) and Eugene Genovese (1968) who devoted their professional lives to studying the Black experience have described the difficulty as follows: Within the dualistic African American experience, there has been a side inescapably part of the larger American experience and also a side inescapably "national" and separate from the American experience. White scholars who study African Americans write largely as external observers of the Black experience while Black scholars write largely from within the experience. These points of view—which we can label external and internal, respectively—are both necessary for a complete understanding of the African American experience. If they are to be incorporated together in the work of one scholar, it is much likelier they will be found in the work of a Black scholar than a White scholar.

It seems to follow then that my biography of Horace Mann Bond is just that, a White's interpretation of the life of an African American, an interpretation driven by the concerns of an outsider who made every effort to understand that life as much as he could, but an outsider nonetheless. In no sense did I write the "definitive" interpretation of Bond's life. Other interpretations, particularly ones by African Americans, could and should differ in tone and substance from the work I produced.

A return to my own life, as it intersected with issues raised in writing Bond's biography, adds another dimension to this work. The major theme of *Black Scholar* is the tension between scholarship and administration in the career of Horace Mann Bond. I contend that Bond was an excellent scholar of African American history and education whose scholarly career was stunted when he became a college administrator. Administration diverted Bond despite his constant efforts to pursue the scholarly vocation.

Further, I argue that Bond did not become an administrator simply by his own choice. A Black scholar in Black colleges, he was effectively prevented from competing for faculty positions at White colleges and universities, positions that would have encouraged and rewarded him for his scholarly accomplishments. Black colleges offered few positions for scholars, particularly in the history of education. Most Black college faculty members teach several often large classes a semester. In the academic pecking order, the faculty member from a Black college was distinctly inferior in status and in pay to the administrators, and especially to the college president. Given this situation and given Bond's ambition to achieve for himself and his family, one should not be surprised that he became an administrator and, eventually, the president of two Black colleges.

Bond's administrative career was marked by initial success but ultimate failure, as he progressed through several roles. While he reached the position of college president, I initially appraised his administrative work as mediocre at best. But my conversations with his wife, Julia Washington Bond, showed me something that I had missed. From my biographical point of view, Bond's Lincoln University years were beset by conflict. Mrs. Bond pointed out, however, that from the family's point of view, these were happy years. "It was a wonderful place to raise a family," she told me.

But every administrative position, successful or not, curtailed Bond's scholarly accomplishments. This tension between scholarship and administration, the ultimate resolution in favor of administration, and the interruption of a promising scholarly career constitute the main story line in my biography. I have no doubt, from a close reading of his professional papers and from talks with several of his colleagues, that Bond knew what was happening to his career and did his best to maintain his scholarly interests under the increasing demands of administrative work. I also have no doubt, though I am less confident that Bond saw it, that his later scholarship was inferior to what he produced early in his career.

The scholar-administrator tension I emphasized in my biography was an experience with which I was personally familiar. Shortly before embarking on the biography, I ended a seven-year period as chairperson of an academic department of twenty-five faculty members from three different academic specialties. In those years, I became increasingly uncomfortable with the amount of time that day-to-day administrative work and worry over its consequences was taking away from my own scholarly output. That discomfort, which led to my resignation from the chair's position and, two years later, a research leave to work on the biography sensitized me to the discomfort I found in Bond's own accounts of his scholarly interests and administrative duties.

Thus, the personal dimension I sought in writing the biography entered *Black Scholar* in an unexpected way. I had been less than acutely attuned to the personal dimension in Bond's life; in fact, this dimension remains notably absent from my biography because Bond removed practically all personal references and excised most of the personal material from his papers before his death. (I noted this problem in the "Preface," but most reviewers persisted in commenting on the biography's lack of the personal dimension.) What was present, however, was an important struggle in Bond's life remarkably similar to one I had just experienced in my own. Some could argue that I made too much out of Bond's scholar-versus-administrator dilemma, reflecting my own circumstances. But I would dispute that conclusion. The tension was definitely there in Bond's life, and he frequently pondered it and its consequences for his own career. Yet I can also see that had the tension been less compelling in my own life, I could have missed understanding and appreciating it in Bond's. Further, in choosing this tension for the theme of my biography I may well have told the reader a good deal more about me than I intended.

Interestingly, the reviews that emphasized the scholar-administrator tension in Bond's life included some of the most favorable reviews the book received (Butchart, 1993; B. Franklin, 1993; Stameshkin, 1993). All these reviews came from scholars who were either then engaged, or had been engaged, in administrative work. All were by White historians of education. I might deduce from this response that I captured a reality which made Bond and his life accessible to White historians of education. Conversely, the reviews of the book by Black scholars, while not uncomplimentary, focused on what was missing in the work (Barksdale, 1993; V. P. Franklin, 1993). V. P. Franklin, for example, concluded that the biography "ultimately fails to define Bond's place in an emerging African-American intellectual tradition in the United States." It is a fair criticism. It also seems to be an aspect of Bond's life and work that could be more fully and fairly covered by an African American biographer steeped personally as well as professionally in that tradition.

Conclusion

In what ways has this biographical study contributed to my own scholarly development? First, both my earlier stated preference for particularity and my suspicion of overarching generalizations have been reinforced. My Bond study confirmed for me the richness and diversity I saw in a single life as well as my own inadequacies when challenged to capture all of its qualities. With regard to generalization, the Bond book did not solve the problem completely. My positing of the scholar-administrator tension as the prominent theme in Bond's life testifies both to the need for some organizing principle in a biographical study and to the subtler aspects, in Bond's case centered mainly on his personal life, that such an organization sometimes precludes.

Second, the study pushed me to consider carefully my own intellectual stance in the light of two current trends in scholarship, Afrocentrism and postmodernism. While I am by no means an Afrocentrist, after twenty-eight years of working in the South, I am sensitive to the needs of African Americans to recover and claim their own history. In fact, I am personally immersed in this process as I recover the ethnic consciousness of the Polish-American immigrant experience. When I read the autobiography of a Mexican American, like Richard

Rodriguez's *Hunger of Memory* (1982), or an account of the tensions in the cultural evolution of twentieth-century Mexican American, like George Sanchez's *Becoming Mexican American* (1993), I feel an empathy based on some personal familiarity with the issues and problems discussed there.

But while I have tried to be open to new methodological and ideological currents in my work, and have sought here and elsewhere to be critical of my own scholarship, I remain unconvinced of the need to make the wholesale alteration in my work postmodernism requires. While I find the notions of perspectivism embedded in postmodernism both attractive and compelling, I find the radical subjectivity embraced by some postmodernists alien. Like Joyce Appleby, Lynn Hunt and Margaret Jacob, authors of *Telling the Truth About History* (1994), I remain committed to the value of the narrative form in history. As they write, "Historians cannot capture the fullness of the past experience any more than individual memories can; they only have the traces or residues of the past, and their accounts are necessarily partial." But they go on:

> We see no reason to conclude that because there is a gap between reality and its narration (its representation), the narration in some fundamental sense is inherently invalid. Just because narrations are human creations does not make them all equally fictitious or mythical (pp. 234-235).

In a sense, then, I take a position on the methodological issue of the particular versus the universal similar to the position I (along with Appleby, Hunt, and Jacob) take on the radical perspectivism suggested by Afrocentrism and explicated by postmodernism. Perhaps I am best described as a chastened modernist scholar, sensitive to the value of the particular and the perspectival at the same time I am reluctant to relinquish the general or the quest for accuracy in historical and biographical description.

Chapter Eight

Trust and Memory:
Explorations in Oral History and Biography

Alan Wieder

"Biography is history made personal."

The biographer brings out this "character of being human" in his or her research. Oral history is a major aspect of biographical work and offers a personal perspective— people's spoken recollections and reflections—to biographical studies. When biography is described as the "human heart of history," I see the process of oral history as permitting a biographer to shape complex issues or concerns of an individual or group of individuals. I view oral history as the heart of biographical research; its personal dimension humanizes the research while also raising and magnifying issues not always a concern in other research methodologies. Moreover, its personal dimension humanizes the researcher.

Recently, I saw "history become personal" through the trust an interviewee placed in me. I came to see as well how this trust demanded certain responsibilities from me as an oral interviewer. An oral historian is always aware of the issues of memory and accuracy as he or she conducts an interview:

> To be sure, memory is a fallible instrument, whether in an interview, a letter, or a written reminiscence. In an interview, however, the biographer-historian has a unique opportunity to ask questions. This can yield significant material, so long as the interviewer is honest and avoids leading questions that trap

the person into saying what the interviewer wants to hear. (Oates, 1991, p. 29)

True enough, but let me take the conversation in another direction and examine aspects of truth and fact and the complexity of memory and human interaction through the interviewer-interviewee relationship. It is the story of sex and controversy—appropriate topics for a commercial biography. Yet I describe not the writing of a biography but, instead, the oral history of a controversial education program in a southern suburb. Perhaps I am in the midst of preparing a biographical vignette; I am uncertain. I am certain, however, that this study has forced me to reexamine the place of the researcher in biographical work.

The Trust
The primary source for the sex education study was a forty-six-year-old man named Hank Chardos, the controversial chairperson of a sex education committee in a South Carolina suburb with a spirited controversy over its curriculum. Chardos was the most vocal supporter of an abstinence-only curriculum; he was also the president of Birthright in South Carolina. I called Chardos to ask if he would speak with me about his committee and the controversy over sex education. I explained I was a professor at the university interested in telling the story of the controversy. He took my phone number and promised to call me back within a couple of days to set up an appointment. What I did not know until months later was that he checked me out before he called back. He spoke with one of my colleagues who happened to be his ally on the sexuality education committee. Then he called back and we scheduled an afternoon interview at his office at the Internal Revenue Service.

I had read many newspaper articles on the controversy before I called Hank Chardos, and I reviewed them on the eve of our first interview. I prepared for the interview as always by sharpening pencils, setting out a new legal pad, and making sure my tape recorder worked. I went to Chardos' office ready to begin the interview for my study. But things do not always go as planned in oral interviewing, and I never took a note or turned on the recorder. Still, this initial meeting was one of the most important interviews I have conducted. Chardos reminded me of the magnitude of a human being agreeing to be interviewed. He reminded me of the trust involved when people tell other people their stories— especially when those stories are taped for later retelling. He reminded me of the responsibility of the interviewer when someone bestows this trust.

At that first meeting, then, we interviewed each other. Chardos was trying to decide if he wanted to share his recollections and reflections, and he asked me questions about my work and my reasons for doing the study. He asked why I wanted to interview him. I described some of my work and explained that I thought the story of the controversy over sex education was important to tell. He listened and decided to let me tell this controversial story. He knew that our views differed ideologically, but he was ready to trust me—or at least he was willing to let me begin interviewing him.

Chardos told me he had turned down other interviewers and reemphasized that he was putting himself on the line. Throughout our interviews, I continued to reflect on this aspect of the human reality of the interview process. Chardos was the teacher at this initial meeting, and his teaching reached deep within me to establish an internal understanding of my own responsibility not to betray his trust.

I began at our first meeting by communicating some self-imposed routines. I told Chardos I would provide him with transcripts after each interview, and he could make comments and correct errors. I also told him I would give him draft copies of the essays I wrote. But I emphasized that the written work would be *my* attempt to tell the story as honestly as possible.

As it turned out, a mutual trust did form. I met with Chardos thirteen more times over the next six months. We met at my office, its walls covered with my black and white photographic portraits of children, from 6:30 to 8:00 in the morning before Chardos had to report to work. He enjoyed the photographs and felt comfortable in this setting. So did I. More and more trust developed, and it remained throughout our meetings in spite of the fact that I often asked him to reflect on his conservative views and consider the liberal position. Most important, though, were his recollections and reflections on his views and the events of the sex education controversy. In retrospect, I am sure that Chardos was ready to trust someone because he wanted to tell his story. I do not mean that he would have spoken to just anyone who came along. I doubt he would have been comfortable aiding a study by someone from Planned Parenthood, for example. He was definitely aware, though, that my views were much more liberal than his and that I did not support abstinence-only sex education.

Hank Chardos displayed an enormous leap of faith entrusting a stranger with his story. I kept thinking of Dick Cavett's interviews with Norman Mailer many years ago when Mailer complained that the interviewer never told the whole truth and always made him look bad—that Cavett and his producers constructed a false reality. With this criticism in mind, I worked to interview Hank Chardos. I had not thought seriously about how sacred the interview process was since the early 1980s when I interviewed those African American families who had allowed their six-year-old daughters to integrate the New Orleans public schools. The sacredness of those interviews was clear because the toll it took on some of the families was heavy. The lesson I learned from Chardos, though, was more transferable and universal to the interview process and to the interviewer-interviewee relationship. Chardos trusted me to do justice to his life and his story, and he has forced me, as well as the students I teach, to keep this sacred trust.

Memory and Interaction

The *International Journal of Oral History* and *Oral History Review* have both published scholarly work on memory, interaction and oral history. The *Journal of American History* devoted its March 1989 issue to history and memory. The editor of that issue, David Thelin, emphasized that the literature concludes that memory is *constructed* rather than reproduced. This perspective, of course, weds memory to interaction and it also brings up other issues: personal versus collective memory and the effects of class, race, gender, ethnicity, culture, geography, age and so forth. How does the present as well as the time between events affect the construction of memory? Why do we construct—shape or reshape; include or omit; recall or distort; separate or combine; and organize or reorganize? These and related questions resist easy or even specific answers. A recent collection of Michael Frisch's essays, *A Shared Authority* (1994), displays the relationship between oral history and memory. Frisch used oral history because of its democratic possibilities, because it is the construction of knowledge by the interviewer and interviewee:

> What is most compelling about oral history and public history is a capacity to redefine and redistribute intellectual authority, so that this might be shared more broadly in historical research and communication rather than continuing to serve as an instrument of power and hierarchy (p. xx).

He thought about titling his book *A Shared Author-ity* since the interviewer and interviewee are partners in the construction of the past. Frisch referred to Studs Terkel's oral history of the Great Depression, *Hard Times*, and noted that Terkel called this "a memory book." Frisch even cited Terkel's quote of Steinbeck's Pa Joad: "He's tellin' the truth, awright. The truth for him. He wasn't makin' nothin' up" (p. 9).

Because oral history books are at least partially "memory books," they raise even more questions. How do people select their memories? What cultural process do they follow? How do we promote self-conscious and reflective memory? What happens to experience on the way to becoming memory? Frisch explained that we probe these questions by understanding who is talking, what they are talking about, and what sort of statements they are making. Frisch expressed surprise when reviewers of *Hard Times* almost exclusively referred to it as a testament to the American spirit. His response illustrates the probing of oral history and memory:

> Anyone who has wondered why the Depression crisis did not produce more focused critiques of American capitalism and culture, more sustained efforts to see fundamental structural change, will find more evidence in the interior of these

testimonies than in any other source I know. By seeing people
turn history into biographical memory, general into particular,
we see how they tried to retain deeper validation of their life
and society, and how they deferred the deeper cultural judgment
implied by the Depression crisis (p. 12).

Frisch addressed questions of class and culture and our
collective and personal present when he considered memory
and oral history. He went further to discuss our recollections
and reflections on the Vietnam War. Frisch referred to it as
"selective amnesia." We might translate this into opposite oral
history poles—glorification or horrification. In the former the
past represents everything that is ideal. An example might be
our representations of the 1950s through *Happy Days* or
Ozzie and Harriet.

The horrifiers, on the other hand, view the past as evil. The
present is good while the past was bad and ignorant. Of
course, this view of the past is inaccurate as well as arrogant. It
also distorts the present. In both cases, one uses memory to
justify one's present view. Frisch whimsically referred to it as
IGNORE-ance.

While possibilities abound within the interview process,
communication between the interviewer and interviewee
sometimes seems impossible. Martin Buber's *I and Thou*
comes to mind in any discussion of human interaction. The
vitality and importance of human beings addressing each
other as Thous—as subjects rather than objects—is the essence
of Buber's recommendations on human dialogue. All of this
is relevant to oral history, and Peter Friedlander (1975) used it
in that context in *The Emergence of a UAW Local*. Friedlander
analyzed the interaction involved in the construction of
history by the interviewer and interviewee. This construction,
of course, connects directly to memory, and Friedlander called
the interview process "critical dialogue."

Friedlander also examined language and the difficulty of
communication, and he concluded that even when the oral
historian and the informant have similar backgrounds, it can
be difficult for them to find a common language. It is
possible. Friedlander did it in his work and the examples here
from my own research show two parties working towards

dialogue, an oral historian working with interviewees mutually to locate historical truth.

This cooperative search is the job of the biographer. The work proceeds with sensitivity and grace for, as Vandiver (1983) stated, "Empathy is biography's quintessential quality —without it lives are mere chronicle. It is the biographer's spark of creation" (pp. 16-17). Yet, empathy is not a trait often discussed in research courses. Oral interviews are an important aspect of this educational research because they offer a personal perspective—people's spoken recollections and reflections. Oral history provides a place for educational researchers and biographers both to hear about the importance of honoring the uniqueness of the human spirit and to experience the trust a subject places in the researcher—to transcend, that is, both the personal and collective blocks that alter memory. This type of interaction—interaction that probes the heart and soul and allows the mind to represent the individual and personal as well as the public and collective—I now see as the human heart of history.

PART THREE

Archival Research and
Educational Biography

Introduction

No documents, no history.
    Fustel de Coulanges

While a good deal of research depends upon data gathered by the investigator, the biographer often relies on documents preserved by others. Diaries can be a blessing; however, biographers gladly examine assorted local newspapers, institutional descriptions, church and civic records and various ephemera once their existence is known. Archival repositories take any form—libraries and museums, attics and garages—any place where people keep large amounts of "stuff" that helps a biographer to create and recreate a life after searching through the clutter of boxes or the extensive listings of a finder's guide. As Leon Edel (1981) wrote,

> I remember finding a fur neckpiece in a box that contained letters of Henry James in the Library of Congress. The fur, I was told, was public property, and it was a question whether it should be quietly burned or properly sequestered. It told me merely that the lady who had received the letters got her archives mixed with her wardrobe. Yet perhaps that mangy little fur had its place. The oddest scrap of paper sometimes takes on an awesome significance after the passage of time. . . No, we must allow papers to accumulate in a laissez-faire spirit. . . . Our concern is how to deal with this clutter. . . . (p. 24).

"Clutter" comes with rules, however, especially when materials are acquired by a repository. Entering an archives for the first time can unnerve the neophyte biographer. The rules become shibboleths to the uninformed. Herbert Hartsook has prepared an introduction for those who wish to draw upon the resources of archives and special collections. Hartsook describes how staff members can greatly assist one's research efforts and how they transform "clutter" into thoughtfully organized and preserved data. Hartsook reaffirms the archivist's motto: "There is little virtue in mere acquisition if it is divorced from intelligent purpose," and he explains these purposes.

The federal government currently generates in four months documents equal in amount to those produced during the first 124 years of *The Nation's* life—that is, from Washington to Wilson. Yet, we learn that not all documents— governmental, institutional, personal—are available to the research community even when donated to a repository. Fair use and its accompanying tentacles of copyright, literary property rights and privacy wreak havoc for the researcher. Avoiding legal jargon, Philo Hutcheson discusses such research questions from his perspective as a higher education biographer and, in so doing, offers common-sense guidance for biographical researchers.

While Hutcheson stresses caveats and concerns for fair use, Geraldine Joncich Clifford describes how one researcher goes about obtaining biographical information of a "somewhat unknown" figure: Edyth Astrid Ferris, a woman researcher who completed a master's degree in 1926 at the University of Iowa. With only this sparse information, Clifford proceeds to describe the preliminary research for the preparation of a biographical portrayal. Edward Beauchamp (1990) has stated that "the field of educational biography is wide open. There are scores of interesting and important men and women in search of a sensitive biographer" (pp. 2-3). As Clifford shows, any "bit" of evidence can serve as a starting point for inquiry and as a way to answer Beauchamp's call for sensitive biographical studies.

This section concludes with a "narrative of transformation," Louis M. Smith's account of an ethnographer becoming entranced by the experience of archival and biographical work. Smith's earlier presentation version of this essay convinced me, in fact, to undertake this collection.

Stephen Oates entitled his 1986 collection of biographical essays "Biography as High Adventure." Smith wonderfully depicts this same spirit with his account of working with the Barlow Papers.

Note

Herbert J. Hartsook delivered a presentation version of his essay at the 1993 keynote session of the Explorations in Biographical Method Conference at the Museum of Education, University of South Carolina. Philo Hutcheson delivered a presentation version of his essay at the 1996 roundtable session of the Archival and Biographical Research SIG of AERA. "The Historical Recovery of Edyth Astrid Ferris" by Geraldine Joncich Clifford is reprinted with the permission of AERA; it first appeared in the *Educational Researcher, 17* (4), May 1988, pp. 4-7. Louis M. Smith delivered a presentation version of his essay at the 1992 keynote session of the Archival and Biographical Research SIG of AERA.

Chapter Nine

Unique Resources:
Research in Archival Collections

Herbert J. Hartsook

Archives and other special collections repositories are homes to unique scholarly resources. Although similar to libraries, critical differences exist in the nature of the materials each type of institution holds. Libraries chiefly make accessible books, journals, newspapers and other published materials. Their holdings are often widely available and circulate for the benefit of their patrons. Archives and special collections repositories chiefly hold unique materials available for study only at the repository; these documents do not normally circulate. Repositories differ dramatically in their individual collecting goals. Most institutions have a clearly stated collection policy outlining their reason for existence and the nature of the material they collect. My institution, The South Caroliniana Library, collects "newspapers, manuscripts, monographs, pamphlets, serials, maps, audio-visual recordings and visual images documenting all aspects of the history and culture of South Carolina." Many special collections repositories have similar, regional collecting focuses. Others have a national focus defined thematically, like Wayne State University's Walter P. Reuther Library, home to the Archives of Labor and Urban Affairs, documenting "the American labor movement, with special emphasis upon industrial unionism," or by historic era, like the University of Michigan's Clements Library, which documents America "from the period of discovery and early exploration in the 16th Century through the 19th Century."

Government records are usually collected and preserved by government archives. Archives are generally defined as repositories of those official records of a government, organization or business deemed to have permanent historic value. The National Archives and Records Service maintains the archives of the federal government. Most if not all states have an archival agency responsible for maintaining the papers of the governor and the records of the legislature, state judiciary and other departments and agencies. Generally, these archival departments do not hold private papers.

Special collections repositories are often affiliated with a college or university and may play important roles in supporting graduate research programs. For example, South Carolina is fairly typical in having a number of repositories located across the state as well as important South Carolina collections held outside of the state by repositories with a regional or national collecting theme, and the Southern Historical Collections at the University of North Carolina and the Library of Congress each hold important South Carolina collections. Typically, repositories collect broadly and try to document the life of the common people as well as the elite. The papers of three generations of a farming family (1850–c. 1920) might be collected to document the concerns and lifestyles of a typical family of that period. Diaries, correspondence, account books, school records and other materials all serve to shed light upon a family, geographic area, style of living or period in history.

A biographer's research subject and travel budget will determine what repositories he or she should contact. The identification of repositories whose holdings might pertain to a topic grows ever easier thanks to such reference tools as the National Union Catalog of Manuscripts Collections (produced by the Library of Congress and recently upgraded to an on-line system), the publication of guides to individual repositories, and recent work to standardize collection descriptions at the national level. National databases describing book and manuscript holdings are gaining widespread popularity and will soon supplant printed guides for locating relevant documentation. The most common of these are the Research Libraries Information Network (RLIN) and the On Line Union Catalog (OCLC), originally known as the Ohio Computer Library Catalog. RLIN contains detailed descriptions of non-book materials including manuscript collections, maps, oral histories, audio-visual records and more, held in and outside of the United States. OCLC contains full bibliographic descriptions for more than 32 million books, serials, manuscripts, audio-visual materials, maps, music scores and computer readable files. Updated daily, OCLC reflects records at member libraries worldwide and the Library of Congress. Finally, many repositories establish home pages on the Internet that include statements describing their collecting policies, hours of operation, names and phone numbers of staff members, descriptions of primary holdings, and in some cases, finding aids and even texts of actual documents.

The Repository and Archival Collections

Archives and manuscripts repositories may appear to be static entities, charged with safeguarding old or even ancient documents. But this impression is superficial. Many repositories strive to document contemporary affairs just as they do earlier eras. Each year, my repository acquires remarkable collections dating from the 18th and 19th centuries, but we also seek out contemporary collections ranging from the papers of key members of our Congressional delegation to those of leading architectural firms and contemporary authors.

One can break archival work down into five broad categories: administration, collection development, processing (the preparation of collections for study), conservation and reference. Each area is important—none more than another —and each has an impact upon the researcher's ability to locate and use the collected documents efficiently. Collection development, also referred to as field work, entails the identification, solicitation, negotiation for and transfer of collections to a repository. Carefully planned field work is crucial to developing significant holdings. Larger repositories may employ one or more persons to locate and acquire holdings central to their repository's collecting theme. In smaller repositories, staff members also involved in administration, processing and reference may share the field work. Collections must be arranged and described before they may be opened for study. This work can be simple and quick or time-consuming and challenging, depending on the size and nature of the collection. The papers of an early twentieth century educator might hold from three to five hundred items spanning sixty years. Contrast that to a typical collection of a prominent contemporary United States senator, which may number two or three million discrete items in formats including paper, photographs, film, audio-recordings and computer records. Processing large complex collections may require several years of work for a team of archivists. The educator's papers will be arranged in simple chronological order and lend themselves to a brief and easily written description. The senator's collection is much more of a challenge. Its arrangement may reflect the "original order" of the collection—the configuration in which the senator maintained the records. If that order is sensible and allows for the ready identification and retrieval of information, it will be retained. If not, the staff will devise an arrangement that provides a suitable level of intellectual control. Finding aids to large complex collections can exceed one hundred pages.

During processing, a collection is appraised at the series, box, folder and, sometimes, even item level. The National Archives retains less than four percent of the records generated annually by the federal government. Manuscripts repositories, in processing a typical congressional collection, discard (or "weed") some forty to seventy percent of the papers. Even in eighteenth century collections, some "weeding" may occur if, in the opinion of the processor, the records have no permanent historic value. One should note here that, by accepting a collection, the repository obligates itself to maintain its information in perpetuity. The focus of archival work is the collection and preservation of the historic record, and that focus has a long time frame. We archivists are as concerned about future generations of researchers as we are the patrons we serve each day. Preservation issues may call for the microfilming or other reformatting of material whose physical condition has deteriorated, like newspaper clippings or thermofax copies, but the informational content will always be preserved.

A biographer's main contact with the institution will be with its reference staff. Reference assistance is designed to link researchers to those collections that pertain to their topic. Larger repositories often employ reference specialists knowledgeable about their holdings, their various finding aids, and related materials held outside of their institutions. Some— typically smaller repositories—combine administrative, field, processing and reference work. This integrative role can provide wonderful bonuses since the researcher comes to know the very person who solicited and processed the collection. Of all staff members, the processor will know the collection's contents and arrangement best.

Scholars should always feel at ease sharing their research topics and strategies with the staff. By sharing this information, they enable the staff to pinpoint those collections likeliest to contain worthwhile material. For a reference staff, the most frustrating patrons are those who are reluctant or unable to describe their topic and research wishes clearly. If possible, write ahead and note your topic, date of arrival and length of stay. The staff can then alert you to any problems while also preparing for the visit. They may even recommend lodging. I, myself, once housed a student while he found more permanent quarters for a month-long visit, providing perhaps an unusual but not extraordinary level of assistance. The reference staff may list or otherwise describe the collections you may wish to study, sometimes even estimating the time the study may require. One visiting scholar who had carefully reviewed our published guide allocated two days for his visit. On the afternoon of the first day he called his office and rescheduled his plane reservations to extend his visit to a week. Later that week, he again rescheduled and spent two full weeks because of the wealth of information he discovered. Had he alerted us to his visit and plans, we could have told him he had underestimated the amount of material we had available.

Those scholars worried about disclosing a "hot" research thesis should know that the Archival Code of Ethics precludes archivists from revealing details of a scholar's work without permission. Archivists will, however, strive to ensure that a researcher does not waste time beginning a project being developed by another scholar. The Archival Code of Ethics of

the Society of American Archivists (1992) also calls for
archivists to answer

> with a spirit of helpfulness all reasonable inquires about their
> holdings, and encourage use of them to the greatest extent
> compatible with institutional policies, preservation of
> holdings, legal considerations, individual rights, donor agree-
> ments, and judicious use of archival resources.

As a researcher, expect the reference archivist to help identify
all collections which may be pertinent to the research subject,
assist in understanding and using the finding aids for those
collection, and retrieve those elements of the collections which
have been requested for study. Nothing pleases a reference
archivist more than a productive research visit, and patrons
may leave confident they have seen everything pertinent to
their study.

Reading Room Etiquette
Archival repositories generally enforce specific rules governing the manner in which patrons request and handle material.
These rules are intended to guarantee the security of the
collections and ensure that no harm comes to the materials.
Researchers should remember that the staff operates with
imperatives in direct opposition to one another: encourage
research into their holdings, yet preserve the materials for
future generations of users. As a result, research typically
proceeds in a carefully monitored environment. These next
remarks summarize standard reading room regulations and
explain the rationale behind them.

A researcher will be asked to complete a user registration
form. A security measure and an important part of the
repository's record keeping, the form often requests a
summary of the patron's research topic. Genealogy is a staple
in archival research; genealogists form a critical patron group.
But most archives identify scholarly research as the basis for
their existence. Genealogists typically make up the single
largest category of users for many repositories; however, they
are a statistical anomaly. A genealogist may visit the repository once and spend an hour or two studying a family Bible,

genealogical notes or church records. The scholarly researcher may visit the repository daily for a week, a month, or even a year, working steadily throughout each day, examining dozens or even hundreds of collections or thousands of items in a single collection. Thus, those engaged in scholarly research should carefully delineate their research interests on this registration form or in conversation with the reference archivist to ensure that they receive the best possible assistance in locating relevant material.

Once registered, a researcher will receive help in orienting himself or herself to the resources held by the repository. This will include an introduction to the finding aids and other tools available to help identify potentially valuable materials. He or she will receive a copy of the institution's rules governing research. Always read these carefully; they will be enforced. The description of archival and manuscripts collections has long been highly individualized, with little commonality among various repositories. This pattern is, however, rapidly changing as the profession has recognized that uniform descriptive practices help both the repositories and their users. The growing use of electronic finding aids ensures even greater uniformity.

Almost all repositories maintain their records in stacks closed to the public. Once a researcher identifies a desired collection, he or she will complete a request form, and a staff member will retrieve the collection from the stacks and bring it to the research area. Nothing circulates, and a researcher may be restricted to requesting a limited number of items, boxes or collections at any one time. Collections are arranged in a precise order and researchers must preserve that arrangement. The use of a limited number of items helps maintain security and also ensures against scrambling the order of the material. If the requested collection or item has been microfilmed, or otherwise reformatted, the researcher will receive that copy. Reformatting is done for a variety of reasons, including the anticipation of heavy research demand, publication or fragility. If a collection has been filmed, often one can borrow the film, either microfilm or microfiche, through one's own library via interlibrary loan. If one must see the original, perhaps to search for a watermark to help date the item or read a phrase that appears out of focus on the film, one should tell the staff. Usually, they will make the original available if the need seems valid.

Many repositories monitor researcher activity closely. One may be asked to leave a briefcase and other articles in a locker and take only blank paper and a pencil for note taking into the research area. Pens are forbidden so that a careless user does not doodle on the original documents. I once watched a distinguished elderly scholar absent-mindedly underline a sentence in a document with a felt tip pen while making a point to an associate. That episode made me a firm believer in the pencil-only rule. If one can take personal items into the area, a staff member may insist upon examining the materials upon departure. Theft is rare, but it does occur. Because of the unique nature of archival material, theft is a constant concern. Insider theft has accounted for a number of highly publicized incidents in recent years, and internal security may be just as stringent as that the patrons experience.

The general rules all center on handling materials with care. If you treat the documents with respect, the staff members will notice and appreciate your consideration. Staff can exercise wide discretion in dealing with patrons, and their good will is priceless. I know associates who have devoted lunch hours or worked into the evening searching for a poorly remembered document that could help a patron. I also know of many long friendships resulting from a shared interest with a patron. Researchers who show a disregard for records, through rough handling or ignoring the rules, are quickly noted and the staff will carefully monitor their behavior. In a worst case scenario, the patron may be denied access to records.

No generally accepted standards exist for photocopying procedures or the amount of material one may duplicate. Archivists sometimes give the impression that we discourage copying but, in fact, nothing could be further from the truth. We realize copying provides real benefits to the researcher and helps to further the goals of the repository. We do, however, see copying abused or used as a substitute for careful research. The worst case I witnessed involved an individual who spent over a year at our library looking at every item among our holdings dating from the period in which he was interested. As soon as he identified a document as relevant to his project, a doctoral dissertation, he added the item to his photocopy order and went on to scan the next document. When he left our city, he had amassed some twelve thousand pages of photocopies. He had to be ignorant of the copies' contents, since he took few notes and seemed not to read the documents with any particular care. This may explain why, almost ten years later, he has yet to complete his dissertation.

Some repositories place copiers in their reading rooms and allow patrons to copy at their discretion. More typically, researchers complete a photocopy request form and staff members do the actual copying for a modest fee that may or may not fully cover the costs to the institution for this service. Prohibitions on photocopying by the public reflect both preservation and copyright concerns. Photocopying is usually prohibited if the fragile condition of the original would place it in jeopardy. In addition to copying of documents, most repositories can supply copies of photographs and audiovisual recordings in whatever format might be required.

Copyright can present complex problems for the scholar. One must never forget that simple possession by a repository does not give the researcher the right to quote and publish. In negotiating the gift of papers, the field archivist will strive to receive both the property and literary rights to the materials, but the literary rights may be withheld if the donor attaches a monetary value to those rights or intends to write for publication. Also, only within the last twenty years have formal deeds of gift come into general use. The rights to older collections may never have been formally transferred; and technically, they may remain with the collection's creator, if living, or the creator's descendants. Finally, donors can transfer literary rights only to those papers they authored, not to letters and other unpublished materials authored by another. Thus, the copyright to John Smith's letter to Peter Jones, in the Jones collection, remains with Smith. It is the researcher's responsibility to seek and acquire permission for publication. The finding aid should indicate whether or not the repository holds literary rights to a particular collection. Researchers are responsible for providing proper citations to documents used in their work. Always seek the advice of the reference archivist regarding a citation. The archivist can help assure that the citation used will direct interested parties to the proper document. References simply to the Jones Papers are of little value if the Jones collection is large or arranged in some complex fashion.

Conclusion

The archival field is changing dramatically. Within the next ten years, expect to see great strides in access as more repositories place collection descriptions, and even whole collections, on-line. A few archives and repositories are currently scanning documents and, if this becomes popular and proves cost effective, scanning could be the next major advance in access to archival collections.

Contemporary collections challenge the profession continually to rethink its methods as we deal with new record formats and the great volume of records being generated today. The rise of electronic media promises freer access but also creates major concerns. In an age seeking "the paper-less office," more collections include computer records and some are composed almost solely of these records. With technology changing so rapidly, electronic records present difficult and worrisome appraisal, storage and preservation problems. How well we grapple with these issues will determine how well we document this and future eras.[1]

Few collections created today resemble those of past generations. Keeping a diary was once a common practice for young and old, men and women, rich and poor. Few now have the time or inclination to keep a daily record of their lives. Letter writing is a lost art in an age of e-mail. First the telephone and now the Internet have made many forms of paper-based communications obsolete. Such "papers" long provided the meat of biographical research, but future scholars will rely on electronic records and other types of materials to study contemporary society. Quantitative analyses will certainly be popular, using the massive and wide ranging statistics created in our bureaucratic world. Congressional collections will also be more important, containing communications received from constituents and other concerned individuals regarding legislation and the "hot button" issues that shape our world. It seems certain that no other sources will offer these intimate expressions from the vast American public on critical issues. Archivists will strive to ensure that the historic record adequately documents our society. Again, this role illustrates the dual—equally crucial, often opposed—duties to serve both current and future generations.

One can look upon archivists as critical conduits to the information researchers seek. Share with them your excitement for research; describe the intellectual framework of your study and the thesis you hope to prove; assist and enable them to help you. Good archivists will enjoy and learn from your visit and will provide you with access to all they hold and maintain.

Note

1. The archival field is still a profession in search of its identity. Most archivists now have specialized training in archival administration and a background in either history or library and information science. The Society of American Archivists [SAA] is the chief professional organization in the United States and publishes *The American Archivist*. The Association of Canadian Archivists publishes *Archivaria*. Both are useful journals, as is *Archival Issues*, published by the largest of a number of regional archival organizations, the Midwest Archives Conference. Archival certification is offered through the Academy of Certified Archivists, an organization created in 1989 to establish standards of knowledge for the archival profession.

Chapter Ten

Fair Use Issues in Archival and Biographical Research

Philo Hutcheson

> We must wait to see what light the Supreme Court will shed
> on . . . the entire muddle which has characterized fair use
> decisions.
> > E. Gabriele Perle, 1992

For scholars interested in archival and biographical research, legal matters often determine and guide the archive experience. At times, certain documents are closed (or "restricted") until a specified date. Other materials can be examined but cannot be quoted in a to-be-published article. On other occasions (as noted in the previous chapter) one may find oneself writing an individual directly to seek permission for publication. As Michael Hill (1993) noted, "The publication of materials gleaned from archival repositories involves somewhat more than simply inserting appropriate quotations and footnotes in your manuscript. Typically, you must obtain permission to publish even short quotations or extracts of unpublished materials from archival repositories" (pp. 69-70). These complications arise from the topics of copyright protection and fair use, privacy and literary property rights.

Copyright protection refers to the legal protection of all works produced by an individual, especially in reference to their commercial value. Fair use refers to the right to use those materials, on a limited basis, for the advancement of learning. Privacy involves those legal rights to and restrictions placed upon documents in collections that control the use of and access to materials; these restrictions stem from an individual's presumed right to live a life free from unwarranted publicity. While five restrictive categories pertain to privacy, a biographer's research often becomes complicated by one of the four forms of invasion of privacy—namely, intrusion upon an individual's solitude or private affairs. Privacy issues, though important, are not the focus of this essay. Literary property rights acknowledge the fact that authors hold title to the expression of their ideas even though the "carrier" of these ideas—for example, paper or audiotape—may be in someone else's possession. Biographers must obtain permission from the archives or the donor to use the actual content of a document; property rights, the rights of an archive to possess a document in a collection, do not by themselves permit a researcher to quote from the document.

All researchers and biographers should be familiar with the rudimentary issues of copyright protection and fair use. Despite their baffling nature, some working guidelines for the biographer do exist. The United States Congress expects the courts to resolve issues of copyright and fair use on a case-by-case basis. Thus, my comments will be most informative if I draw upon specific cases. One must not make generalizations about copyright protection and fair use issues; moreover, brevity leads to clarity. For those who wish to "conquer the field," however, several works are useful including *Copyright's Highway* by Paul Goldstein (1994); *Unpublished Materials: Libraries and Fair Use* by Angie W. LeClercq (1993); *The Copyright Book* by William S. Strong (1993), which includes a detailed examination of the case of *Williams & Wilkins v. the United States*; *The Nature of Copyright* by L. Ray Patterson and Stanley W. Lindberg (1991); and *Copyright Law for Unpublished Manuscripts and Archival Collections* by Robert Cogswell (1992).

In the simplest terms, copyright protection is a right granted by the Constitution. In the words of the original document, "The Congress shall have power . . . to Promote the Progress of Science and useful Arts, by securing for limited Times to Authors and Inventors the exclusive Right to their respective Writings and Discoveries." The United States

Congress has since passed many acts covering copyright issues; these acts extend protection to inventors and authors while still providing further access to their writings and discoveries. Copyright law is an "intellectual property law," although as a property law, it is an indistinct one. As one jurist observed, it is relatively easy to determine the owner of a leg of mutton, but ascertaining the ownership of the expression of ideas is far more difficult. As Goldstein noted, the basic tension of copyright law is the question of the property owner's rights as opposed to the rights of the user (1994, p. 37). Patterson and Lindberg, however, argued that the critical question for unpublished material is "whether an author may use the copyright to prevent rather than promote the cause of learning" (p. 215). Nevertheless, they observed that commercial interests rather than users' rights tend to wield the greatest influence over the definition of copyright.

Copyright law is nearly 300 years old, and it originally applied to written work and more specifically to the duplication of such work. Beginning in the mid-1800s, the nature of the law began to shift, increasingly covering "imitations and adaptation." By the early 1900s, judicial and legislative actions had begun to provide copyright protection to a wide array of writings and creations until the protection became extensive. Now, in Goldstein's phrasing,

> A letter, a conversation, a shopping list has full copyright protection from the moment it is written down, with no need of registration, deposit, notice, or examination in the Copyright Office. (p. 19)

Unpublished as well as published materials in a wide variety of forms clearly fall under the aegis of our current copyright laws.

In late 1960s and early 1970s a major copyright case, *Williams & Wilkins v. The United States*, involved duplication and fostered the confounding situations that researchers now find themselves in. The case arose when a publisher of medical journals sued the National Library of Medicine and National Institutes of Health for photocopying articles. Although the 1935 Gentlemen's Agreement between "library and publishing representatives" allowed single copies for scholarly use not intended for profit, the National Library of Medicine was producing multiple copies of articles. Various library associations supported the National Library of Medicine with *amicus curiae* (friend of the court) briefs, while the publisher associations supported Williams & Wilkins. While the 1974 Supreme Court ruling favored the National Library, a new question arose: Given the private nature of photocopying (as opposed to the public nature of printing, for example) and the low revenues involved, would the United States Congress establish liability? The copyright laws had traditionally protected the author's property as a commercial interest; now private reproduction might replace retail benefits and, if so, could a specific party be held accountable for the loss of profit?

In 1976, the Congress passed a revision of the 1909 copyright law. The 1976 Copyright Act gave copyright owners "the exclusive right to control the reproduction of their works," *including private copying of unpublished materials.* The interpretations of this explicit language have, however, been ambiguous, and the Congress has chosen to study the situation rather than act upon it. On the issue of copying, the 1976 Act states that:

> the fair use of a copyrighted work . . . for purposes such as criticism, comment, news reporting, teaching (including multiple copies for classroom use), scholarship, or research, is not an infringement of copyright. In determining whether the use made of a work in any particular case is a fair use the factors to be considered shall include:
> (1) the purpose and character of the use, including whether such use is of commercial nature or is for nonprofit educational purposes;
> (2) the nature of the copyrighted work;
> (3) the amount and substantiality of the portion used in relationship to the copyrighted work as a whole; and
> (4) the effect of the use upon the potential market for or value of the copyrighted work (17 USC, 107).

Both the courts and businesses have been able to define narrow circumstances for such copying. But no scholar (or professor, for that matter) should interpret Section 107 without further clarification. Scholars may now connect with the on-line archive of the Stanford University Library and the Council on Library Resources. The Stanford site seeks to keep scholars abreast of "fair use" issues. The site is http://fairuse.stanford.edu/.

Several court cases have specifically addressed private copying problems, and all are significant for biographers. I will discuss only some of the cases; the texts cited in the references for this chapter provide additional details on these cases as well as others. In the case of *Harper & Row v. Nation Enterprises*, the United States Supreme Court decided that *The Nation* magazine could not use as-of-yet unpublished memoirs written by former President Gerald Ford for *Time Magazine* and Harper & Row. Of particular interest to the Supreme Court was the set of economic questions pertaining to the value of the unpublished work. Given *The Nation's* extensive use of quotations and the considerable value of President Ford's writings, the Court was convinced that *The Nation* had violated the unpublished material's copyright. It also found a difference between scholarly use and profiteering, so that each instance of fair use must still be considered *sui generis*—that is to say, individually as if it were a unique set of circumstances (LeClercq, 1993, pp. 111-113). Curiously, the Supreme Court ignored Section 107's express granting of fair use to newsworthy topics (Gorman, 1991), a reminder to researchers that they should not attempt their own interpretations of the law. Subsequent judicial decisions have generally attended to the *sui generis* criterion the United States Supreme Court set forth in *Harper & Row v. Nation Enterprises*.

The idea of fair use often confuses. Since unpublished material is often important to research, a scholar may naturally want permission to include that material in a to-be-published work. Yet this is precisely where aspects of literary property rights become a concern. Simply because an archive possesses certain materials and provides access to them, a researcher does not necessarily have permission to quote portions from or even paraphrase the materials. The Salinger case is instructive in this matter. In *Salinger v. Random House, Inc.*, biographer Ian Hamilton had access to letters written by author J. D. Salinger, from which Hamilton quoted extensively. Hamilton had agreed to notify the universities that held the letters if he quoted from them, and they were, in fact, under copyright protection. Salinger learned of the biography and registered a copyright to the letters; Hamilton subsequently changed his use of the letters, greatly reducing the number of quotations and substituting paraphrases. A district court ruling denied that Salinger's copyright held, accepting in part Hamilton's argument that the doctrine of fair use applied. On appeal, however, the Second Circuit Court ruled that the 1976 Copyright Act explicitly included unpublished letters and that the letters had substantial literary and commercial value (some half million dollars), reversing the district court decision.

An important distinction regarding the fair use of copyrighted unpublished materials arose in *Wright v. Warner Books*. The widow of author Richard Wright sued Warner Books for the publication of a biography of her husband. The district court ruled that the biographer used the unpublished letters to establish facts in Wright's life rather than for their literary value per se, that the number used was reasonable, and that no economic damage had occurred to the potential market for the copyright owner, Mrs. Wright. Here again we find a curious component of copyright law: The estate of an author (family members, for example) may hold the copyright for published or unpublished works. The court also ruled that in contrast to Hamilton's use of Salinger's letters in archival repositories other than Salinger's own, Yale University had expressly purchased the Wright holdings for scholarly use. The Second Circuit Court affirmed the lower court ruling, although it focused on slightly different issues. Of particular interest to biographers, the appellate court found that a "critical biography"—or, perhaps more accurately, a "factual biography"—indicated that the use was fair (LeClercq, 1993, pp. 118-119).

In both *Salinger v. Random House, Inc.* and *Wright v. Warner Books*, the court rulings regarding institutional protection of copyright holders should place biographers on their guard. While archives are responsible for notifying users regarding the status of literary property rights (at times called "publication rights"), they are not liable if the users fail to contact the owners, or the copyright holders, asking to use the materials (LeClercq, 1993). Thus, if one is conducting archival research, one should read the archive forms carefully both for the basic rules and for copyright restrictions. Some archives insist that one secure permission to quote from their materials, even in papers presented for conferences. I have found that archivists always tend to be helpful in these matters and, if difficulties arise, provide advice for making a "best effort" attempt to contact probable literary property right holders.

Donors, heirs and executors may retain literary property rights for any materials donated to archives; however, field workers succeed most of the time in gaining these rights for their archives. Archivists help determine any special restrictions donors (or their families) may place on donations, and researchers must live by these stipulations. These restrictions may include special permission to use the materials from both the donor (or heir or executor) and the archive. As in the case of access, restriction practices vary among institutions. While these forms suggest some variation, the more complete the statement of restrictions on fair use, the less potentially liable the institution leaves itself. Regardless of institutional variations, the courts are clear on the matter: the user is liable.

Creeping litigiousness has now entered the staid, cerebral world of archival and biographical research. We must attend to the consequences of copyright and fair use, privacy, and literary property rights issues while respecting the rights and wishes of those who produced the works we wish to reproduce and while honoring the rights and wishes of those in the role of guardian. At times, the problems may seem overwhelming; however, what is most important for the biographer is the recognition that these issues exist and the willingness to ask the repository's archivist and curator to help resolve them. Perhaps this seems too complicated in relation to the ease of other forms of qualitative and quantitative research. Nevertheless, for researchers and biographers, the thrill of reading primary documents far outweighs the associated problems.

The Historical Recovery of Edyth Astrid Ferris

Geraldine Joncich Clifford

Edyth Astrid Ferris was nominated for the projected American Educational Research Association volume on *Women in Educational Research* by the Dean of the University of Iowa College of Education because, in 1956, Ferris's estate gave $15,000 to the College "For the purpose of assisting other women to prepare themselves for careers in educational research." The income from this modest endowment has been used periodically ever since to provide small tuition grants and emergency loans to women graduate students in education.

By letter I asked the Dean's Office staff, the College of Education Alumni Society, and the University of Iowa Alumni Association to try to answer the following, predictable questions: Did Edyth Astrid Ferris earn any degrees at the University of Iowa? If so, when and in what fields or specializations? Is there any record of with whom she studied at Iowa? Is there any record of her home town including a street address? Do financial records remain that provide the name and address of the lawyer (executor) who communicated the Ferris bequest? These inquiries produced only the following information: Edyth Astrid Ferris was awarded a Master of Arts degree in education, with a specialty in child development, in 1926. The title of her thesis was "Play Apparatus and Motor Coordination Development in Seven and Eight-Year-Old Children in Three Johnson County Schools." Commencement programs (still on file) gave her home address as 177 First Street, Independence, Iowa. Next, standard biographical directories were consulted: *Biography Index* (the volume for 1955-58), the pertinent volumes of *Who Was Who in America, Who's Who of American Women, Who's Who in the Midwest, Notable American Women,* and *Contemporary Authors,* along with specialized biographical reference works: *Leaders in Education, Biographical Dictionary of American Educators, American Men and Women of Science, Dauntless Women in Early Childhood Education, Biographical Encyclopedia of Scientists, Names in the History of Psychology, The Women of Psychology,* and *The Psychologists.* In none of these was she listed. *Bio Base,* a microfiche periodical cumulative master index, did not list her. Neither was her name found in the card catalogues in the Teachers College Library of Columbia University—which reportedly has the nation's second-largest collection (after the Library of Congress) of the literature on education.

At the University of Iowa, College of Education catalogues and publications of the period were scoured for clues. The university published, for example, *Iowa University Monographs in Education* beginning about 1926 and University of Iowa Studies in Education somewhat later. This produced some information and promising clues about where Ferris's interests fit in the Iowa scheme of things in those years. The faculty teaching child development and elementary education courses between 1920 and 1926 were identified and their activities noted. One, Beth Lucy Wellman, was a research assistant professor associated with the Child Welfare Research Station at the University of Iowa (then routinely referred to by its official name: The State University of Iowa) from 1925-1929. She was promoted in 1929, and still listed in *Leaders in Education* as being at Iowa through the 1940s. I next read a very brief history of the Child Welfare Research Station; this included titles of master's and doctoral theses researched under the sponsorship of the Station. The Station was created by the Legislature "to conduct research on the development and conservation of normal children, to disseminate the findings so gathered, and to train students to do further research and teaching."[1] This list confirmed Edyth Astrid Ferris's association with the Station.

The publications of the Child Welfare Research Station for that period were recovered and searched. A footnote to a Wellman study in a 1927 publication named Ferris and three others as having assisted Wellman in gathering and analyzing data on motor control, which was a popular subject of the time judging by the above-mentioned historical survey of the Station's research output. A subsequent request for the business records of the Station (administered separately from the College of Education) brought the information that an employee named E. A. Ferris worked at the Station, under varying titles, in 1925-1926 and 1928-1933. The University's personnel records revealed no one by that name thereafter. In the depths of the Great Depression was she laid off or did she leave voluntarily, perhaps for doctoral studies or a better position?

Meanwhile I addressed letters to Independence, Iowa: to the Public Library, the Town Clerk, and the County Clerk of Buchanan County, requesting help in locating information on Miss Edyth Astrid Ferris. (Despite my knowledge of the social conventions of the time—that married women seldom pursued higher education—the possibility belatedly occurred to me that "Ferris" might be a married and not a maiden name.) This appeal brought me only one item, from the county library: a photocopy of a page from an historical gazetteer of Buchanan County, listing residents in 1930, the date of the publication. Two families with the surname "Ferris" were identified. (The 1930 U.S. Census reported Independence as home to 3,642 Iowans [Branom, 1932].) The librarian's accompanying note said that no families by that name were currently living in the town, and her inquiries to elderly library patrons yielded only one uncertain recollection: of a long-widowed Mrs. Ferris who had moved back to be with family in Racine, Wisconsin, "some time before Roosevelt." (Independence is 60 miles west of Dubuque, the Mississippi River, and the Wisconsin border; Racine is, however, across the state, on Lake Michigan.)

Since I possessed a street address it was possible to consult census records, which are organized geographically by address and not by name. I traveled to the federal records depository in Burlingame, California, to examine the manuscript censuses (officially called "Population Census Records") on microfilm. The 1920 census being unavailable until 1990, I consulted the 1910 federal census. It uncovered the following facts: a Mr. Samuel Henry Ferris and Mrs. Bertha Grisholm Ferris (he a shopkeeper born in the United States, she a housewife born in Germany), the names and ages of four Ferris children (three attending school), plus Jacob Green, and one Green child (an infant) resident in the household. Edyth Astrid Ferris was the second of the children listed, age 15 and a half in 1910. Her birthdate was given: February 10, 1895. The names of other Ferris children were noted for possible future use.

Because there was no newspaper published in Independence during the 1920s and back files of the county "Weekly" had been destroyed in a courthouse fire in 1937, I wrote to the Iowa State Department of History and Archives in Des Moines for help, with an offer to reimburse a staff member for searching Buchanan County history for these Ferrises. An archivist sent me a bill for $31.20; information from the Department of Vital Records that Edyth Astrid Ferris was born in Independence on February 10, 1895; photocopies of two clippings from the Buchanan County *Patriot—Recorder,* both for 1919; and a commencement program for the Buchanan County Union High School for June 1911 which listed Edyth Astrid Ferris as one of the five members (four girls and one boy) of the graduating class. The first newspaper clipping for 1919 reported that

> Samuel Henry Ferris of Independence died of the Spanish Influenza on May 3. He was born on January 18, 1866 in Buffalo, New York. Mr. Ferris was a respected citizen of this place and leaves a grieving family and many friends and business acquaintances.

And the second, an item from a social column for December 28, 1919, reported that "Mrs. Bertha Ferris is enjoying out-of-town company for the holidays from her daughter Edith who attends college in Cedar Falls and from her sister Mrs. Lucile Artz of Kenosha, Wisconsin."

What did Edyth Ferris do in the eight years between her high school graduation in June 1911 and her reportedly being a college student in December 1919? The search started with the entries for Iowa in the American Council on Education's volume *American Universities and Colleges* (American Council on Education, 1983). The college in Cedar Falls was the antecedent institution of the present University of Northern Iowa: Iowa State Teachers College, when Edyth Ferris was there. An exchange of correspondence revealed that Edyth A. Ferris (of Waverly, Iowa) received a Bachelor of Education degree in June 1919, having entered only the previous year. The same reference work revealed that Waverly was the site of Wartburg College (a union of five Lutheran colleges, one of which was, until 1920, Wartburg Normal School).

Wartburg records further revealed that Edyth A. Ferris was a student there during 1916-17 and 1917-18, taking the advanced course in teaching and special work in kindergarten education, then a subject of raging interest among educators, especially women. It was quite probable that she subsequently transferred to the State Teachers College because it had a pre-kindergarten and regular and extension courses in child development and parent education, in a consortium arrangement with the Child Welfare Research Station at the University of Iowa ("Preschool Laboratories," 1929).

Five years remained unaccounted for. But given what is known about normal school students in that era—that many were experienced teachers before matriculating for degrees—the strong probability was that she spent at least some of that time teaching, most likely in that section of eastern Iowa; she had, after all, never gone farther than eighty miles from Independence, even to attend the University at Iowa City. The search was expedited by the fact that Wartburg records show a Miss E. Farris entering from Waterloo, Iowa. Ten times larger than any place she had ever lived before, Waterloo had graded schools. Existing records do list her as a teacher of the primary grades during the years 1913-1916. No other information was found on that point.

The search led back to the State Department of History and Archives, with the request that the County Superintendent of Schools' annual reports for the years 1911-1913 for

Buchanan, Benton, Blackhawk, Bremer, and Fayette Counties be searched for lists of teachers of the rural, ungraded schools—the kind that would have hired, as teacher, an inexperienced girl right out of high school. Miss E. A. Ferris was indeed reported as teacher of a District School in Blackhawk County, at Gilbertville—about twenty-five miles southwest of her parents' home in Independence, for the 2 years in question. The surviving alumni newsletters from Iowa State Teachers College, next consulted, show her subsequent career until she entered the State University of Iowa for graduate work in September 1924. She was a first grade teacher from 1919 to 1924 in the Training School (sometimes called Practice or Model School) attached to the Teachers College. The search was halted at this point.

Summary and Conclusion

We know Edyth Ferris's birthdate (1895) and approximate death date (1956); her education from high school through the M.A. (1926); and her professional career prior to graduate work: 9 years spent as a teacher, in ungraded and graded schools, including five years in a "training" (or "model" school). We can see her experience increasingly centered on the education of young children, and expressed in her thesis topic and probably in her relatively brief career on the staff of the Child Welfare Research Station of the University of Iowa. Subsequent research—capitalizing on leads such as her Wisconsin relatives' names and locations, her mentor's name and career (Beth Lucy Wellman succeeded, in 1949, such well-known past directors of the Station as Bird T. Baldwin, 1918-1928, and George Stoddard, 1928-1942), her executor's name, her past experience as a predictor of her future employment—might reveal her going on in her career as an obscure educational researcher.

What positions for a woman of her background were available to persons of Edyth Ferris's generation of educational researchers? A likely place was in the research bureau of a city school district—usually meaning a testing or statistics-gathering agency. The directors of such bureaus were the group that founded what became the American Educational Research Association. She might have worked in the

United States Bureau of Education, which already had, in 1919, 91 professional employees and 133 office workers (Lykes, 1975, p. 79), perhaps working on the pioneering National Survey of the Education of Teachers which was published in the mid-1930s.

There were occasional openings on the research unit staffs of some major universities such as Teachers College's Lincoln School, where Beth Lucy Wellman worked before going back to Iowa in 1925, or its Institute of Educational Research where Edward L. Thorndike used foundation money to employ men and women research assistants, some of whom made careers there. The 1920s saw several child development research institutes founded, some with money from the Laura Spelman Rockefeller fund at the University of Minnesota, University of California, Teachers College-Columbia, and at Toronto and McGill. There was the Gesell Clinic at Yale, the Merrill-Palmer School in Detroit, and the Bureau of Educational Experiments (later Bank Street College of Education), all of which had research staff working on early childhood education in this period.

There was more irregular and peripatetic employment available on large scale research projects. The best known of these to historians of education were Lewis Terman's longitudinal studies of the "genetics of genius," Ben Woods' testing project that led to the National Teachers' Examination, and Ralph Tyler's evaluation within the *Eight Year Study* for the Progressive Education Association. There were a few staff positions in state departments of education (the larger ones had a hundred or more professional employees before World War II), in the Russell Sage Foundation, or in the Research Division of the National Education Association that published the *NEA Research Bulletin* from about 1922 (the majority of its small permanent research staff were women, at least during some of its history). Professional organizations were multiplying and they had need for a small, versatile staff that could combine professional with clerical and editorial work. Edyth Ferris could have pursued her interests by working with the Child Study Association of America or on the Monographs of the Society for Research in Child Development that began appearing in the mid-1930s.

In none of these places was she very likely to get her name known and her contributions recognized. Neither was she free to choose the subjects of her research and how they would be studied. As Margaret Rossiter (1982) found in her study of women scientists of Edyth Ferris's generation, however much formal training they acquired and however well qualified they were, women researchers in virtually every discipline made most of their contributions as unrecognized and often exploited research assistants. It is even more probable that Ferris ceased being an educational researcher altogether, returning to the primary grades as a teacher or, perhaps, to an instructorship at a state teachers college where she would never enjoy the time or the encouragement to pursue research.

We will never know because Edyth Astrid Ferris is a fictional character, a product of historical imagination.[2] She is a composite of the thousands of women who passed through teaching and, then, in large numbers but still little regarded, into study in the departments of education of America's colleges and universities during the years when educational research was assuming its future shape and preparing to burgeon with the post-World War II boom in higher education (Clifford and Guthrie, 1988). This was a company of women who have been, until now, almost entirely unremembered, unacknowledged, unappreciated, and unstudied (of the 12 persons portrayed in *Leaders in American Education* [Havighurst, 1971] only one woman—Ruth Strang—was included). As suggested by this illustrative case, their historical recovery will not be an easy task. But by ending their silence on this subject the origins of educational research will begin to say something—rousing, I hope—to the women researchers now in training, who are the new majority in many of our graduate programs in education, and to those male researchers who are ready, with these women's help, to break the cake of custom.

Notes

1. *The Institute of Child Behavior and Development: 50 Years of Research, 1917-1967* (1967). See also "Iowa Child Welfare Research Station: State University of Iowa, The 40th Anniversary, 1917-1957" (1959).

2. The names of, and facts associated with, persons, places, organizations, and collegiate institutions are genuine; the "facts" connecting them to E. A. Ferris are fictional, however.

Reprinted with the permission of the American Educational Research Association; *Educational Researcher, 17* (4), May 1988, pp. 4-7

Chapter Twelve

On Becoming an Archivist and Biographer

Louis M. Smith

I am an "uncertified archivist" and an "uncredentialed biographer"—hence the quotation marks surrounding the words. But as I complete my first full-length biography, my wife Marilyn and I also look back with satisfaction at "our archive," one whose 38 boxes now reside in the Manuscripts Room of the University Library in Cambridge, England. Even though I am pleased with these accomplishments, I am even more pleased that it is a working archive. The catalogue we made is useful in getting in and out of the materials. Now I want to tell you a little of how we did what we did—this, our adventure—into the worlds of archival work and biographical research.

Over the last decade I have been working on a biography of Nora Barlow, granddaughter of Charles Darwin, author of four books on the Darwin papers, and a founder of the "Darwin Industry," as the scholarly work on Darwin is now called. Those four books, one written as she turned fifty, a second when she was in her sixties, a third in her seventies, and a fourth in her eighties, were the early intriguing data that convinced me she would be an interesting and important subject for a biography (Barlow, 1933, 1946, 1958, 1967). Other reasons for her importance and my interest came later.

Another very important general item regarding my interest in biography arose from an earlier project. With my colleagues Kleine, Dwyer and Prunty I had been studying school innovation and reform (L. M. Smith, et al., 1986, 1987,

1988). One part of this had focused on the life histories of the teachers and administrators of the Kensington School in the Milford School District, a part of St. Louis County. That project had left me with a desire to go beyond the abbreviated life histories based mostly on extended interviews and move into a full biography (L. M. Smith, in process). I had thought my subject would be a local educator. But along the way I had been reading some of Darwin and the voyage of *HMS Beagle*, and I had found Nora Barlow. I had written to her for information on Darwin's sisters' letters to him during his five years on the Beagle and also I had inquired about the lost Darwin letter from the Galapagos. That inquiry brought a letter from Nora's son Horace Barlow, a research professor at the Kenneth Craik Physiological Laboratory at Cambridge University. A visit to England for a Classroom Action Research Network (CARN) International Conference gave me a chance to visit with Professor Barlow and the Cambridge University librarian Peter Gautrey. I learned about the Manuscripts Room of the University Library and its enormous collection of Darwin papers, and I learned that the young Nora Darwin had been a genetics student of William Bateson and a long time friend of the Bateson family. She and Mrs. Beatrice Bateson had gone to Bali in 1936 when Gregory Bateson and Margaret Mead were first married. To an anthropologically oriented educationist and social scientist, the story became "curiouser and curiouser." When I read of Nora's childhood in the priceless little book, *Period Piece: A Cambridge Childhood* (Raverat, 1952), I was hooked.

Discussions with the family for permission came after I wrote a prospectus. The process involved a series of face-to-face meetings. One of the key latent issues was that Nora was 100 years old and in declining health. She also had a study full of rare books—and boxes and boxes and drawers and drawers full of papers, letters and documents. In colloquial terms she was "a pack rat" and no one of the family had the time nor the energy to do anything with the materials. Yet they did not want to throw them away. I came along wanting to write a biography, and I was both interested and willing to sort through the materials. Also, I did not know quite what I was getting into.

I came with some advantages, some general and some specific to the archival task. I have written and published extensively, which suggested that I would be both able and likely to finish the biographical project. My vita was helpful here. Beyond the general paper credentials, I had done a number of qualitative research projects which produced large quantities of data—file drawers upon file drawers. Each project presented its own problems of data management and its own kind of solutions. I have written several books based on these varied kinds of records and files. As an academic I have faced the organization and reorganization of several decades of accumulated files for my courses and teaching. Sorting and resorting these produced a huge amount of tacit learning, so I would argue, learning that became important in the Barlow archival work.

Starting the Archival Task
One of my first concerns was whether there was enough material to write a biography. When my wife and I first saw Nora's study, our answer was an immediate "yes." We felt we were in some combination of rare book library and an old storage closet. Volumes of rare botany books dating back to the seventeenth century vied with a piano, old carpeting and draperies, assorted pieces of furniture and boxes and boxes of unknown contents. A quick scanning of boxes of letters and manuscripts answered the question of enough material.

The second and later question was "Where to start?" Anywhere seemed a reasonable answer. Actually, we started mostly with an effort to make some working space around two chairs at a table in the study. We literally had to move boxes to make room for ourselves. Without realizing it in these beginning moments, the archival task was to take parts of three summers: a six week period in 1987, a month in 1988, and three weeks in 1989. In addition, we worked briefer times during other visits to educational meetings in Cambridge.

Early on, we made small practical decisions which, in retrospect, I believe were very important. We decided that we did not want the hodgepodge of old grocery boxes, cardboard file drawer boxes and assorted other cardboard containers that contain much of my old data, records and research materials.

We bought acid-free archival boxes. They gave the final results a "neat and tidy" appearance. Eventually we had 38 of these. Subsequently, we have been re-doing our own basement and loft storage with similar boxes.

We enjoyed another advantage or two regarding archives. Early on, actually during the 1987 AERA meeting in Washington DC, I had looked for Nora Barlow letters in the Margaret Mead Collection in the Madison Building of the Library of Congress. There I learned about "linear feet." Margaret Mead's collection involved almost six hundred linear feet of shelved materials—that is, two football fields long of filed materials, and I learned about "catalogues," that notebook that tells the researcher "what's where." And I learned about "letters to" and "letters from."

And I relearned, really re-accented, the power of chronology as a practical principle and eventually as a principle congruent with biography. Actually, I had been concerned very early in my educational research with "classroom processes," events over time. Chronological record storage has been an important practical principle and an even more important theoretical principle for me. In anthropologists' terms, the diachronic has been too often sacrificed to the synchronic, process subordinated to structure. I now believe that history is the core social science and that historical method is close to "the" fundamental method of social science. By this I mean at least two things: First, as C. Wright Mills argues, an historical dimension must pervade all imaginative social (and educational) research. Second, in a hierarchical structure of social scientific methods history will prove to be the most abstract and general, the top of the pyramid, so to speak. Tracing all that out is another and longer story, one that belongs elsewhere. But in that Washington D.C. experience I also found over eighty letters to and from Nora Barlow and Gregory Bateson and Margaret Mead. And that was a real find!

And I learned about feeding dimes into the photocopy machine in the Library of Congress. Library security also came into my view. When one enters the rare book room there, no papers come with you. When you leave the room, all of your notes are on library paper and the photocopies are checked page by page. That kind of control I found startling and led to a number of reflections on libraries and archives around the world. But the principal image remained of how libraries handle archival data. My wife and I were not quite the dozen trained and experienced individuals who worked several years on the Mead collection, but we had some provocative and helpful particular images floating through our heads.

In our work in Nora Barlow's study, Marilyn and I soon fell into a pattern of working together, a relationship we jokingly called "Tonto and the Lone Ranger." She was the Lone Ranger, in that she would scout about and unearth piles of materials and items from those piles. Many of these would come to the table where I sat, with her excited comment, "Look at this one!" each with the appropriate exclamation point. And before I could get that first one logged, she would return with another and another. She moved quickly and excitedly and I labored slowly, but excitedly also. And, yes, I was Tonto. I sat at the table doing the "scut work," writing labels on envelopes and stuffing letters and documents into the appropriate envelopes. (Do you realize that "Tonto" means fool in Spanish?) In a sense she was having all the fun and I was doing all the chores. In desperation I would often cry halt and go to the kitchen and fix a cup of coffee. We worked this way day after day, usually parts of five or six days a week during those summers. Great fun!

One of the most powerful substantive outcomes of that kind of work was a gradually evolving sense of who Nora Barlow was. For a biographer it was expensive in time but priceless for coming to grips with the subject of the biog-raphy. I can't emphasize that enough. Nor can I quite under-stand how others go about doing biographies without that kind of "hands on" experience, as some educators describe teaching and learning alternatives. Division of labor is impor-tant in many activities. For me "becoming an archivist" was an early phase on the way to "becoming a biographer." And that was important for another of my agendas: the gradual extension of ethnographic field work into the domains of biography and history. I began to talk about my intellectual activities with the Barlow project as "doing ethnographic biography." The archival activity was field work in the best

sense of ethnography: we were in another culture, participating, observing and trying to understand this woman Nora
Barlow and the huge array of artifacts she had left behind.
The result was a more integrated conception of qualitative
inquiry including history, biography and ethnography.

Another important consequence was the gradual and
mostly inductive categorization of materials toward an orderly
storage system. In our initial attempts, we filed letters by
individuals, one envelope per person. When the envelope
became too full, we started another, clustered now by years,
early and late. Eventually, with some individuals, the correspondence became too full, and we did one envelope per year.
And, as with letters from Nora's husband Alan, some periods
were so plentiful we did a month by month sort and store
system. Initially, too, we had a box for letters and a box for
manuscripts. These then differentiated into separate boxes of
letters for immediate family, for extended family, and for
professional colleagues. The manuscripts differentiated into
published and unpublished, with separate envelopes for
supporting materials such as notes and galley and page
proofs. And we had boxes of her books. The ones we kept
were those that had interlinear or marginal pencil notes or
those in which she had pasted letters or reviews. And finally
when time ran out we had several boxes of miscellaneous and
essentially unsorted materials, most of which seemed less
important but which we did not want to see thrown away.
Eventually we had a rough catalogue of the boxes and the
clusters of boxes.

During this time we had another major asset. From time to
time we would talk with Peter Gautrey, the long-time keeper of
the Darwiniana collection in the University. My general
question was, "How do 'real' archivists do all this?" My
specific questions involved items such as "Do you separate
'letters to' and 'letters from' or do you mix them?"
Eventually we organized them separately. Later, during the
analytic work, I would often pull both files, and read the letters
chronologically and interactively. But this was made difficult
for there were other "pools of data" from other libraries and
other sources that were not part of the archives we developed.
For example, Nora had given several boxes of materials to the

library years before. These were already there and catalogued independently. I did not even begin to redo their earlier work, although at times I wanted to. But my major point is this: Our informal chats with trained librarians were very helpful. The archival work intertwined with several other more ethnographic procedures and events. Nora Barlow continued to live in her house while we worked during those first two summers. Unfortunately, at 100 she was both deaf and intellectually not competent. The only comment she made that seemed to have some meaning to it was the remark, "What a mess," as she walked by the study with the help of her house-keeper. But we became acquainted with the housekeepers and nurses, with Nora's children and their spouses, and with some of her grandchildren who would come by from time to time. We showed them what we were about, we raised questions about particular items we did not understand, and we talked with them at coffee and lunch on occasion. Our knowledge and understanding increased and increased, in some ways even beyond the long open-ended taped interviews we had early on with members of the family. "Being around" and doing the archival work set the occasion for more ethnographic, partici-pant observer efforts. I found this to be a valuable connection.

So, wanting to do a biography led me into becoming an archivist. Doing the archival work not only set the stage for returning to the biographical task, but in a very fundamental way the archival task became an early part of doing the biography per se. I did not know all that when I began. In retrospect it seems very important. I believe that I am almost ready to conceptualize this archival work as "managing multiple messes" and to build on Donald Schon's conception of the reflective practitioner. But that, too, will take me too far afield here.

Serendipity and Joy

Serendipity and joy seem to run together and perhaps connect to motivation, although the latter makes the interpretation a little more instrumental than I intend. Serendipity and joy seem part of becoming an archivist, as two stories, among many, illustrate.

Perhaps it was an old childish wish, lurking semi-consciously in one's background, that one might discover some rare find in the attic of grandma's house, but one day as Marilyn was "scouting" through an old clothes box, the kind that a man's suit might have come in, she made the big "find." The box was on the floor of the study, along the north wall, not quite under the window. And it was covered by, really buried under, some old curtains and draperies, and contained a variety of odds and ends including some old baby's clothes. As she worked her way down she came to a flat package covered with plain whitish beige wrapping paper. In it was a picture of the young Charles Darwin, what looked to be a pencil sketch. We marveled at it, and also we were frightened by its potential value. We called the CUL librarian Peter Gautrey. His reaction was severalfold: "Is it the one that had been lost for years and found in the basement of the botany building in 1929 by Nora and the chair of the botany department?" I answered, "I think so," for I had seen and filed a letter a few days earlier relating the incident.

Then Peter said, "It is probably one of the very good photos that was made of the picture." Nora had used the sketch as the frontispiece of her first book, her edition of *Charles Darwin's Diary of the Voyage of the Beagle*. I said to Peter, "It really does look like a pencil sketch." He agreed to come look at it the next day. As we repackaged it, Marilyn offered one of the best one liners of her life when she commented, "Maybe I ought to get a pencil eraser and see if it erases." The next day Peter arrived, and we unpacked it and he "oohed and aahed" over it. The sketch was an 1840 picture done as a study before George Richmond did a formal oil painting. I asked him the value of the sketch. He did not know, but told a story of a dozen or so Darwin letters that the library had purchased recently that had cost the library some 15,000 pounds. I asked him if there were wealthy collectors of Darwiniana, and he indicated there were. Speculative visions of prices of fifty to a hundred thousand pounds in an open auction went through our heads.

Since then, the sketch has found its place in the Manuscripts Room and hangs in the area near the table where the "Darwin Letters project" is underway, that is, the multivolume publishing of all of Charles Darwin's correspondence. The tag identifies it as being found in the basement of the Botany Building in 1929. We chided our librarian friends that there should be a second tag under that one, "Rediscovered by Marilyn Smith, 1987, in a clothing box in Sellenger, the home of Nora Barlow." Also in that same box was a complete set of the printer's original proofs of William Blake's "Book of Job." You can imagine the stir that *that* discovery created. But that story is too long to tell here.

I must, however, relate the story of the Leonard Darwin letters, for it makes an additional general point or two. I had read, I believe in some materials on the statistician and geneticist R. A. Fisher (he's the man who invented analysis of variance and covariance for those of you who haven't labored in the statistical vineyards and gardens), that the Leonard Darwin letters were at the University of Sussex. Leonard was one of Charles Darwin's sons and an uncle of Nora's. The answers to my inquiries to the Sussex library had just arrived; they indicated the letters were not there. I was telling this woeful tale to librarian Peter Gautrey one day in his office and raising the question of what to do and where to go. At a desk nearby was another librarian, working quietly, yet sort of listening to our conversation. She started to smile shyly, not quite wanting to intrude, yet needing to, and said, "We have them here." And that is how I met Margaret Pamplin, another archival librarian. Later she introduced me to her friend and colleague Mike Cattermole who had recently finished a book on Nora's father, *Horace Darwin's Shop* (Cattermole and Wolfe, 1987), an account of the Cambridge Scientific Instrument Company. He had gotten the letters from a special project on scientists underway in another part of Sussex University. I was surprised at the connections and lack of connections and the knowledge and lack of knowledge about small pieces of the archival world. Later, we looked at the cardboard box containing the letters and found dozens between Nora and her Uncle. This, in turn, unraveled part of a major question, "Who are the key people Nora talked to during her long career?" But the major point I want to make here is that, in effect, I had made contact in a small way with the group of people exploring Darwiniana. Mike is working on a biography of Leonard Darwin, with a focus on his early years. Later, we found correspondence of Nora's and her sister Ruth that indicates that the Leonard Darwin letters "belong" to the Cambridge University Library. That poses some additional interesting issues in archival work. The social world or community of archivists and biographers is fascinating.

Becoming an "archivist" does have its memorable and satisfying times. As a part of "doing ethnographic biography," finding the Richmond sketch and finding the Leonard Darwin letters became "just" two more stories of serendipity in the inquiry process, a continuingly joyous professional and personal activity.

An Unexpected Problem:
Mixing the Archival and Biographical Tasks
Early on, while engaged in the initial part of the biographical work, I seemed to be fumbling about more than was usual on a research project. I kept bumping into myself, feeling awkward in doing the task. Only later did it strike me that I was mixing, and thereby confusing, the archival task and the biographical task. The situation was this. As we sorted Nora's papers, insights and bright ideas arose regarding both substantive and methodological issues. In my earlier ethnographic work, my label for these has been "interpretive asides." Now, in this new setting and project, I wasn't easy about where and how to note them. Sometimes I would begin a sort of field note, other times I would enter the asides into my diary record, and on yet other occasions I tried to dictate them as summary observations and interpretation notes. As usual, I have records, reflections on the records, and reflections on the reflections, *ad infinitum* if not *ad nauseam*. This time, the recording process was not easy.

Eventually, I found the issue to be two interrelated problems. In part, doing the archival work is a busy set of active personal actions, creative and constructive, whereas doing ethnographic data collection is usually an observational task—sitting and taking notes as an outsider. Constructing the archive, I believe, is closer to doing action research on one's own teaching. It is hard to take notes in the middle of teaching. I did not see those similarities and differences then. The second problem involved two sets of files: the archival record of Nora's papers, letters and documents, which would remain in Cambridge, and a second set, the photocopies, my handwritten excerpts, and my more usual ethnographic records that would eventually go back to St. Louis with me. These would become part of my working files at home, the data for analysis, interpretation and writing. "Normally," in my usual field work, the only important data set was the one I accumulated about the project for myself. This was the file that I would use for whatever essays, reports and books I would write. My file of substantive Nora Barlow documents pales next to the huge archive that is now stored in Cambridge, and that has created one of the most difficult problems in writing the biography. No matter how much I have photo-copied, the "real" records remain in Cambridge—and else-where. I seem to feel that I need to "be there" to do the real work.

Now, as I think about the issues, they seem not to be an "archival" problem, rather a problem in the mixing of the ethnographic, archival and the biographical tasks. And the issues seem to be problems in the similarities and differences in doing biography, ethnography and action research. A transfer of training problem? All this was a surprise and a troublesome one at that. Now I try to teach my students about the distinction between creating archival records and the researcher's use of records. Now I would phrase the issue as a not so small but important piece of practical lore in doing this kind of ethnographic biography. A more cynical view might be that I overindulge myself in too many layers of reflections upon reflections in the practice of doing qualitative research. Has this interest become a kind of fetish?

Conclusions

Sometimes I ask myself, "What have I learned about becoming an archivist and how will this refine my work as an ethnographer?" Several concluding thoughts come to mind. First, I am struck with the similarity of archival work to many of the activities that made up my earlier and continuing life as an educational ethnographer. Putting order into a mass (and a mess?) of qualitative data, this time collected and saved by someone else, is very similar to getting my files of field work data—notes, summary observations and interpretations, interview protocols and documents—organized into some kind of intelligible form that I could move in and out of at a later date for analytical purposes. Now, especially, documents upon documents are the focus. The archival catalog grew slowly and inductively with the practical and conceptual problems of sorting concrete documents.

Second, these archival activities began the move to other related kinds of generalizations: I began to talk and write about "doing ethnographic biography." This had a mighty assist from reading Catherine Drinker Bowen's provocative work—her experiences as a biographer and several of her biographies. *Adventures of a Biographer* (1959) and *Biography: The Craft and the Calling* (1968) are superb methodological books. The summer we spent living at Girton College, I took along and read her *Miracle in Philadelphia* (1966). It added one more image to my enlarging store of Bowen stories and ideas.

Third, I return to the concepts of "vivid images" and "collegial dialogue" as important to new phases in one's development as a research craftperson. This time I was interested in becoming a biographer and archivist. Bowen's accounts, plus a couple of days in the Library of Congress with the Mead collection, and conversations with Peter Gautrey and Margaret Pamplin among others, have been helpful beyond belief. It doesn't take much, but the brief experiences have been exceedingly helpful.

Fourth, solidification continued in the generalization that history, biography and ethnography are of a piece. Their logical structure and practical activities as methods of inquiry are very similar, so it seems to me. Should some of us who traditionally don't hang out together, begin to do so? Should these several forms of inquiry be taught together? "Yes" is my brief answer to both questions.

And finally, C. Wright Mills (1959) argues for the mixing of one's personal and professional life if the sociological imagination is to be actualized. The archival work was carried out with my wife Marilyn. It was the largest piece of this kind of joint professional activity we had ever done. (Most of the time she directs and teaches in the Grace Church Preschool in Kirkwood, Missouri.) This mixing of personal and professional seems to have occurred in a way not quite envisioned by him or us. It added an important dimension to becoming an archivist and our lives in general.

For me, all this is what "becoming an archivist and biographer" is about. Overall, my argument in this essay has been relatively simple. I believe that qualitative research is a large relatively untapped domain of multiple strands of inquiry. Ethnography and biography, arising in different intellectual communities at different times in history, have much to say to each other. By telling one small story of an ethnographer coming to be a biographer in the specific context of developing an archive—and becoming an archivist in the process—the similarities become readily apparent. This kind of grounding in the activities of one social scientist extends the kind of abstract argument and theorizing that has appeared in recent collections of essays on qualitative inquiry. The particular and the general, the abstract and the concrete both come together in a simple but important way. On another occasion, the large array of methodological issues—e.g., paradigmatic stances, kind of theory, goodness criteria, subjectivity and objectivity, art of interpretation, nature of empirical materials—needs to be addressed explicitly, that is, individually and synthetically, rather than implicitly and mostly concretely as I have done here in the joining of biography and ethnography. But here, in this essay, it is joy, serendipity and high adventure that carry the poignancy of demanding intellectual tasks.

PART FOUR

Educational Biography as Dissertation Research

Introduction

Biographies populate the commercial market, emerge from the academic presses, and comprise a portion of the dissertations in history and English departments. A growing number of education doctoral students, too, now select biographical studies as a way to fulfill requirements for graduation in a variety of areas—from history of education to curriculum & instruction and educational administration. Their reasons for choosing this dissertation research range from the carefully planned to the haphazard. Yet, whatever prompts a student to embark upon a biography dissertation, the ensuing adventure includes the excitement and fear inherent in any research endeavor. The contributors to this section discuss the pleasures and the conceptual traps into which they fell as they wrote such works.

Katherine Reynolds' essay explains her wish to do more than merely "dissertate"; she sought to bring her experience as a journalist and researcher to the academic forefront while completing doctoral work in higher education administration at the University of Utah. The experience became much more than producing a scholarly document; Reynolds sought biographical method as a way to achieve "grace"—artistry with language—and to understand "truth." With the experience came a refined conception of facts and accuracy. She reflects Frank Vandiver's (1983) demand for accuracy: "[B]iographers honor facts; biographers honor, too, personality and character and must do no violence to either" (p. 11). As Reynolds concludes, "By writing a dissertation that was a biography, I was able to enjoy the creative work of the artist

and to employ the methodological precision of the scholar."
How do biographers select their subjects? The reasons and
motives vary, yet one rarely questions the willingness of the
subject. Imagine an educator who would be neither pleased
nor flattered to be the subject of a dissertation. Tony Reid,
who completed his doctoral work at the University of South
Carolina in the area of elementary education, found an ideal
subject but, unfortunately, did not learn of her unwillingness
to cooperate until he was committed to writing. He discovered
that gaps in the archival record did not occur haphazardly;
missing documents were meant to be missing. Reid's efforts to
justify his work added a useful dimension to the interpretation
of his biographical subject.

Lynda Anderson Smith, currently a doctoral student in
curriculum & instruction at the University of South Carolina,
found herself in the opposite situation: Her subject is more
than willing to be the focus of a biography and continues to
express that enthusiastic willingness with each passing
semester. While Smith acknowledges Edel's caveat that "No
good biography can be written in total love and admiration,"
she finds herself caught in a "dangerous liaison." Her situation, while not yet resolved, displays the reflection one wishes
of any aspiring biographer.

English academic G. M. Young once wrote that historians
should read the documents of an age until they can hear the
people speak. While completing doctoral studies in the area of
curriculum and foundations, Thomas Horton decided to take
Young's suggestion one step further by engaging the active
historical voice. Horton sought not merely to research a life,
he sought to "reawaken" a life and era and in so doing move
the dissertation experience to new levels of meaning and
significance.

Edwin C. Epps viewed biographical method as an
opportunity to explore a notion of "truth" and "teacher
stories" by examining the context of one of the more noted
stories, Pat Conroy's *The Water is Wide*. As he addresses the
rhetorical question "Was it fiction or biography?", Epps
delighted in exploring a narrative written by a teacher who is
also a novelist, a teacher who writes "with the elegance, grace,
and power uncommon in our current literature."

Are these five cases typical of doctoral students who write dissertations? Perhaps not. Would other academics who have completed biographical dissertations—for example, Geraldine Joncich Clifford, Robert V. Bullough, Jr., Mary Ann Duzbeck, Alice Yeager, and many others—tell similar stories? Perhaps so. What we can assert during this time of expanding research methodologies is that biographical dissertations offer fruitful opportunities and possibilities for the maturing researcher.

Note
Katherine C. Reynolds delivered a presentation version of her essay at the 1996 roundtable session of the Archival and Biographical Research SIG of AERA. Tony Reid delivered a presentation version of his essay at the 1993 keynote session of the Archival and Biographical Research SIG of AERA. Lynda Anderson Smith delivered a presentation version of her essay at the 1996 keynote session of the Explorations in Biographical Method Conference at the Museum of Education, University of South Carolina. Thomas Horton and Edwin C. Epps delivered presentation versions of their essays at the 1995 keynote session of the Explorations in Biographical Method Conference at the Museum of Education, University of South Carolina.

Chapter Thirteen

Finding Facts, Telling Truths, Achieving Art

Katherine C. Reynolds

Like all other doctoral dissertations, a biographical dissertation is primarily a scholarly work, distinguished by its vow to seek and report what is true and committed to methodologies that reflect the paradigm of its academic discipline. When this grim fact of Ph.D. candidate life occurred to me—somewhere between dissertation topic selection and proposal writing and after reading and enjoying hundreds of biographies throughout my life—I immediately felt constrained. I selected the biographical medium because I thought it would grant a certain degree of artistic license not generally available in dissertation writing.

Furthermore, I had selected as my subject the iconoclastic founder of Black Mountain College, John Andrew Rice, not because I was interested in his entire life, but because I was intrigued by his thoughts about education and how he expressed them in print. I wanted to recall his brilliance and wit, as well as applaud his courage during the height of the Depression to start a new college that would become one of the most boldly experimental institutions in the history of American higher education. I preferred to skirt the facts of his womanizing, his insensitivity and his arrogance. I believed I could be selective in my research by limiting my aim to an "educational biography," which would illuminate Rice's thoughts about education and his life as an educator.

Yet, even the preliminary evidence quickly suggested that the audacious and uncompromising side of Rice's personality affected his students and colleagues as much as his Socratic eloquence did. His arrogance toward his associates and his fondness for women eventually led his faculty colleagues to demand he end his association with Black Mountain College, which ended his life in education. Everything about John Andrew Rice the person seemed inextricably intertwined with John Andrew Rice the educator.

Reviewing what biographers have written about their work, I discovered another idea for limiting my biography to intriguing educational ideas and anecdotes while avoiding the "deadly morass of irrelevant narrative" (Namier, 1962, p. 161). From Arnold Rampersad (1991), the biographer of Langston Hughes, I learned that "basically, biography is the art of approximation" (p. 63). Armed with an acknowledgment of the limitations, I drafted a proposal for a dissertation entitled "John Andrew Rice: Approximation of an Educator." Among my five dissertation committee members and one outside examiner, four returned the draft with question marks beside my title. A fifth was less subtle, penning in red, "Nice try, Katherine, but it sounds like a partial work."

At this point, it was too late to turn back. My initial research for a draft proposal about a partial work represented sunk costs in time and effort. Additionally, I still found much to admire and to discuss about John Andrew Rice. Although he was emerging as a disturbingly imperfect human being, he had initiated an important experiment that still reverberates (forty years after the college closed) as an institutional example of innovative answers to enduring questions about the means and ends of higher education. My only option was to produce a biography that would live up to the expectations of a scholarly volume, right down to every fact I could accumulate and truth I could uncover, with maybe some artistry worked in during the writing process.

The rest is history—the history of finding facts, telling truths and achieving art. Along the way, I did manage to complete a biographical dissertation and sign a contract with a university press for the book version, *Visions and Vanities: John Andrew Rice and the Black Mountain College Experiment* (in press). More important perhaps, along the way, I embraced the concept of biography as the search for a life's truth through the determination of fact. In doing so, I found that the facts about a life do not necessarily pose insurmountable obstacles to artistic and literate presentation. Seemingly dry, unadorned facts create patterns, symbolism, metaphor and meaning with surprising frequency, even when they are arranged without chronological alteration. Hesketh Pearson may have been right in speaking of the biographer as an artist who "by the mere process of selection is forced to distort the facts" (in Kendall, 1965, p. 129). The biographer does not, however, take advantage of the predicament by deciding that the inevitable distortion may as well be forged into fascinating but unsubstantiated tales. Instead, the biographer answers the challenge to seek truth through facts that do not compromise artistry and to present truth with artistry that does not compromise facts.

In my dissertation, fact finding became the data collection stage, often resulting in similar "data" from numerous sources, yet with conflicting "facts." The process of determining fact became the foundation on which I built a study that sought to represent a life fully and truthfully. Truth seeking was the stage of evaluation and analysis of the data. Artistic endeavor occurred at the point of presenting the data on paper.

Desperately Seeking Facts
The most basic facts about John Andrew Rice and Black Mountain College are readily available. Several books and many articles about the college recount how Professor John Andrew Rice ignited a big fracas at Rollins College in Winter Park, Florida, in 1933, by publicly speaking against the college administration and its policies. When Rollins president Hamilton Holt demanded Rice's resignation and fired some of his faculty sympathizers, Arthur Lovejoy and the American Association of University Professors joined the fray to condemn Rollins (and reprimand Rice) and strike an early blow against academic censorship. Rice and a handful of faculty members and students left Rollins and decided to create their own college along highly experimental lines.

So far, so good. But that is just the vague outline of the situation. I needed to determine how much of the shape of Black Mountain College was Rice's and how much to credit to others. How long had Rice and others been thinking about doing something like this on their own? Who had the idea of putting the practice of art at the center of the curriculum, and who hired Josef Albers to spearhead the effort? How did the administrative arrangements (no trustees, faculty governance and student representation in policy making) come about? Why didn't John Andrew Rice simply find employment elsewhere when he was ousted from Rollins, as he had when he was forced from faculty positions at the University of Nebraska and the New Jersey College for Women? How did family members, friends, early educational experiences and other educational thinkers influence Rice's (1937) commitment to a holistic philosophy of liberal education reflected in his insistence that, "What you do with what you know is the important thing; to know is not enough?" (p. 595).

Two of the original Black Mountain faculty members were still alive in 1992, and I interviewed them both. I also interviewed several of the first group of students and Rice's son, Frank, who was 16 years old at the time of the college's founding and who acted as his father's chauffeur during a summer of touring possible college sites and recruiting interested faculty members and students. I found a tape of an interview with John Andrew Rice (who died in 1968); I found letters in archives at Rollins College, North Carolina State Archives, Swarthmore College (where Rice's brother-in-law Frank Aydelotte was president), and elsewhere. All supported the vague outline of how Black Mountain College started but diverged on the details of who did what, when and how.

This is where the biographer must cast a net widely and re-cast it many times. Although I could not use the whole of the material I collected, I found the overlapping information essential to assuring informed choices about what is accurate. In my case, the wide casts netted me interviews with 33 family members, friends, colleagues and students of John Andrew Rice, many of them very senior citizens. At least ten of them later gave second, third and fourth interviews during which they explained conflicting information, broke through clouded memories, or amended earlier statements. I made frequent use of the journalist's tool for getting the facts straight by confronting such differences as "You mentioned this event as happening at X location; but when I talked with another former student, he said it happened at Y location. Can you shed any light on that?"

Biographer Arnold Rampersad (1991) warned about three kinds of interviews: "One with people who know something and don't want to help you; another with those who know something and want to help you; and finally, most dangerous of all, with those who don't know anything and really want to help you. Unless you are extremely careful, extremely scrupulous in using the interview form, you are inviting trouble" (pp. 59-60). I encountered all three types in my work, although the vast majority knew something and wanted to help. Interestingly, the four who fell into the first category were all women; I am not certain what that means. I believed I was greatly assisted by the commitment of Rice's two sons and a grandson. These three individuals shared personal information of a most sensitive nature to help me understand John Andrew Rice. They submitted to numerous in-person and telephone interviews and exchanged letters, family photos and e-mail with me throughout the 18-month process of researching and writing my dissertation.

Biographical information about any subject rarely resides in a small geographical area within easy reach. But, skimping —using information from only a few of the more accessible sources—is no option in scholarly biography. Going into debt is a very real option. How I longed to join that group of biographers who preface their books with copious thanks for foundation grants, faculty development funds and departmental clerical assistance. The expenses of conducting a nationwide data search forced me to move much slower on my research than I would have liked. I traveled to interviews and archives only when I had other business in an area and spent much time waiting for copies to arrive from archivists or hired assistants at various collections.

Trolling for Truth

There is a place for intuition in the movement from gathering multiple perspectives of "fact" to telling truths—a sixth sense about what rings false and what just might need one last verification. For example, when several family members told me that in the early 1960s John Andrew Rice received a contract and an advance from a university press for memoirs he never finished, I thought it sounded odd and out-of-character for any publisher dealing with a fine writer who was nevertheless quite old by that time and had not even produced a proposal. My journal tells me I made nine phone calls digging for the truth, locating former editors of the press in their retirement. A similar situation developed when documents and interviews suggested that Rice majored in eighteenth century literature while studying for a Ph.D. at the University of Chicago. In the process of getting a Ph.D. myself, it made no sense to me that someone with a Tulane bachelors degree in Latin and Greek classics and an Oxford first in jurisprudence would undertake a Ph.D. in yet a third field. Finally, armed with a next-of-kin signature from son Frank Rice, I was able to obtain a copy of the Chicago transcript showing Ph.D. studies with a major in Greek and Latin language and philosophy.

While intuition can be valuable, re-checking with original sources or peers who might hear a phrase ring false is better. I sent my draft chapters to everyone who had helped provide information for them, and I was often saved from either accidentally misconstruing information or including information that changed as memories sharpened. I recall thankfully that some, like Rollins and Black Mountain student Norman Weston, even read the nuances between the lines. Weston called me to say, "You've quoted me accurately, but what you selected to quote tilts things toward Rice's faults and not enough toward his absolutely crucial leadership role in making Black Mountain College happen." Together, Weston and I worked out a solution that he felt best reflected his student observation of the enormous force of Rice's personality in shaping Black Mountain College.

Still I occasionally reached a dead end without any confidence that I could discern the truth. For example, some sources were convinced that Rice's inappropriate relationship with a Black Mountain student was a steamy affair eventually uncovered by Rice's wife. Others emphasized that nobody ever saw anything physical and the relationship likely stopped at infatuation. In cases like these, I admitted to ambivalence and let my readers hear both sides in quotations from my differing sources. While a biography will become equivocal and meaningless if it leans too heavily on letting the readers decide for themselves, a case for including conflicting information exists.

But Is It Art?

After perusing only a few dissertations, I realized that bringing artistry to the page has yet to become an academic requirement. The formulaic list of chapters prevails over creative arrangements, and style seems readily defeated by the unyielding requirements of official manuals and university thesis editors. No wonder John Andrew Rice ended his Ph.D. work at the University of Chicago short of his dissertation rather than face the dictates of the notorious thesis czar, Kate Turabian! I had, however, a chance to produce a different sort of work. After all, a dissertation committee demanding an inflexible adherence to introduction, literature review, methodology and so on, would hardly have approved the idea of a biographical dissertation in the first place.

Somehow I needed to create a volume that combined engaging writing with the craft of dissertation research. After a half dozen chapter outlines, I hit on one that worked best for me and my committee members. My review of literature and explanation of methodology became one long appendix entitled "Research Resources and Methods." In it, I discussed my use of preliminary, primary and secondary sources, as well as my strategy for data collection, organization and analysis. This is where I demonstrated my knowledge and use of approved historical research methods and the steps I took to help assure validity and reliability. Additional appendices listed my interview and document sources and my interview guide. In my introduction, I listed my research questions, discussed why it was important to get to know the life of John Andrew Rice, explained the format of my dissertation biography, and acknowledged those who had supported and assisted me in the dissertation process.

Finally, I was ready for the real biography, eventually told in eight chapters that captured John Andrew Rice's life and an epilogue that analyzed his contributions. The art, if there was to be any, meant considering ways to arrange enormous amounts of material in a way that would be coherent, but not necessarily chronological. Life as a march of days, months and years readily defeats artistry. Life as patterns and meanings inspires the artistry of design and metaphor. Easy to think about; hard to implement! John William Ward (1970), biographer of Andrew Jackson, called this point of organizing for artistry the "shuffle, cut and deal stage of scholarship— sorting and resorting, trying to find some pattern, some lines of relationship around which to organize what one thinks one knows. This still seems to me the most important moment in the act of writing" (p. 212).

In my search for patterns, I immersed myself in thousands of pages of source literature, documents and interview transcripts. From the reading and re-reading, patterns began to emerge. The final product, my eight chapters, does proceed chronologically, or at least in order of time, but not in a balanced way. In other words, three chapters represent Rice's seven years at Black Mountain College; only one represents the first sixteen years of his career life. Within each chapter, I subordinated chronology in favor of relating important events or demonstrating important patterns. This decision allowed me to avoid the sing-song accumulation of chronological occurrences and to tell a life with style, rather than write the diary of one man's activities from year to year.

I was selective about what to quote, what to include at length, and what to mention only briefly. Does this mean my "artistry" compromised my "truth"? Maybe, but maybe not. I know that I committed myself to the idea of a scholarly biography and that I searched at length for facts that could form the basis of truth. I reported those fully, although I gave most attention to those who helped answer my questions about the educational philosophies of John Andrew Rice. Others I used more incidentally as contextual information.

By writing a dissertation that was a biography, I was able to enjoy the creative work of the artist and to employ the methodological precision of the scholar. The biographical form gave me an opportunity to be a detective, a romantic and a highly disciplined researcher all at once; and after 18 months, I was still interested and enthusiastic. More than ever I appreciated the wisdom of John Andrew Rice's (1967) own comment: "I've always said you couldn't write history, but you could come close to it if you knew all the people and knew the way they behaved."

Chapter Fourteen

Willing Biographer, Unwilling Subject

Tony Reid

Biography can be a treacherous art. It is not enough that biographers must sort through great mountains of archival information and find a meaningful life in them. No, they must also beware of those facts. Perhaps the subject destroyed some unflattering information. Perhaps the subject wrote a slanted diary with an eye to posterity. These are evident pitfalls. But one under-reported obstacle to the biographer is the subject who deliberately destroys all her personal papers. Such was the case with Laura Zirbes, as I found out after I began my dissertation research. This essay discusses the problems I faced in writing a biography of a subject who was unwilling to be studied.

Laura Zirbes (1884–1967) was one of the "Dauntless Women" of American education. With 61 years of teaching experience, she was perhaps the greatest authority on elementary education of her time. As it is for most people, I considered a biographical approach helpful for understanding her because her personality influenced her approach to her job. But for Zirbes, the connection was also strong in the opposite direction as she worked hard to make her personal life reflect her professional beliefs. Thus, to understand why she did not wish to be studied is, in essence, to seek to know her character.

Fresh out of normal school, Laura Zirbes began her teaching career in Cleveland in 1903 at the age of 19. Two weeks later, she revolted. She took her teacher's manual into her principal's office and said, "Do I have to use this thing?"

The principal answered sagely, "What would you do instead?" Laura, who had as many as 56 immigrant children in her class, told her principal exactly what she would do "if I didn't have to be told what to do by a book that was written by somebody I didn't know, and who never saw the children I was teaching." Zirbes found the manual to be "no good, it got in the way. And the minute I put it aside and got their Americanization and their growing in my mind, and went straight for that, something happened" (Zirbes, 1962).

Zirbes placed children first and had the courage to follow that instinct. We know little about the curriculum Zirbes used during her first years as a teacher, but in her later speeches and books she told of a time when "lockstep teaching" dominated. Increasingly she abandoned the fixed curriculum, so much so that the math supervisor scolded her for being "too analytical," reprimanded her for deviating from drill methods, and charged that "You certainly do not make a good cog." Zirbes, angered, replied, "Cog? Cog? I don't think the Lord intended me to be a cog!" (Zirbes, 1958, p. 211).

Zirbes was afraid of nothing. When she was nine her father, a Baptist preacher, told her that the organist was going to have a baby and that Laura would have to learn to play the organ for church. Laura, who couldn't play a note, accepted the challenge. "All right," she said, "do I do it next Sunday?" (Barkan, 1952, p. 115). Within a few months she had taught herself to play. Naturally, then, when she was a fresh Ph.D., and William S. Gray offered her the chance to help him write the Scott-Foresman basal readers, she turned him down. Possible fame and fortune were no match for her principles (Jacobs, 1991). Basal readers, she believed, were not the way to teach children to read, and she would not be a party to them. Perhaps she remembered from her father's sermons "For what is a man profited, if he shall gain the whole world, and lose his own soul?"

In 1928, Zirbes joined the staff at Ohio State and made it her mission to establish the elementary teacher education program there. The Summer Demonstration School and the University Elementary School were two of Zirbes' most important innovations. While laboratory schools were hardly a new idea, Zirbes deserves credit for insisting that hers be an experimental school rather than just a teacher training school. In the 1950s she pioneered the Language Experience approach to reading, was active in Action Research, and became a national leader in the creativity movement leading to the publication of her best book, *Spurs to Creative Teaching*, in 1959.

As I began to research the life of Laura Zirbes, it quickly became apparent that no collection of her personal papers existed. How then (I asked myself) could I write a biography? Could I produce only a shallow exegesis of her 242 articles and books? Ohio State held only one small folder of biographical material and none of her prized collection of taped speeches. Then in the archives of the Association for Childhood Education International (ACEI) at the University of Maryland I found some letters and several of her tape recordings. With the help of Paul Klohr, her former colleague and student at Ohio State (Klohr, 1996), I began to track down her students and colleagues, eventually interviewing 42 of them. These contacts would lead me to some invaluable primary sources. Lorrene Ort graciously shared with me her private collection of more than a hundred personal letters Zirbes had written to her between 1955 and 1967. Virginia Macagnoni gladly shared another large collection of letters dating between 1957 and 1967. Lorraine Lange contributed letters and other unpublished materials. Fred Helsabeck found his forgotten correspondence with Zirbes from between 1961 and 1965, as well as correspondence with friends of Zirbes after her death as he led the effort to place her on the ACEI Roll of Honor. All these letters provided insight into Zirbes' personal thoughts, albeit chiefly during the period after her retirement. Together with the interviews, they fleshed out her character, her personality and her values. The real Laura Zirbes, who had been just a shadow behind her writing, began to come into view.

But in the midst of all this revelation, the thunderbolt struck: Zirbes did not want to be studied. Soon after I wrote my first inquiry letter to Lorrene Ort, I left on vacation. I returned two weeks later to find the phone ringing; it was Ort (1991a), eager to discuss Zirbes. Standing in the kitchen I knew I had to take notes, but on what? I took a small notepad off the refrigerator and started writing. I filled 16 pages. But the biggest news was on the first: Zirbes had destroyed her own papers. It had happened in 1960 when, after a heart attack, she moved out of her own house into a friend's house. Instead of donating her papers to the university, she asked her friend Louie, the garbage man, to throw them out. Ort recalled that they included papers on two of Zirbes' innovations, the University School and the Walhalla House nursery school. At the same time, Zirbes also gave a lot of her dresses to Louie since his wife was about her size. Did Zirbes' life work mean no more to her than her dresses?

For an instant I was shocked that Zirbes would destroy her own papers and half doubted it. But in the next instant, I knew it was true. Naturally she would do that. Her whole philosophy pointed to just such behavior. For one thing she was genuinely modest. As she once said, "I wasn't raised to brag about anything; one just did it" (Barkan, 1952, p. 118). She never sought status and she abhorred status seekers. She shunned organizations where she felt the members were mainly interested in office holding and status. She often worked anonymously, writing unsigned articles or contributing large checks to the ACEI's Building Fund. She minimized the importance of her own contributions to the field. Her writing is full of descriptions of how a teacher handled a situation or of a program someone developed without revealing that she is talking about herself. (I know this only because internal evidence occasionally allowed me to tie the story to something I had already confirmed about her.)

I also recalled that Zirbes considered the past unimportant, a somewhat odd belief considering her thorough understanding of history. What mattered to her was not how we got here, but where we are going (Ort, 1991b). In fact, Zirbes was so intent on fighting the past, on overcoming tradition and fixed ways, that she saw little use in studying history.

Finally, and most importantly, Zirbes was convinced that a solution developed for one situation should never be imposed on another situation. This belief in *sui generis* situations lay at the core of her philosophy. A child-centered theorist, she believed that every teacher must be in tune with her particular students and teach them according to their specific needs and interests. What was appropriate for a third grade class one year might be inappropriate for next year's third graders or inappropriate for third graders in another school or another state. How, then, could her solutions from the 1930s suit the needs and interests of students in the 1960s or the 1990s? A colleague recalls that someone once told Zirbes she should write a book and put down all her ideas. Zirbes responded, "No, I might change my mind entirely!" (Utterback, 1991). Zirbes had fought all her life against traditional, fixed methods, and she resisted the idea that her solutions might become the new tradition unthinkingly accepted by future teachers. No wonder she destroyed her own papers!

So, I faced a philosophical and perhaps an ethical dilemma: Should I write a biography about someone who probably would not have wanted it written, and whose ideas had constantly evolved throughout her life? She had once told Lorrene Ort, "I do not want all this re-hashed." How could I ignore her request? It was neither a selfish nor an ill-considered request; it came from a woman who lived her convictions. It grew out of the courage of the nine-year-old willing to teach herself to play the organ. It reflected the conviction of the fresh Ph.D. who turned down a lucrative offer from one of the leading scholars and publishing houses of her day.

My respect for her convictions worsened my quandary. I knew that Zirbes had an extraordinary sense of principles and a unique understanding of who she was and where she wanted to go. My friends did not believe me when I said that I even "talked" to her, but it was true. With someone so principled, who was I to violate her wishes? But what about my own goals? I had chosen Zirbes for a subject because of those very qualities; I liked her values and her spunkiness, so vivid in contrast to the bland education landscape. I liked the idea of studying a woman, and I liked the idea of studying someone in my own field, elementary education. Zirbes was more than just a theoretician; her forte had been to make developmental philosophy work. She had much to teach me.

I worried about the dilemma, and in the course of my subsequent interviews with her friends and colleagues, I often raised it. They all agreed that Zirbes should be studied, despite her wishes, because they had grown weary of hearing about today's "new ideas" that she implemented forty or sixty

years ago. Educators today re-learn many of the same principles that guided Zirbes. As James Hymes (1991) noted, many
educators are discovering these ideas as if for the first time.

This rationale clicked. I had been trained as an historian,
and now I recalled that—at least among some historians—one
reason we study the past is to learn more about the present.
Here I found a strong reason to study Zirbes. The construc-
tivists and whole language advocates of today share much with
the Progressives. Will they make the same mistakes the Progressives made? They are already under attack, just as the
Progressives were. Should not they listen to the voice of Laura
Zirbes, who fought and lost the same battle once before?

Zirbes gained insights today's reformers do not fully
grasp. She understood that since teachers teach as they were
taught, those who teach teachers must examine their own
methods. She understood that teachers are not trained, they
are educated. She understood that if you ask a teacher to work
without a pre-planned curriculum, at least you should let her
see the new system in operation to convince her it can work.
The Progressives used laboratory schools for this purpose;
today we slowly rediscover the value of model schools. She
knew that unless *teachers* keep growing professionally, they
become mere *schoolkeepers*. She knew that teaching was
science *and* art. She knew how important it was for children to
work together democratically, to tackle real problems and to
develop the habits of analyzing and assessing their own work.
These many valuable lessons Zirbes still teaches.

Zirbes should also be studied as a woman who succeeded
in a man's world, in the face of staggering prejudice. Though
things have changed, women can still find inspiration in a
powerful model like Zirbes. I am glad my three daughters and
my son have come to "know" Laura Zirbes. I am glad I have
come to know Laura Zirbes. As an elementary school principal I find her common sense and her blend of practicality and
vision relevant to my daily life. I can ask myself, How would
Laura Zirbes react to this situation? What questions would she
ask? How would she seek to move forward? I feel no com-
pulsion to do what she did (and I know that she would not
want me to), but it is helpful to examine my ideas in relation
to hers.

Scholars may become impatient with these selfish and present-oriented reasons alone. Yet, to put it simply: We study history to understand what actually happened. When I thought about it that way, I realized Zirbes had no say in whether she became the focus of a study. She was but an actor on the stage, not the playwright. We want to know what actually happened, and we cannot allow one person to remove her contributions from consideration.

So the ultimate reason I saw for studying Laura Zirbes was to glean more knowledge of her era. She made many contributions to her times, and I am content with my decision to profile an unwilling subject. On the general level, I am convinced that writing a biography is an appropriate way to study education and to refine one's abilities as a researcher and writer. On the particular level, I am content that Zirbes would understand my reasons and perhaps agree with me— even though we would no doubt argue and I could hardly expect her to change her mind entirely. I studied Zirbes because she is part of our past and part of our present. The philosophy of developmental teaching had to be learned from a master teacher, and passed from one teacher to another in an apostolic succession. Her greatest legacy is these thousands of teachers. Many of them, in turn, taught others, so that Laura Zirbes' influence carries on in countless classrooms, even among teachers who have never heard her name. She has now become, as James Hymes (1991) observed, part of the unconscious mind of education today. Since she belongs to all of us, we must come to know her better.

Chapter Fifteen

The Biographer's Relationship with Her Subject

Lynda Anderson Smith

Recently, I thought about how I feel at the end of a long day of rifling through dry, dusty archives as I continue my research on Robert Gilchrist. I read for endless hours, then at last, I have a glimmer of insight into my subject's character or uncover a precious bit of new information. These discoveries and insights become enmeshed in speculation and wanderings, and the gentle elation brings to mind the Lerner and Loewe lyric: "What a rare mood I'm in! . . . It's almost like being in love."

While perhaps inappropriate reflections for a dissertation student, I feel qualified to use those words to describe the relationship between the biographer and her subject. Paul Mariani (1984) agreed when he said: "Writing biography is . . . rather like falling in love. At some point we must have seen something like a greatness in our subject, or if not that at least a uniqueness . . . an achievement, or . . . a special peculiarity in the life, a hunger at least for something, an ideal, however flawed, which draws the biographer on day after day" (p. 31). Infact, writing biography can be exactly like falling in love. What biographer has not felt the same exhilaration, excitement, attraction and then the joy of discovering that the two of you agree on many important matters, that you share beliefs, ideas and interests. What a thrill it is when you begin to identify with your subject, when trust, commitment and even ownership begin to develop and grow! It really is almost like being in love.

If the subject is dead, the relationship tends to be one-sided, with the biographer in control. But what if the subject is living? And further, what if the subject is eager to develop the relationship? What if the subject is more than just "ready, willing and able"? Might the situation then become a biographical "dangerous liaison?" These rhetorical questions are hardly rhetorical for me. I am grappling with those questions right now because my biographical subject is living, anxious to have his biography written, and cooperative to a fault.

In 1991, Dr. Robert Spence Gilchrist donated his professional papers to the University of South Carolina Museum of Education. At the time I was searching for a dissertation topic that would lend itself to a creative research methodology and the idea of using the archives to write an educational biography interested me. Gilchrist and I had several things in common: He had been a practitioner, as am I, for nearly all of his career in public education (from 1922 to 1967), and he had been involved, as am I, in progressive education, core curriculum and unit teaching. I saw an additional advantage to choosing Gilchrist as my research subject: He is interested in working with a biographer and is willing to cooperate in any way he can.

While I was at first interested, I was also a bit apprehensive about tackling the project. I considered myself too objective, impersonal and reserved to write the life of another human adequately, to elicit "the warmth of a life being lived." Writing a research paper is one thing, but writing a life? No. I concluded that biography was best left to historians, psychologists and detectives. Over the next year, I considered several other topics, yet nothing seemed to engage my interest quite as strongly as the possibility of a Gilchrist biography had.

As Catherine Drinker Bowen (1968) suggested: "Perhaps what the biographer needs is not love as much as identification with the hero. Whether or not one likes one's subject, it would be fatal to choose a hero with whom one could not identify. . . . Something in the subject's life has touched the biographer's own experience, even though the deed came no closer than a wish" (pp. 66-67). Gilchrist's professional life certainly struck a familiar chord in my life; I felt that we were somehow connected as fellow educators over time. Because we share viewpoints and hold many of the same educational beliefs, I felt that this connection would allow me to present dual perceptions of the field of curriculum: one rooted in present practice and one rooted in the past. With these thoughts in mind, but still reluctant and with reservations about my ability to develop a relationship with my subject, I decided in 1992 to write an educational biography of Gilchrist.

After reading Gilchrist's published works, studying the archival documents, and finally interviewing him face to face in March of 1993, I found "falling in love" with one's subject an apropos description of my condition. From the beginning, I had no problems establishing a cordial relationship with my subject. Indeed, far from having the objective distant research orientation I thought might frost and distort my work, I find myself in danger of violating Leon Edel's (1959) second "principia" for writing lives: "[B]iographers must struggle constantly not to be taken over by their subjects, or to fall in love with them" (p. 29). The danger now is not impersonality but subjectivity caused by fascination with my subject. From the moment I told Gilchrist "I do," I have been asking for trouble.

Yet, the more I find out about Gilchrist, the more I admire him. Actually, the interview clinched it for me. He was friendly, charming, amusing and helpful. What more could I ask? Unless I am careful, my dissertation will turn into hagiography —the life and times of Saint Robert! Who would approve that? Certainly not Gilchrist, who is professional enough to respect whatever version of the truth my research justifies. Certainly not my committee members, who demand scholarship and thoughtful research, not emotional blubber. No, unless I curb my infatuation, my work may sink into mediocrity.

Overfascination is far from the only problem that can surface in a personal association with one's subject. Any attraction requires a close involvement with the object of one's admiration. Frank Vandiver (1983) suggested that the biographer cannot remain in contact with the subject for long and avoid feelings of empathy—"biography's quintessential quality." Of course, the danger is not that I may become too involved with my subject since writing a truly objective history of another person's experience is impossible. Rather the danger lies in over-identification. A natural consequence of the intimate contact between researcher and subject is empathy, the ability to understand and share another's feelings. But empathy can easily become sympathy, a patronizing feeling of approval, as the biographer becomes more and more involved in the relationship and begins to "root for" the subject. The biographer begins to feel that she can actually predict the subject's feelings and emotions. She begins to believe that the two of them think alike. She takes criticism of her subject personally, ardently defends his behavior against any question, and begins to deny facts that do not fit the image she has created. The result is as much a distortion of the subject's life and the biographer's intentions as too little involvement and too much objectivity would produce.

The following example demonstrates how a biographer maintains an empathetic perspective as he deals with the unexpected behavior of his subject. During the research for his biography of Martin Luther King, *Let the Trumpet Sound*, Stephen Oates (1982) discovered that King had engaged in several sexual indiscretions. Oates (1991) wrote, "While I do not condone infidelity, I tried to understand it in my subject, to be compassionate about his troubles—his needs and loneliness and the constant temptations—that led him astray" (p. 30). Oates was relieved to discover that King felt guilty about his behavior. Believing the indiscretions did little damage to King's integrity as a public figure and failed to detract from his significance as a national leader, Oates did not try to conceal or justify his subject's behavior. Rather, he decided to present it as an example of King the human being, with the same flaws, frailties and shortcomings many others possess. In short, Oates used empathy as the creative spark to illuminate his subject's humanness. Another less experienced biographer might have allowed empathy (understanding) to turn to sympathy (protection) in a similar situation.

Marc Pachter (1981) noted that when the biographer loses herself in her subject, she gives up "the distance that allows the writer to become something more than the agent for a reputation. . . . [I]t is the force of the subject's personality, its power to fascinate or to dominate, which binds the biographer. The threat is all the greater when biographer and subject know each other" (p. 9). This problem is mine as Gilchrist and I reconstruct the past together, a luxury biographers whose subjects are dead do not enjoy. Because we hold similar beliefs about many aspects of education, over-identifying with him is especially easy. We already have much in common; I already like him as a professional and as a person; and I already find myself wanting to overlook or discount anything that fails to match the vision of his life I am forming. The question I might ask myself is whether I could react as Oates did if I found disappointing or unsavory behavior in Gilchrist.

Not wanting to disappoint or displease the object of one's admiration can be an insidious consequence of choosing a living subject. Because I admire Gilchrist, I want his approval of my work. I want him to be proud of what I have written and to admire me, too. My dissertation now has two criteria for success: My committee must approve it, and so must Gilchrist. In fact, his opinion of my work may supersede the opinions of others. It is, after all, *his* life I am writing. What could be worse than falling short of the expectations of someone whose life you admire? The temptation to write what the researcher knows her subject would like to read can be irresistible. But to embrace and present a sanitized one-dimensional view of that life would be to smother it with love. The attraction becomes fatal if allowed to obscure the truth through embellishment, overstatement or omission.

Writing biography is an intensely personal experience. Linda Wagner-Martin (1994) noted that "once a biographer has chosen a subject and dedicated herself to investigating and researching the life in question . . . , she does merge in some ways with the subject" (p. 167). This merging becomes a synergetic marriage, a partnership formed from joint interest and for mutual benefit, a collaboration and a combination of minds and hearts. I have had company in those dusty archives; Gilchrist has been there with me, looking over my shoulder, illuminating the corners of his past. He and I together have stepped into the time machine and have become caught up in the educational events of receding decades. As a result, I will come away with much more than the knowledge of a neoteric research technique. I will have shared in the recreation of another's life story, something one cannot accomplish by qualitative data analysis or statistical inference.

Whether a relationship is amorous, familial, friendly or professional, as is the case of researcher and subject, too much love can indeed be a "fatal attraction" when it comes to biography. Fascination and over-identification with the subject, combined with the desire to please, can distort the biography and destroy impartiality. Not that I strive for absolute objectivity. Quite the contrary, scientific detachment belongs in a case study not a biography: "Let objectivity and distance be relegated to the preface of the biography or to the notes of the index" (Mariani, 1984, p. 30). We come to know our subject in a special way, based on a combination of admiration for, interest in, and curiosity about someone else's life and our own life experiences. As a practitioner of the art of life-writing, however, I strive for accuracy by tempering love with logic, by mitigating fascination with reason, and by balancing subjectivity with objectivity. That range of emotions and feelings between the two extremes is where the proper relationship takes me.

Chapter Sixteen

A Search for Prose That Recreates the Past

Thomas B. Horton

Resurrecting a life story from the past differs from researching the history of a contemporary person. Both tasks compel
the researcher to look beyond what is merely apparent—what
is easily known. Researching a contemporary life imposes the
burden of sifting through a multitude of first-person accounts
and an accumulation of personal trivia. Then, too, the living
current of prevailing opinion often divides along at least two
lines of interpretation of the character's contributions. When
biographers plunge through the decades and centuries to
recapture a nearly forgotten life story, however, they dwell in
the recesses of lonely archives amid rows of Hollinger boxes
that contain the dusty fragments of long forgotten ventures.
From the flaking pages of old diaries to the eulogies in
crumbling newspapers, one meticulously reconstructs a voice
cloaked with the passion of another time. Absent are the living
peers and adversaries who can guide one to this or that
anecdote. Gone forever are the thousands of pertinent yet
unrecorded minute acts of humanity that lend meaning to
existence. Biographers of past subjects are alone with their
musings, and they must piece together meaning and reconstitute the vitality of a bygone time.

That lonely search has become my adventure. By
combining my love for education and a desire to reconnect
with its heritage, I chose biographical research to adduce meaning from facts I might find from the past. When I set out in
search of Moses Waddel (1770-1840), the eminent South

Carolina educator, I began a journey both back into time and into my own imperfect comprehension of the competing, sometimes conflicting, currents of political, theological and philosophical thought so evident in the Federal period of American history. Along the way, I found the essence of biography to be going beyond the obvious into the informed imagination where the subject breathes and speaks and the reader senses the fervor of forgotten struggles and reconnects with lives and ideas once lost but lost no more.

Years ago, I read Coit's (1950) Pulitzer Prize winning biography of John C. Calhoun, and I came across a reference to Moses Waddel and his famed log cabin academy, Willington. I stored the reference and when I decided to re-search this once legendary educator, a phrase from Catherine Drinker Bowen's (1966) preface to *Miracle at Philadelphia* came to mind: "If the story is old, the feelings behind it are new as Monday morning. If all the tales are told, retell them, Brother. If few attend, let those who listen feel" (p. xii). Perhaps I, too, could bring back a colorful personality and a compelling story complete, with both passion and vigor and tedium and earthiness.

My search for Moses Waddel led me to the area of his birth near Statesville, North Carolina. There a Presbyterian Church librarian pointed me to old church records. Five miles from town, a state historical society marked the nearby loca-tion of the site of Waddel's grammar school, a famed colonial classical academy. I found his name referenced there as one of the prominent graduates. University libraries provided useful background on my character, yet Waddel's personality remained elusive. I knew by then that this son of Scotch-Irish immigrants had been deeply influenced by the Calvinist teachings of his youth, but at this point, I took a detour in my research to familiarize myself with the patterns of Scotch-Irish immigration to America and the strong reformation heritage of the Calvin movement that strongly influenced these pioneers. Somewhere in this all-consuming search for meaning it occurred to me that Moses Waddel's story had its own voice complete with its own vocabulary, sentence struc-ture and syntax. I was in the Library of Congress reading Waddel's microfilm diary and book of sermons, for he was a teaching divine of the frontier era, when the feeling came to me that his story needed retelling, yet his original voice should be preserved.

I wrestled with the dilemma of whether or not storytelling has a place in serious scholarship. Yet, I became determined to capture the flavor of a prose style that utilizes nineteenth century phraseology drawn from careful readings of period literature. When I wanted reassurance, I turned to Stephen Oates (1986) who stressed that a writer has an obligation to convey a feeling for the subject through diction:

> Because it must make the people of history live again, pure biography must be more than the compilation of research notes—more than the presentation of what one has gleaned from letters, interviews, journals, diaries, reminiscences, and other contemporary accounts. The prose of the biographer must radiate a sense of intimacy and familiarity, quite as though the author himself had lived the life and walked the ground. And this is a quality that can only be acquired by visiting the landmarks where one's subject lived and died. In the course of writing about John Brown, I journeyed across eastern Kansas where the civil war of 1856 had flamed, taking notes on the landscape, the murderous thunderstorms, and the howling winds that lashed the area where Brown's Station was located, and comparing these to descriptions recorded in Brown's time. As I stood rooted to the spot, the sounds of Bleeding Kansas—of artillery salvos, pounding hooves, shouts, and gunfire—echoed in the windy trees around me. And I could almost see Brown and his guerrilla band as they rode across the prairie to ransack proslavery homesteads and fight proslavery men (pp. 129-130).

In my biography of Moses Waddel I strove to recreate the atmosphere of the nineteenth century frontier academy recitation hall. Leon Edel (1959) observed that "No biography is complete unless it reveals the individual within history, within an ethos and a social complex" (p. 14). I wanted my readers to share Waddel's tension as he was torn between the two compelling drives in his life: preaching and teaching. Using the writing style of the subject's own era is one means of capturing the time and the essence of that struggle.

I prepared myself to write about a nineteenth century educator by reading much of the literature presented in the preparatory school curriculum of the day. In an age that stressed classical studies through translation of copious lines of Latin and Greek into English, I knew I could benefit by reading Homer, Ovid, Virgil, Cicero and Petrarch—though I did read these in translation. Not content with merely familiarizing myself with the preparatory school curriculum, I became immersed in the milieu of nineteenth century life of upcountry South Carolina. Old newspapers on microfilm provided glimpses into everyday life. Diaries and letters of contemporaries rendered flavor to the period. Oratory was a prized art in those early days of the Republic, and many fine speeches of the nineteenth century are preserved in archives. They exhibit tendencies toward eloquence, verbosity and flowery sentiment. Teresa Iles (1992) spoke of life writing as being "full of the interconnected pains and pleasures" (p. 2). For coming to terms with who Moses Waddel was to his students and parishioners, I had to feel the pains and pleasures of his time. Since Waddel taught many famous men, John C. Calhoun, Andrew Crawford, Hugh Swinton Legare, Augustus B. Longstreet, James L. Petigru, Alexander Stephens to name a few, I was able to find a treasure trove of memoirs from his students. From their writings, I pieced together anecdotes that shed light on the mood and temper of the log cabin classical academy.

Pulling the pieces of a life together involves a lot of mundane detective work as any researcher knows. "Gleaning" is a term that surfaces often as information from libraries, archive and public records offices begins to meld in one's mind. Then comes the time when the information search must end and the writing must begin. Note cards spill out on a desk, photocopies of countless pages get clipped together, a photograph or two might mean nothing to anyone save the researcher, a pebble and a leaf collected from the old home site—such are the fruits of months of inquiry. I know Waddel has uttered no sound since 1840. How shall I tell his story to the world? He is from another time entirely, and he worked to disassociate himself from the age in which he lived—old Puritan that he was. Biographers can look backward in a patronizing way, but that strikes me as self-righteous and pompous. Rather, just as an actor gets himself into character and becomes that character on screen or stage, a biographer, too, can choose to cast a subject's life story in a historical voice that uses a prose style reflecting the era and the life story.

But where does one begin to acquire historical voice for a subject? I drew from my literary interests first. I have always enjoyed Victorian and nineteenth century American prose. I knew that a flowery descriptive phrase of eight words describing a phenomenon in the nineteenth century condensed to three words in the twentieth. Yet, without being burdensome, I believed I could convey Moses Waddel's story subtly through language that he would have recognized, and that the power of language could evoke a feeling of the scent of wood smoke and fresh cut pine from the days of the frontier.

I read the journals of the period, the newspapers, the novels (Calvinist preacher, Moses Waddel despised novels as the ultimate frivolity), the lengthy letters and diaries. Every researcher does that. One nineteenth century writer, William Gilmore Simms, the novelist referred to as the "American Scott" and the "James Fenimore Cooper of the South," influenced more than anyone else my determination to induce my reader "to feel the history," as Catherine Drinker Bowen prescribes. His prose style pulls readers into the setting and invites them to be unobtrusive observers and at times partisans in the unfolding drama. If I could imitate Simms' sentence structure complete with dependent clauses and descriptive verbs and flowery adjectives, I might achieve the "spark and glow" Stephen Oates (1991) alluded to when he said: "the writing of biography is a literary art requiring special skills. It is as demanding as fiction—maybe even more demanding, since the biographer's imagination is limited by fact. He is an artist on oath. He is a sorcerer who rubs facts until they spark and glow with life. . . . To stimulate his subject's life, the biographer relies on the magic of language" (p. 15).

In William Gilmore Simms' *The Scout* (1854), a work of historical fiction set in South Carolina in the 1770's, the author's rich prose style pulls the reader into his narrative:

The stranger, as he leaped upon the solid earth, appeared of a noble and commanding presence. In shape he was symmetrically and vigorously made. Tall, erect, and muscular, his person was that of one who had been long accustomed to hardy and active exercises. In his movements there was a confident ease —the result equally of a fearless spirit and a noble form— which tallied well with a certain military exactness of carriage; commending his well-finished limbs to the eye, while conveying to the mind of the observer an impression, not less favorable, of the noble and firm character of their proprietor (p. 18).

Simms employed abundant adjectives and adverbs in a complex sentence structure to convey mood. Simms' contemporary, James Fenimore Cooper, in *The Last of the Mohicans* (1826), is equally descriptive, if not quite as verbose:

The words were still in the mouth of the scout, when the leader of the party, whose approaching footsteps had caught the vigilant ear of the Indian, came openly into view. A beaten path, such as those made by the periodical passage of the deer, wound through a little glen at no great distance, and struck the river at the point where the white man and his red companions had posted themselves (p. 36).

These works of fiction, characteristic of early nineteenth century literary expression, trap peculiar moments in time and preserve them, flavor and all, for posterity.

Mason Locke Weems, known as Parson Weems, another early nineteenth century American literary figure, wrote a highly romanticized life of Washington that popularized many colorful, if fictionalized, anecdotes about the first president. Weems collaborated with Peter Horry of South Carolina in the 1820's to write his *Life of Francis Marion* (1824). Examine a paragraph of Weems' biography of Marion:

Presently day appeared; and, as the dawning light increased, the frightened militia began to discover the woods reddening over the crimson with the long extended lines of the British army, which soon, with rattling drums and thundering cannon, came rushing on to the charge. The militia, scarcely waiting to give them a distant fire, broke and fled in the utmost precipitation.

Whereupon Gates clapped spurs to his horse, and pushed hard
after them, as he said "to bring the rascals back." But he took
care never to bring himself back, nor indeed to stop until he
had fairly reached Charlotte, eighty miles from the field of
battle. I remember it was common to talk in those days, that
he killed three horses in his flight (p. 105).

Note the cadence and choice of expression, almost quaint by
more modern standards: "rattling drums," "thundering
cannon," "scarcely waiting to give them a distant fire." In
"Reassembling the Dust," Paul Mariani (1984) observed that
"What we want after all in a biography is the subject alive and
moving, and if this means evoking the Muse of the novelist as
well as the more familiar Clio, that is all to the good" (p. 30).
Weems brings back the thunder of horses hooves, the swirl of
dust, and the gripping sense of fear as Gates propels himself
away from a certain date with the hangman's noose. Weems
gives us "the life and not the marble tribute."

In my portrayal of Moses Waddel and his nineteenth
century academy, Willington, I sought to recreate the mood of
the best of early American secondary education by employing
the kind of descriptive prose and sentence structure familiar
then. My intention was to make my modern research effort
congruent with the voices of the past. No longer were we
separated by a chasm of word usage and syntax. Examine, if
you will, the opening sentences of Chapter Three with a description of the area where the Willington Academy became
one of America's most prestigious schools:

The wide Savannah River meanders stogidly by the slight
knoll on which was nestled the bustling village of Vienna.
Across the way one could make out the houses, sheds, and
docks of two of the newly laid out towns, St. Petersburg near
the confluence of the Savannah and Broad Rivers, and Lisbon
on the west bank of the Broad. Not far up river was the little
port of Southampton. A hint of Europe, if in name only, still
flavored this frontier corner of America. The daylight hours in
Vienna were rent by the sound of axes and crosscut saws. The
scent of fresh-hewn lumber stacked on wharves greeted the
casual stroller just as nearby rafted river skiffs knocked and
bumped monotonously in the gentle waves (Horton, 1992, p.
110).

Let the mind disengage for the moment and be transported to another time and place where human interaction occurred at a less hectic pace than in this internetted computer age. The archaic language recreates the character's peculiar life story. The phraseology, and occasional archaic spelling help convey the appropriate mood. In fact, after immersing myself for months in the prose style of another era, I acquired a sense of the syntax and descriptive vocabulary. How does this effort benefit the researcher and the reader? What does recreation of historical voice accomplish that traditional research fails to accomplish? I experienced another subtle dimension to scholarly writing and, in so doing, I refined my perspective as historian, biographer, ethnographer, teacher and educator addressing important contemporary issues. I took Maxine Greene's (1995) advice to "release the imagination." Creating an active historical voice does, in fact, facilitate an act of transcendence, a going beyond the mere trivia and trappings of human existence into the tone of an era. One no longer merely superimposes ancient subject matter onto a modern interpretive context. Hearing an historical voice, the reader understands more of the characters in their own terms. In many cases the narrative, by being more descriptive, is more readable than the sterile prose style of modern theses and journals. An active historical voice pulls the reader into, not just a life, but an era complete with sounds and aromas, and it encourages a further look into the turmoils of other times.

The active historical voice is an alternative writing style that brings creative diversity to the developing art of educational biography. In her biography of William Bull, colonial governor of South Carolina, Geraldine M. Meroney (1991) said, "unless history speaks to the human condition it becomes only the plaything of pedants" (p. vi). This dimension of historical writing speaks to the human condition. I believe that an historical voice enhances biographical writing by taking the reader to the era of the action rather than bringing the action to the era of the reader. Catherine Drinker Bowen admonished storytellers to make those few who listen "feel," and we researchers who use the voice of the time employ one more compelling component in the complex of strategies known as educational biography. I make no claim to speak *for* Moses Waddel; however, I have re-presented his era, and I have listened and faithfully recounted a forgotten, yet educationally significant life story. In so doing, I have heard the great man speak—not as from the tomb, but as from the battered schoolmaster's desk at Willington.

Chapter Seventeen

Is It Fiction or Biography?

Edwin C. Epps

With the 1965 publication of *In Cold Blood* Truman Capote claimed to have presented the literary establishment with the first—some would say still the best—representative of a new literary genre, the nonfiction novel. Described on its dust jacket as "a contribution toward the establishment of a serious new literary form," *In Cold Blood* told the story of a gruesome quadruple homicide in the small town of Holcomb, Kansas, by treating the narrative novelistically instead of journalistically, the usual strategy in such reports. Capote rendered scenes with a painter's eye for detail; he developed characters that compelled the reader's attention as much as they repelled it; and he created memorable dialogues, which although gripping and presumably true to the real personalities involved, were often reconstructions or based upon a novelist's feel for what must have really occurred. The book caused a sensation and was followed by a sensational film treatment.

In the thirty years since, the "nonfiction novel" and its permutations have become commonplace. Writings as diverse as Norman Mailer's *The Armies of the Night* (1968) and *The Executioner's Song* (1979); Carl Bernstein and Bob Woodward's *All the President's Men* (1974); John McPhee's many pieces for *The New Yorker* and such subsequent books as *Oranges* (1967), *The Crofter and the Laird* (1970), and *Looking for a Ship* (1990); and Carol Shields' *The Stone Diaries* (1993)—all serve as examples of successfully rendered novelistic nonfiction, fictionalized biography, confessional autobiographical quasi-memoir, nonfiction-like novelization based upon historical record managing to tell engaging stories.

I belabor the point and provide a quick compendium of sub-genres within the type to set a context for the story of my own encounter with Pat Conroy's *The Water Is Wide* (1972a), a nonfiction novel (one might say, though Conroy never has) that describes his year on Daufuskie Island in 1969 and 1970. In Conroy's story I found an opportunity to explore the biographical method as dissertation research and as a means of establishing some idea of educational "truth" in a way a little different from that explored in the more traditional "teacher stories" of those who were *not*, as Conroy was, also novelists.

The problem with any such work, first of all, is what to call it. All of Conroy's novels draw heavily upon his own family and personal histories, a fact that the writer both acknowledges and considers to be an inevitable consequence of his own authorial personality. As he once told an interviewer,

> When I began to write I decided to disguise everything. If I made my father an Air Force officer it's very different than a Marine Corps officer. I knew a great deal more about Marine Corps officers. Also, if I made him a ground officer that's very different than a pilot. But, I kept coming back to why don't I just write about a Marine Corps fighter pilot from Chicago who married a woman like my mother? Writing fiction is difficult enough without putting additional problems in your way. So when I wrote *The Great Santini*, I was writing out of real autobiographical territory. People do feel they know me, and it's a natural product of the first decision I made when I started writing fiction (Walsh, 1989, p. 200).

Or, in slightly different words, "I find myself imprisoned in the sensibilities I was given" (Walsh, 1989, p. 201). Enough reviewers of Conroy's work have adduced this aspect of it to establish the awareness as underlying any discussion of his books.

I had this awareness of the place of autobiography in Conroy's work when I began my research into his year on Daufuskie Island; indeed, it was one part of his style that attracted me to *The Water Is Wide* and which drew me to every book he published thereafter. Even so, I was unprepared for the nearly universal tendency of reviewers of the book that was to become the film *Conrack* to regard it as "the truth." Jim Haskins' (1972) review in *The New York Times Book Review* termed the work "an autobiographical account of [Conroy's] own awakening" (p. 10); Matthew Hartman (1972) wrote in *Library Journal* that Conroy "has woven a pleasant story that reads like [not is!] a novel" (p. 2388); and James Buckley's (1972) review for *America* extended for 500 words without once even suggesting that Conroy so much as pretended the book to be fictional, throwing Conroy into such unimpeachably nonfiction company as Herbert Kohl, Jonathan Kozol and John Holt. Later critics agreed, calling the book "basically autobiographical" (Willingham, 1980, p. 56) and a work of "autobigraphical non-fiction" (York, 1987, p. 40).

Certain aspects of the novel at publication also argued against the book as especially clever fiction. For one thing, the blurb printed on the front and rear flaps of the dust jacket, while using the island's fictitious name "Yamacraw" as the setting for the action, shifted confusingly from present to past tense and back again. Also, the first edition includes very real photographs of Pat Conroy and the students he taught; these later appeared as part of a feature story in *Life* magazine (Conroy, 1972b). Then, too, quotations from a lesson in progress in the Island school adorned the front cover; the rear cover carried the comment, "The material on the book jacket was taped in the classroom by William Keyserling. Photographs by William and Paul Keyserling." Both William and Paul Keyserling are actual persons who took their photographs and made their tape recordings on Daufuskie Island and in Conroy's classroom during the year he taught on the island.

In light of these observations, even the most cursory reading of the book and the slightest reflection compelled the conclusion that my first research task—and perhaps my most important task—was to separate the wheat from the chaff of verisimilitude. How much of what seems to be based on fact in the "novel" was so based? Without a serious attempt to answer this question, there seemed little point to ask such others as, Did Conroy "help" his students on the island during his brief time there? What "help," if any, did his students really need? and What, if any, are the broad educational policy implications of Conroy's experience as a teacher on Daufuskie Island in Beaufort County, South Carolina, in 1969 and 1970, at a time of nationwide political turmoil and following close after the start of local desegregation?

I examined the names in the book in an attempt to separate out those of real individuals from invented names for characters who might or might not be based on real persons. In the former category I was able to identify almost two dozen people who appear in the book under their real names and in their actual relationship to Pat Conroy (Epps, 1993, pp. 80–83 ff.). To advance my research, I attempted to contact these individuals and succeeded in several instances. As a result, I discovered a fact potentially both invaluable and problematic: Pat Conroy inspired (and inspires today) strong reactions in people—fierce loyalties and equally fierce antipathies. To his friends' credit, no one tried to gloss over the flaws in Conroy's personality—"stubborn," in fact, was a common epithet issuing from both friends and foes alike—and to his enemies' discredit I found an uncomfortably common tendency to dismiss negative portrayals and conclusions in *The Water Is Wide* as the misperceptions of a callow, unbridled, youthful neophyte, or worse. As an additional complication, I came to like and admire those who I found to be Conroy's strongest champions: Bill Dufford, Gene Norris and Reverend Mike Smith, for example. I also developed a tendency to suspect those who quasi-officially represented the school system of Beaufort County: relatives of former administrators, for example, and former district office consultants. In both situations, I had to sift my predispositions to assess the information they gave me.

Then came the real individuals represented more or less faithfully as characters under fictitious names. Among these I found the former Assistant Superintendent of Beaufort County Schools and Conroy's colleague at the island school, the characters named Ezra Bennington and Mrs. Ruth Brown in the book. H. Emmett McCracken, the real-life counterpart of Ezra Bennington, died within weeks of the start of my research just a few miles from my own home. Julia Johnson, Conroy's actual fellow teacher, had suffered a mental collapse after years of apparent suffering from her portrayal in the book. Unfortunately, then, I missed my chance to interview both of these central actors in the drama. Still, others supplied valuable information about them, as a result of which I could confirm that, whatever its actual basis in fact, Conroy's portrait of Bennington was the grossly stereotypical caricature it seems to any student of literature. One observer at the time called him "paternalistic at best" but then added that "disinterested" was a better word for his attitude toward the students on Daufuskie (Sklar, 1992); in the book, he seems by contrast almost consciously malevolent. One of Conroy and Mrs. Johnson's former students verified for me the woman's essential humanity: "Mrs. Johnson was a true disciplinarian! She was big on covering the basic expected guidelines of the textbooks. She commanded control over her students. *I loved her very much*" (Simmons, 1992; emphasis added). Other members of the school community observed, "I believe Mrs. Johnson did her best" (Powell, 1992) and that she "worked with the children over things that were vital to their survival. . . . We were lucky to have her over there" (Anders, 1991). Even one of Conroy's friends told me, "Pat's portrayal of her in the book was I thought a little much" (Sklar, 1992).

What of Conroy's depiction of the educational condition of the children he taught upon his arrival? Few who have read *The Water is Wide* can forget the dramatic catalog of their deficiencies:

> Some of them could barely write. Half of them were incapable of expressing even the simplest thought on paper. Three quarters of them could barely spell even the most elementary words. Three of them could not write their names. Sweet little Jesus, I thought, as I weaved between the desks, these kids don't know crap. Most of them hid their papers as I came by, ashamed for me to see they had written nothing. By not being able to tell me anything about themselves, they were telling me everything (pp. 28-29).

The catalog is dismal, despairing, hopeless and made even more damning by the fact that the students were *middle school* children, not kindergartners or first graders. From the self-righteous, we-can-conquer-the-world-and-solve-all-its-problems perspective of the early seventies these kids are the literal

embodiment of disability and disadvantage. From other perspectives, however, things look less bleak—a lesson that I
learned early as I considered the various illuminations a given
situation might reflect. As one of the former students told me,
"Generally the students were mixed. We had some very bright
students that could stand in any school setting. [Conroy] down-
played the intelligence of these students" (Simmons, 1992). A
newspaperman from Columbia concurred, quoting "a spokes-
man" at Beaufort High School (Conroy's own alma mater,
the school the Islanders attended after completing the eighth
grade) to the effect that once they left the Island for continued
secondary schooling on the mainland, "They're just like any
other kids" (Krell, 1972, p. 1-B). A district reading teacher
also told me both that the students were far better off than
Conroy depicted them and that he had not had the spectacular
successes with them many readers infer from *The Water Is
Wide* (Powell, 1992).

All in all, as I learned more from those who had been
either participants in or contemporary observers of the events
reconstructed in *The Water Is Wide*, I became more firmly convinced of the truthfulness of two conclusions. First, Conroy's
dispute with the Beaufort County Board of Education and its
representatives is pretty accurately depicted when compared to
the historical record. Interviews with principals and observers,
the journalistic accounts of newspaper reporters at the time,
the School Board Minutes, and the court record of the hearing
on Conroy's appeal of his dismissal all substantiate the basic
plot of the novel, the sources of the conflicts, and the reasons
for that dismissal. Second, Conroy's depiction of characters in
some instances is far removed from the actual personalities
upon whom he appears to have based his characters. This
latter feature of the book might, of course, simply reflect the
novelist's need to tell a good story and to keep his audience
entertained by creating memorable people; in other words, the
demands incumbent upon the artist outweigh those incumbent
upon the chronicler. If such is the case, one is fully justified in
viewing the book on the whole as a "nonfiction novel" or
something like it.

As I undertook my study of Pat Conroy's year on
Daufuskie Island with all its tribulations and triumphs in terms

of the ways they appear in *The Water Is Wide*, I knew I would also have to examine Conroy's life up until the year 1969. His book relates some of the circumstances of his teaching before Daufuskie, his friendships with colleagues and mentors, and his prejudices and gradual moral enlightenment during the age of desegregation and the anti-war movement. If these factors could have shaped either his decision to go to Daufuskie in the first place or some of the instructional decisions he made "across the water" on Daufuskie, then the biographical component of my study would loom large. Some of the same kinds of factors after all shaped my own career as a teacher and those of many friends who had begun teaching in the early seventies as I did. Might it not be possible to validate my private experience—to say nothing of understanding it better —through an understanding of Pat Conroy's very public experience? Better still, might it be possible to suggest at least inferentially through my approach that since education is a quintessentially human undertaking it must also be a thoroughly complex one, fraught with the possibility of mis-understanding, unmeant wrongheadedness, misinterpretation, and occasional refusals to see the light at many stages of the process precisely because of the inescapable play of personality and the burdens of personal history interwoven in the endeavor?

I thought so at the outset and do now after reflecting for nearly three years on the process and product of my study. In 1993, I concluded my dissertation with the following paragraph:

> Did Pat Conroy make a difference in the skills levels of his Daufuskie students? Did he raise their test scores? Did he enable them to make more money as adults? Who knows? Who could possibly know? More to the point, who cares? In the final analysis that's not what it's all about (p. 225).

What is, however, important about Conroy's experience on Daufuskie is the human energy spent fighting the good fight and the almost willful obstinacy of some in refusing to recognize that was what was going on. In the end, the person Pat Conroy could do no other than set in motion the chain of events that led to his own dismissal; his professional self lay at the mercy of his biography. He paid a high price for his entrapment in his personality, and the teaching profession lost a wonderfully gifted talent. In another sense, however, the profession also found a powerful, elegant voice in the process. *The Water Is Wide* is hardly what we think of as a "teacher narrative." It is both more and less. More in the sense that the teacher, not his students, writes with the elegance, grace and power uncommon in our current literature; less in the sense that the focus ultimately is the person and not the analysis of the profession. But the profession needs such people, and the book itself justifies this conclusion.

Conroy's experiences on Daufuskie Island informed his teaching in a way so basic as to be obvious once I knew of his life. His sense of fair play, so strong throughout *The Water Is Wide*, grew out of his own family experiences, the influence of several male role models in his youth, his four years at The Citadel, and the era of social and political unrest into which he was born. His personal integrity, his devotion to truth and righteousness, and his loyalty to friends grew out of these same influences. If such a person *had* to be sent to Daufuskie, the best candidate would be a young man like Pat Conroy whose own life gave him the sensibilities to attempt to understand his students, to respond to them honestly, to learn from them, and then to communicate what he had learned— including the frustration and pain and sadness inherent in both the situation and his role within it—to others eager to learn and to serve as he had. Doris Kearns (Goodwin) (1981) wrote that: "A biographer's original angle of vision also encompasses an image of the place and the time span within which the subject's life story is played out. One would hope that the fascination most biographers feel toward the person extends equally to the place and the time" (p. 94). My fascination with place and time gave me an opportunity to separate fact from fiction, the lesson I learned on my journey into educational biography.

PART FIVE

Implications for the Field of Education

Introduction

We conclude *Writing Educational Biography* with four exploratory essays from contributors asked to speculate on how
biographical studies strengthen work in the field of education.
While I would wish the question moot and the answers
obvious, the current state-of-the-field of educational research
requires such a discussion. In twenty more years, I hope an
"implications for the field" section would describe the impact
of an assortment of full-length biographies and how they have
extended our understanding of the past and present and
offered insights into the foundations of education, teacher education, qualitative research and various other educational concerns. At present, however, implications must rest upon how
biographical and autobiographical research *assists* and *enhances* forms of educational inquiry. Narrative and case study
clearly lead educators to fresh insights into schooling and the
educating of teachers; however, these contributors were asked
to explore additional topics that could be brought into the
educational conversation through biographical research.

Janet L. Miller acknowledges the importance of "narrative
voice" but calls for educators to move beyond the linear and
static conceptions of self: "[W]hat is clear to me is that no one
—neither the educators whom we study through historical or
current biography, nor educators whom we study through
primary works, nor we as educators working together—speaks
in a constant and unchanging voice." Miller sees biographical, autobiographical and narrative forms of inquiry
enabling educators and researchers to "construct, deconstruct,
employ and deploy versions of ourselves as teachers that

challenge any one unitary version of who we are or would be as educators."

William Ayers poses the question, What do you do? "To answer," he maintains, "is, in part, to build a narrative of a life being lived, to speak of agency, to name oneself as social and public, in relation to others, and to be moving forward." He underscores the power of biography and public voice by acknowledging its appropriateness for teachers and students of teaching: "Biography is about passion and commitment, prescription and choice, freedom and responsibility, the individual and the crowd, now and then, life and death. Reading biography can help us locate ourselves; reading biography together can introduce a powerful touch-point for pulling a community together."

Jean Clandinin and Michael Connelly examine the role of storytelling in schools and universities. The importance of storytelling lies in the act of educating others beyond the mere telling per se. Clandinin and Connelly fear that the "rush to narrative and storytelling" may fall to mere faddism when, in fact, for them "the promise of storytelling emerges when we move beyond regarding a story as a fixed entity and engage in conversations with our stories."

This section concludes with a quantitative researcher's perspective. Lorin Anderson re-examines the purpose of research and discusses the delineated, static, isolated "research tribes." Anderson wonders if biographical inquiry can engender discourse and establish community. He challenges biographers, with their integrative methods and their willingness to judge and critique their work, to expand the conversation of the educational research community, to renew discourse and to point conversations in new directions.

These, then, are the possibilities for educational biography at the present. I hope that this collection, with its complex, wide-ranging conceptions of educational biography, will nourish the growing interest in biographical studies in education.

Note
Janet L. Miller and Jean Clandinin delivered presentation versions of their essays at the 1994 keynote session of the Archival and Biographical Research SIG of AERA. William

Ayers delivered a presentation version of his essay at the 1995 Witten Award for Distinguished Work in Biography/ Autobiography Lecture at the Museum of Education, University of South Carolina. Lorin W. Anderson delivered a presentation version of his essay at the 1996 keynote session of the Explorations in Biographical Method Conference at the Museum of Education, University of South Carolina.

Chapter Eighteen

Biography, Education and Questions of the Private Voice

Janet L. Miller

The nature of biographical inquiry, as described by biographer Stephen Oates (1991), is "delicate because it strives to elicit from cold fact the warmth of a life being lived" (p. 5). That delicate nature is one reason biographical, autobiographical and narrative inquiries have increased and come under scrutiny in recent years as viable forms of educational research. Even for those of us who engage in such inquiries, that delicate nature also points to the precarious, perhaps impossible act of eliciting "from cold fact" any one final, complete and coherent version of a self and "the warmth of a life being lived."

Now, I have to think that few people enter the field of education because of a fascination with cold facts. I hope and believe that most of us come to teaching and educational research primarily because of our interests in and concerns about human beings. Moreover, because of these interests and concerns, we most often place "the warmth of a life being lived" at the center of our curricular and pedagogical deliberations and enactments. So, forms of inquiry that include the biographical can help us construct versions of teaching and learning that transform curricula, pedagogy and educational research from "a world of lifeless data and impersonal force into a landscape filled with living people" (Oates, 1991, p. 7).

At the same time, the delicate nature of biographical work invites criticism from those who, it seems, are content with

"cold facts" and see no need to elicit from them "the warmth
of a life being lived." For example, responding to public pres-
sures for accountability, some educators continue to prescribe
versions of teaching and learning as a series of linear and
measurable skills to be mastered. Their accounts of students'
successful (or unsuccessful) mastery of those skills rarely
include descriptions of or inquiries about the students' and
teachers' struggles, fears, hopes and desires that accompany
any learning and teaching experience. They view such
responses as "private," and therefore both separate from and
less important than "public" demonstrations of "official"
and "objective" knowledge.

When institutions as well as public opinion reward only a
measurable version of teaching and learning (and insist on a
separation and a higher valuing of the public over the private),
educators may find our research and practice frozen in the
immutable glaze of cold facts. Drawing too close to the
warmth of a life risks a melt-down of objective facts. It also
risks a melt-down of the presumed possibilities of prediction
and control about the processes of teaching and learning as
well as about the living people who enact these processes.

At the same time, eliciting from cold facts the warmth of a
life is hardly a straightforward act. Any work that embraces
the warmth of a life being lived must also risk melt-downs: In
biographical, autobiographical and narrative work, those melt-
downs pool around assumptions about access to and representations of the personal and the private of that life. For,
while biographical work enlivens cold facts, it is, at the same
time, often filled with befuddling, partial, paradoxical and unknowable aspects of a self:

> The word "self" . . . names an essential elusiveness, an organi-
> zation in being that is inexplicable, that cannot be represented
> or located (Bollas, 1995, p. 157).

Thus, the biographer, the autobiographer, the storyteller
and the educational researcher must confront often contradictory, fragmented and incomplete interpretations that point to
what is unknowable about and within any individual. The
warmth of a life, even if elegantly and minutely elicited from

cold facts, may have melted those cold facts into shimmering pools that splash and spill into one another, blurring any one version of the self and its truth or voice.

Biographical Work and Teachers' Lives

I have worked with teachers in graduate education for the past eighteen years, and I currently teach in a graduate program in which teachers work together for two years in cohort groups. Because of our extended time together, we can bring the warmth of our individual and collective lives as teachers to bear on the cold facts of our formal educational studies.

Within this context, we use forms of biography, autobiography and narrative to examine historical and contemporary expectations about teaching, learning, research and curricula. Tensions that currently pervade theories of biography and autobiography—tensions around the presumption that there exists one singular truth or version of self—also pervade our studies of curriculum and instruction. For example, we examine the effects of narrow and unitary versions of teacher or student on our work as educators. Or we examine ways in which predetermined curriculum packages limit our sense of what and who constitute knowledge.

We also use biography to grapple with those tensions created by adherence to one linear version of truth, or knowledge or self. Biographies of educators usually provide a number of entry points into those tensions: They can provide historical perspective on and critiques of current organizing principles and educational philosophies that insist on one version of school restructuring efforts and curricular reforms. They can provide examples of how particular historical, cultural, economic and social forces helped to shape varying and changing conceptualizations of teacher, or student, or curriculum. They can provide insight into how educators, influenced by particular historical moments and contexts, constructed versions of themselves as educators. They can provide contexts for questioning how the biographer has constructed both herself and her subject through and in language.

I find these uses of biography compelling, and I believe it is important that such biographical, autobiographical and narrative work avoid romanticizing or essentializing ourselves or others as individuals. Rather, I believe such work can help us show how we have come to teach and learn by examining social, cultural, historical influences, and framings of our particular educative processes and beliefs.

Thus, my passion for biography as a form of educational inquiry grows when I can trace how its apparent cold facts connect to and are influenced by particular historical, social and cultural contexts. As well, I wish to posit the uses of biography in education as one way of examining the discourses we have available to us at particular times and in particular contexts to construct the voices that point to "the warmth of a life being lived."

Working from and through these perspectives, what is clear to me is that no one—neither the educators whom we study through historical or current biography, nor educators whom we study through primary works, nor we as educators working together—speaks in a constant and unchanging voice. Rather, what the elongated nature of our cohort work together as well as biographical studies provide are countless examples of how voice—as a way of conceptualizing a single, essential version of a public or private self—dissolves. Instead, our voices—as supposed representations of who we *are* as educators—simultaneously can change, disappear, multiply, become muted, get muffled by a litany of cold facts.

So like the biographer, we have to interrogate various versions and constructions of our voices and selves; for as Oates (1991) pointed out, those constructions, like the biographer's data, are "full of evasions, duplicities, and contradictions" (p. 10). Further, and even more challenging, how might we begin to consider the paradox Bollas (1995) posed "that part of the core of us is an apparently absent presence rather than an articulate, active subject . . . an internal object that is sensible, that can be felt, even though it has no voice" (pp. 151-152).

Grappling with this paradox, we can use biography, autobiography and narrative to construct, deconstruct, employ and deploy versions of ourselves as teachers that challenge any one unitary version of who we are or would be as educators. Further, grappling with the paradox of self as an "essential elusiveness" that has no voice, such work could enable teachers and teacher educators to make more complex any simplistic notions of practices that promise the discovery, recovery or restoration of real, true and authentic voices and selves.

Questions of Identity

Given the work in which I engage with teachers, I believe that any educational inquiry that involves the uses of biography and autobiography must attend to conceptualization, questions and paradoxes of self and voice. I'm persuaded by current theories in the fields of literary criticism, anthropology and psychoanalysis, among others, that question absolute, whole and static versions of cold facts about the truth and experience. These theories also question the total knowability of the self and the unity of voice. Such theories, especially informed by psychoanalytic and feminist perspectives, also point to issues of power, language and subjectivity that circulate between and among biographer and subject, autobiographer and self, the researcher and the researched. These perspectives take into account the postmodern moment as, in Marshall's (1992) words, "an awareness of being-within a way of thinking, . . . of being-within, first, a language, and second, a particular historical, social, cultural framework" (p. 3). These perspectives thus call attention to language as a constituting factor in the artificial separations, hierarchical orderings, and essentialist constructions of public and private, theory and practice, self and other. Consider Weedon's (1987) formulation here:

> Language is the place where actual and possible forms of social organization and their likely social and political consequences are defined and contested. Yet it is also the place where our sense of ourselves, our subjectivity, is *constructed*. The assumption that subjectivity is constructed implies that it is not innate, not genetically determined, but socially produced. Subjectivity is produced in a whole range of discursive practices—economic, social and political—the meanings of which are a constant site of struggle over power. Language is not the expression of unique individuality; it constructs the individual's subjectivity in ways which are socially specific. . . . Unlike humanism, which implies a conscious, knowing, uni-

fied, rational subject, poststructuralism theorizes subjectivity
as a site of disunity and conflict, central to the process of
political change and to preserving the status quo (p. 21).

The implications of such perspectives are paramount for
educators who want to use biography, autobiography and
narrative as forms of inquiry in teacher education and educational research. Teachers and researchers must address issues
of identity, subjectivity and power relations that circulate
through and in language as well as human interactions. These
issues, at the very least, draw attention to the warmth—indeed,
the heat—generated by the unpredictability, the multiplicities,
the confusions, and the unknowable in a life being lived. For
example, Betty Bergland (1994), working with postmodern
theories of autobiography, has asked crucial questions about
conceptions of self and language:

> [D]o we read at the center of the autobiography a self, an essen-
> tial individual, imagined to be coherent and unified, the origina-
> tor of her own meaning, or do we read a postmodern subject—
> a dynamic subject that changes over time, is situated
> historically in the world and positioned in multiple discourses?
> . . . Do we assume a transparent language implying that a
> speaking subject automatically conveys in language an in-
> tended meaning that is immediately apprehended, or do we
> understand that the discursive practices in which the speaking
> subject is situated and positioned shape possible utterances,
> which remain fragmented and partial, inadequate to represent
> the "I" who speaks? (p. 134).

In educational research and in teacher education, many of
us who choose the warmth also choose to address such
questions and tensions, and our uses of narrative, biography
and autobiography as forms of educational inquiry have a
particular focus. We use these inquiries in ways that highlight
how the personal and the private voice, for example, are
inextricably bound up in varying social, historical and cultural
influences on and constructions of the self and the truth.

Biographical Work and Voice
Working with and in the complexities generated by "the

warmth of a life" compels us, then, to consider the many ways in which we and others hear and conceptualize our voices. On the one hand, those called "expressionists" in composition theory argue for a notion of voice as both inherent and emerging within the individual. Expressionists often encourage the development of the "authentic voice" in student writing and encourage forms of personal writing, including the biographical and autobiographical, as means for tapping into a voice that is faithful to a student's self.

Other theorists, like Klaus (1994) for example, working from postmodern perspectives that challenge any essentialist notion of one and true self or voice, attempt to show how a conception of authentic voice avoids both historically and socially located circulations of power *and* the unconscious as powerful forces that mediate who can speak:

> Such expressions as "having one's own voice," or "having an authentic voice," or "having a distinctive personal voice," or "having the immediacy of a real voice" predicate so intimate a connection as to imply that voice is a fully authentic expression and reflection of self. The grammatically singular form of such expressions also tends to suggest that voice is singular not only in the sense of being distinctive or unique, but also in the sense of being a single, unified entity in and of itself (p. 114).

Bergland (1994) discussed additional difficulties of equating voice with one essentialized version of an individual or a group of individuals: "I suggest that we need to question any easy relationship between discourse and the speaking subject, particularly the assumption that *experience* produces a *voice*— that, for example, *being a woman* means speaking in *a woman's voice*" (p. 134).

One way of questioning the relationships among discourse, power and the speaking subject is to investigate the consequences of even categorizing the multiplicities and complexities of a life being lived into such rigid notions as public and private voice. Feminist theorists (e.g., V. Ross, 1991) have noted the reinforcing of unequal power relations that become attached to the essentialist separation of a private voice from a public voice:

[T]he private life [and voice] . . . is that which we are trained
to "leave at home" or "leave at the door." It occurs "outside"
the institutions' self-constituted public space; brought
"inside," it provokes shame, embarrassment, the taint of
naiveté and unsophistication. It must be suppressed, displaced,
or sublimated into our work. Private life [and voice], within
the academy, is held at bay by such literary-pedagogical clichés
as "emotional baggage," a traveling metaphor in flight from
the affectively feminine and concretely domestic (p. 139).

Biographical, autobiographical and narrative forms of
educational inquiry could point to the ways in which our
educator identities and voices are never just—or even—public
or private. These forms of inquiry can demonstrate that voices
are never just pre-existing and awaiting discovery, never fixed
and unchanging, never easily separated into distinct and
"naturally" existing realms of public and private, never im-
mune to specific social and historical conditions.

Thus, biography that points to the flux as well as the
unknowable in a voice and self might help educators resist one
definitive and measurable version of the successful student or
teacher, for example. Such conceptions of biography might
help educators challenge easy prescriptions for classroom
management, organization and philosophy that guarantee that
everyone's voice will be heard, or that everyone's self will be
realized.

Further, the unknowable, the partial, and the contradictory
about and within a self further complicate notions of the
private. The work here then is more than just to resist any
hierarchical ordering and binary separation of the private
from the public. The work for those of us who wish to use
biography and autobiography as forms of educational inquiry
must also include challenges to conventional constructions of
the private.

Such conventional constructions reinforce a notion of an
essential self always able to know that self consciously, and to
access and verify—even in such private forms as the journal or
the daybook or the diary—the truths of that self. Such constructions hardly enable us to confront the point that "some
are positioned in closer proximity to truth depending on their
relation to other terms of value: gender, class, race, and

sexuality, among others" (Gilmore, 1994, p. 107). Nor does a conventional conception of the private enable us to grapple with "the paradox that part of the core of us is an apparently absent presence rather than an articulate, active subject" (Bollas, 1995, p. 151).

All of these theoretical positions point to the complexities of working with biography, autobiography and narrative as forms of educational inquiry. Especially because teacher education and educational research are currently replete with examples of teachers who have found their own voices and thus have become "empowered," it is crucial that educators examine how such linear and developmental notions reinforce static and always knowable versions of self and voice. We use such versions of self and voice too easily in the service of delimiting equally knowable versions—the cold facts—of curriculum, teaching and learning as well as of the power relations inherent in their constructions and processes.

Conceptions of teachers' voices as multivalent, as capable of contradicting, juxtaposing, layering, and speaking (or not speaking) from multiple and concurrent positions, do not support single and unitary versions of finding or developing or keeping a voice or a self. Rather, as Bollas (1995) pointed out, these conceptions point to versions of self and, by extension, voice that acknowledge the unknowable:

> As conscious selves, we have an intriguing relation to our mental contents, some of which are part of a moving or dynamic inner presence that we experience but cannot put into words except by partial derivatives. Freud certainly knew this. His descriptions of the unconscious and later of the id are references to an *it* within us that we cannot put into consciousness. . . . I think that one of the reasons "self" is an apparently indefinable yet seemingly essential word is that it names its thing: saturated with *it*, the indescribable is signified (p. 148).

If we can agree that a self can be only partially and incompletely represented and never fully known, a notion of the private voice as easily accessible and capable of full development also becomes problematic. Such a position raises serious questions for those in education who would use biography and autobiography as vehicles for discovery or illumination of an already existing, fully formed self and voice.

At the same time, the uses of biography and other forms of educational inquiry that "elicit from cold facts the warmth of a life being lived" *do* enable us to challenge any fixed or predetermined notions of who we are and what it might mean to work as educators. Like Oates' version of biography, then, such work provides more than just cold facts about the multiple tensions that characterize the role of teacher, for example. It also presents myriad complexities in both investigating and representing the warmth [and confusions, contradictions, commitments and the unknowables] of a life being lived. At a time when so much teacher education and educational research focuses on standards and on teaching as a set of delivery systems, biography as an educational practice generates material and processes that we educators can use to dislodge unitary notions both of our selves and our voices and of prescriptive systems of teaching and learning. Such work could also enable us to acknowledge that the processes of teaching and learning always interrogate the unknown—that is, the meaningful unknown.

Chapter Nineteen

I Search, You Search, We All Search: Biography and the Public Voice

William Ayers

So, what do you do?

Well, I began teaching in 1965 in a small free school associated with the Civil Rights Movement. From that day until this, although I have worked at many different jobs and pursued a wide range of passions, I have thought of myself first and foremost as a teacher. To be more accurate, I think of myself in pursuit of teaching, searching for teaching, attempting to teach. "I am a teacher" sounds a lot more settled and certain than I have ever felt. Even now each year begins in dread and wonder, and every class bumps along to an idiosyncratic rhythm of hope and unpredictability. I struggle to keep up, worry about the paradox of teaching subjects I neither fully know nor understand, live whole lifetimes inside perfect moments of discovery and surprise. And so I teach.

Throughout most of my teaching, my life partner has been an attorney (in pursuit of equity, perhaps, or justice), and I often find myself at lawyer parties. Those parties thrive on small talk, and invariably a lawyer will bump into me somewhere between wine and cheese and, mildly curious, ask, "So, what do you do?" Depending on the year I have replied, "I teach kindergarten" or "I teach high school." I always get the same response: a frozen smile, a patronizing look, then something crashingly noncommittal like, "Oh, that must be interesting." Then the inquisitive lawyer sidles off in search of someone interesting. Lawyers find something unspeakably odd about a normal person, and in particular a man, teaching kindergarten.

When at last I tired of this ritual, I devised a snappier and more forceful response:

Lawyer: "So, what do you do?"

Me: "I teach kindergarten. It's the most intellectually demanding vocation I've ever had."

This response causes a surprised pause, a kind of head-snap as the lawyer tries to reconcile three words: "teach," "kindergarten" and "intellectual."

Partly, what I had in mind, of course, were the ways in which teaching—when one does it well, when it focuses on the profound mysteries and events of life—demands thoughtfulness, wide-awakeness and sustained curiosity. I was thinking as well about how a five-year-old's questions can lead one into complex and important places: Why do rubber balls bounce? Why does spilled apple juice make the floor sticky? Why is *your* skin pink? Why is that woman sleeping in the park? Why is the sky sometimes blue and sometimes black?

More than any of this, however, what I had in mind were the ways in which a teacher must focus on the lives of children, becoming intensely aware of these unique, dynamic, complex and three-dimensional creatures, learning the hearts and minds, the dreams and capacities of each one in order to be the most effective teacher possible. This is excruciatingly difficult, intellectually demanding work.

I never got to say all of that, of course, because the inquisitive lawyer—once his head had snapped, once he had paused a beat or two—invariably cast me the same pitying look and the same reply, this time with emphasis: "That must be *very* interesting."

And so I again adjusted my standard response, and after a while the exchange went like this:

Lawyer: "So, what do you do?"

Me: "I teach kindergarten. It's the most intellectually demanding vocation I've ever had, and if you ever tire of making six figures and want to do something useful with your life, you might want to become a teacher."

* * *

So, what do *you* do? Alfred Kazin (1979) claimed that

> The deepest side of being an American is the sense of being like nothing before us in history—often enough like no one else around us who is not immediately recognized as one of our tradition, faith, culture, profession. *"What do you do, bud?"* is the poignant beginning of American conversation. *"Who are you?"* What am I to expect from you? put into history's language means that I am alone in a world that was new to begin with and that still feels new to me because the experience of being so much a self—constantly explaining oneself and telling one's own story—is as traditional in the greatest American writing as it is in a barroom (p. 76).

The most common question framing our social and cultural life asks for more than a job description. "What do you do?" after all, follows twenty or more years of answering a prior question: "What do you want to be (when you grow up)?" These questions require thought and reflection and, then, some priority-setting. They encourage a normative response, a sense of oughtness, and they assume a sense of possibility, of choice, of projecting toward a future. To answer is, in part, to build a narrative of a life being lived, to speak of agency, to name oneself as social and public, in relation to others, and to be moving forward.

It is also, of course, to stretch beyond oneself and to place a particular life in an abundance of other lives. This is where "breathing biography," as my friend Jonah Raskin calls it, can help. Breathing biography means participating in America's great folk epic, the telling and re-telling of the stories of our lives. Biography is about passion and commitment, prescription, and choice, freedom and responsibility, the individual and the crowd, now and then, life and death. Reading biography can help us locate ourselves; reading biography together can introduce a powerful touch-point for pulling a community together. Raskin calls reading and writing biography essential for teaching and learning, and points to literature departments that focus on the lives and works of Ernest Hemingway or Toni Morrison, nursing schools where

students compile life and health histories of patients and their
families based on intensive interviews and research, and
journalism classes where students complete assigned profiles
and obituaries of the famous as well as the unknown. In my
ongoing struggle to become a teacher, storytelling (my own,
that of my colleagues) and re-telling (this is how Herb Kohl or
Sylvia Ashton-Warner or Jim Haskins or Jamie Escalante or
Pat Conroy faced a familiar crisis or similar situation) provide
both inspiration and practical guides.

Raskin describes a conversation with Phyllis Rose, author
of *Parallel Lives* and editor of *The Norton Book of Women's
Lives,* who talked of loneliness as "having a memory and no
one to share it with"; he concludes that writing and teaching
biography can point to the creation of a genuine intimacy, a
kind of family of students and teachers exploring together
"the human geography of memory and experience."

Biography is particularly appropriate for teachers and
students of teaching. It can provide a window upon hundreds
of subjects and disciplines, open a dozen doors, point to
thousands of entry points for inquiry and study. It can also
portray specifically the complexity, the power, the idiosyncratic wondrousness of teaching. Teacher biographies show us
moments of transcendence, of greatness, lived in the every day
of classroom life. At their best, teacher biographies resist the
smooth and the cliched in favor of the rough-edged reality we
actually face. Catherine Bateson (1989) pointed out that

> there is a pattern deeply rooted in myth and folklore that recurs
> in biography and may create inappropriate expectations and
> blur our ability to see the actual shape of lives. Much biogra-
> phy of exceptional people is built around the image of a quest,
> a journey through a timeless landscape toward an end that is
> specific, even though it is not fully known. . . . The model
> that is held up for young people is one of early decision and
> commitment, often to an educational preparation that launches
> a single rising trajectory. . . . These assumptions have not
> been valid for many of history's most creative people and they
> are increasingly inappropriate today. The landscape through
> which we move is in constant flux. (pp. 8-9)

Teacher biographies and biographical research in education can provide examples of possible lives—dynamic portraits of teachers working and making choices in an imperfect world, living in landscapes of fear and doubt, holding to a faith in the craft of teaching and in the three-dimensional humanity of their students that allows them to reach a kind of greatness against the grain. This kind of greatness, when nuanced and layered and textured, highlights what could be but is not yet, and helps us set our own course as teachers.

* * *

Adrienne Rich (1979) described three prototypical ways we middle class Americans choose to live in our cities—and we might expand her example to include how any of us chooses to live in the modern world. The first choice she calls the paranoiac, to live as if the city or the world is all danger, all dread and to live then behind triple-locked doors, always to carry mace, never to look a fellow citizen in the eye, to scurry hurriedly here and there, and to hunker down inside an isolated and protected apartment. The beauty of this choice is that the city cooperates so readily: it really can be a scary place.

Rich's second option is solipsism—to create, if you can, an island of privileged self-indulgence, and then to pretend that this little space is equivalent to the whole city or the entire word. Some people taxi from their health clubs to the opera to the condo and say, without a hint of irony, "I love this city" and who deplore the problems of the city or the rest of the world but never really ask, "How did it get that way?" or "What is my responsibility?" or "What can I do about it?"

The third and best choice, which Rich found difficult to name, compels one to look at the city as a site both of hope and difficulty and to ask "What can I do?" This choice requires one to become more than a visitor, more than an accidental tourist in one's own life. Rich called it something like the city as lover. She was not speaking of a romantic love, but rather the love one feels for someone else who is locked in a struggle for life. Here is this person—sick, perhaps dying, injured or preyed upon—and your love is also your struggle, not always pretty, but always human, always crucial.

What will you do?

What are you doing out there?

Each of us is born and there is an assembly already there to welcome or at least meet us. We first experience intimately a social surround in the hands of those who care for us, who feed and clothe us. Soon this intimate world bursts open and we are aware of something larger, something pulling us forward. We press our faces against the window pane, then we open the door. Annie Dillard (1987) described awakening to "a going world" (p. 56), an existing community, a society to step into that is up and running, filled with color and noise and texture, coming from somewhere and heading toward who knows where else. We are creatures of that going world, and we are also soon enough creators of it, simultaneously object and subject.

Being thrust into a going world is to confront the objective and to face the facts. For example, I never chose my parents, siblings, gender, nationality or physical condition. I never chose to be born to the blinding light of Hiroshima or to live my entire life under the stench of war and the threat of nuclear annihilation. These frameworks are part of the going world.

But I do—indeed, I must—choose who to be, how to act, what to do in light of the facts of life. Once nuclear bombs enter my consciousness, for example, I can choose to support mutually assured destruction, to oppose proliferation, to fight for abolition, and to do a lot else. I can put my head in the sand and ignore the whole thing, which is itself a choice, and not an uncommon one. In each case, I choose, and in choosing I become a subject in that going world. I am, then, more than an object, a victim, a client, a consumer. I can choose to become an actor.

The experience of choice, of possibility, occurs within the hard edges of peril and pain and, for too many, hopelessness. After all, we in the United States comprise just over five percent of the world's people, yet we control over sixty percent of the world's wealth, an outrageous inequity we enforce with the most powerful military machine ever assembled. Looking down the barrel must be harrowing indeed; it must narrow the options precipitously. Our own choices occur in a world that includes Liberia, where ten-year-olds shoot each other with

American-made weapons; Guatemala, where legions of children die of preventable diseases while American corporations extract the nation's wealth and natural riches; and the west side of Chicago, where a child can get a gun and a packet of crack cocaine easier than a job or an education. It includes the homeless and the hungry, the addicted, the discriminated against, the battered woman, the abused child. With this in mind my late, beloved brother, Haywood Burns, used to say that solidarity and service are the rent we pay for our space on earth.

Am I in arrears?

Is the rent overdue?

The modern world presents particular predicaments and issues its own demands. Our choices attract opposition. Lisa Delpit (1996) writes of her daughter's struggle to be herself in a world intent on scripting her life, forcing her to be a thousand things other than herself, erasing her altogether if she resists. Part of the modern predicament is the reduction of human beings—three-dimensional, trembling and real—to categories we can aggregate, label, put on a shelf, pin to a board. Nowhere is this practice more evident than in our schools. Indeed, the shared language and common sense of our schools is hardly about education at all—it is about sorting and judging, grouping and stereotyping, classifying and labeling. We speak knowingly of children who are B.D., E.M.H., L.D., T.A.G., V.F.C., At Risk. We speak of "B" students and "C" students, as if initials correspond to an objective fact "out there." We speak of students who are "on the fourth grade level" as if there is an actual Platonic ideal—The Fourth Grade. (The wholesale acceptance of this silly myth, incidentally, explains why every fifth grade teacher in America is angry at every fourth grade teacher, every high school teacher is angry at every elementary school teacher, and every college teacher is angry at everyone else. The kids, they say, arrive below "grade level.") Common sense, it turns out, is more insistent and dogmatic than any ideology or fundamentalist sect. Meanwhile, the children become invisible, lost in the blizzard of names they never call themselves.

Cynicism and dogma, then, pervade public speech and public life in the modern world. On the one hand one feels the dreadful sense that nothing one does can possibly make a difference, that every choice is futile, every act hopeless. Those who speak of something larger, something hopeful in public life, are brought down, their shortcomings or weaknesses put on gaudy display as if only perfect people may speak, and—Catch 22—we have no perfect people. Nothing matters.

The other hand beckons with the lure of pure truth, of dogma, the shrill insistence on absolute rightness. In *The Life of Brian* Monty Python portray a reluctant savior as he greets masses of acolytes:

"I am not your Savior," he shouts from the rampart.

"You are not our Savior," they repeat compliantly.

"You are not sheep," he cries.

"We are not sheep."

"You have minds of your own," he continues.

"We have minds of our own."

Then one in the crowd turns to his comrades and says quietly, "Funny, I don't feel like I have a mind of my own," to which they reply, "Shut up! You have a mind of your own."

It's funny but also a terribly common experience. Certainty in a world of uncertainty is tempting. Calm in chaos, fixity amid dynamism, stillness within the storm we can all understand the desire. But dogma is always deadly; it is the antithesis of reflection, the end of questioning, the murder of thought. The big dogmas Americanism, jingoism, racism, Marxism leave their bloody fingerprints everywhere. But the daily dogmas, the glib and menacing arrogance of easy belief, have the power to wound as well.

* * *

Biography at its best can provide an antidote, for it involves the search for identity and meaning within multiplicity. It embraces active choice making at the intersection of private and public. It resists objectification, portraying the importance of individual experience and personal narrative inside a social surround, a cultural web, an historical flow.

Biography and autobiography in teaching (and teacher education) provide multiple entry points to learning and multiple pathways to success. They encourage students to understand their lives in larger frameworks, to set and reset directions. Telling a life or retelling another life is, in part, an exercise in plausibility. Biography posits possibility, uncertainty, dialogue, the next utterance. J. M. Coetzee (1986) believes that "in every story, there is a silence, some sight concealed, some word unspoken" (p. 14). There is a sense of unfinished business, of a future still to come, of a next word.

In a school for returning dropouts a talented teacher I know named Deborah Stern (1995) uses a lot of poetry, biography and autobiography as catalysts for reflection and growth. In a unit on personal responsibility she used (among dozens of other poems) a poem by Rainer Maria Rilke that speaks of one man leaving home in search of his own spiritual goals, while another man accepts the everyday duties of home and family allowing his children to achieve dreams he had denied himself.

Stern encourages her students to write their lives in the style of any of the poems they happen to like. Monique— fifteen, pregnant, drug involved—liked Rilke and responded this way:

> Sometimes a woman stands up during her pregnancy
> and goes to the clinic, and walks out a few hours later,
> because of a future that stands somewhere in her own mind.
> -------------------
> And her parents and her boyfriend curse her as if
> she was dead.
> -------------------
> And another woman has the baby,
> lives there, inside the diapers and days of baby-sitting
> so that her boyfriend can go out into the world
> toward a future, which she had to forget.

Stern and Rilke had given Monique a vehicle to tell her story in her way, to rise above stereotypes, and yet to locate herself in a larger social world.

Biography and autobiography invite you to take stock and to project: Here is what someone else has done; what might I do? It asks you to understand yourself as agent: Here's what I have been made; here's what I make of what I have been made; here's what I will do with what I have been made. It can push beyond second-hand intimacy toward an engaged individual living toward something larger.

What will I do when I grow up?

What will I do with my life?

These questions seem to me as good to ask myself now at fifty-two as they were at two or twelve or twenty-two. My eyes are open. I know that misgivings follow every authentic choice, that every "yes" is also a "no," that standing aside is itself a choice. Teaching is part of the real work of the world. At their best, teachers can give and fear not. Biography can help them.

Chapter Twenty

Asking Questions About Telling Stories

D. Jean Clandinin and F. Michael Connelly

We find storytelling and narrative everywhere in the educational literature these days. National education conferences schedule sessions and papers devoted to the topic; specialized conferences on narrative and storytelling flourish. Schools and school boards have also adopted the idea of having teachers tell stories on professional development days so as to reflect on their practices. Narrative methods of inquiry and research writing have gained legitimacy in educational studies. Narrative is heavily debated in the pages of our academic journals. Narrative, once methodologically novel, is becoming familiar. Teachers feel listened to, researchers find themselves doing something human, and we sense that each feels closer and more in tune with one another as researchers collect and tell teacher stories. Some people tell us that schools now look less strange to researchers and universities look less forbidding and judgmental to teachers. But the very ease by which stories appear to bridge theory-practice gaps should be a signal to the cautious. Events in our own teaching-research lives now alert us to the dangers, and in this essay we ask some pointed questions about telling teaching stories.

The legitimacy of narrative and storytelling, both in academic and practical circles, has always raised a measure of skepticism. Furthermore, a host of questions arise in classrooms and in the literature, questions like "Who tells?," "Who owns a story?," "What makes a good story?," "Whose story is being told?," and "What is the purpose for telling the story?" These questions and more deserve to be asked. For our own purposes, we have explored them (Clandinin and Connelly, 1994; Connelly and Clandinin, 1990), and they are no longer uppermost in our minds.

Asking Questions About Telling Stories on the Landscape

Recently, we have begun to think about narrative and education and, more specifically, about the professional knowledge landscapes on which both school teachers and university teachers work (Clandinin and Connelly, 1995, 1996). Lodged between the two, school and university, our teaching and research compels this consideration. Considering stories in terms of professional knowledge landscapes throws light on what might be accomplished in educational studies through the use of autobiographical and biographical writing. When we began to think about stories in this light, we were less sure about the educational rationales for the value of storytelling. We sometimes disliked the educational consequences that seemed to follow from some of our storytelling experiences. As a result, we decided to stand back and rethink the place of storytelling and narrative on our professional knowledge landscapes. In so doing we make explicit here a somewhat different sense of the value of storytelling, narrative and biography in educational studies and in educational practice. As may become evident, this rethinking springs from our own inquiries, our own "re-storying" of our educational lives.

We give our teaching and inquiry over to exploring questions of the relationships between theory and practice, of the relationships between teachers in universities and teachers in schools, and of the relationships between schools and universities. In our research and in our work in teacher education, we try to imagine more collaborative ways of working with schools. Narrative inquiry and storytelling have a central place in our collaborative work because we see the pursuit of these activities as directly connected with life and education. Narrative and storytelling allow us to link teachers' and children's lives with a concept of education. It is *education* that is at the core of our enterprise and not merely the telling of stories. We see living an educated life as an ongoing process. People's lives are composed over time: biographies or life stories are lived and told, retold and relived. For us, education is interwoven with living and with the possibility of retelling our life stories. As we think about our own lives and the lives of teachers and children with whom we engage, we see possibilities for growth and change. As we learn to tell, to listen and to respond to teachers' and children's stories, we imagine significant educational consequences for children and teachers in schools and for faculty members in universities through more mutual relations between schools and universities. No one, and no institution, would leave this imagined future unchanged.

As we imagined spaces in which we could engage in these collaborative relationships, we were drawn to the metaphor of a "narrow ridge" found in Martin Buber's (1957) notion of a community of otherness. Buber's concern was to conceptualize communities in which people with different points of view thrive. He imagined the community of otherness as located on a narrow ridge, a place of tension between two gulfs where there is "no sureness of knowledge" but only a "certainty of meeting." From the ridge there is the possibility of response without the withholding of self. The ridge allows the possibility of "overcoming otherness" in a lived unity that is the community.

One way of imagining the relationship between schools and universities is to imagine a narrow ridge between the two institutions. We can imagine the professional knowledge landscape of schools on one side of the ridge and the professional knowledge landscape of universities on the other side; school teachers' lives on one side and university teachers' lives on the other. Thinking of a narrow ridge between the professional knowledge landscapes of schools and universities as a possible space for collaboration sets the stage for our questions about telling stories.

Telling Stories in University Classes

We base almost everything we do and think about on our teaching. Most of that teaching occurs in the university though some of it occurs in schools. Our common ground as authors is graduate teaching and our graduate teaching forms the basis of our discussion. What we have to say, however, resonates with our work in such other settings as schools, school classrooms and, with Clandinin's work, in pre-service teacher education.

In our graduate seminars, students tell stories of their lives and their teaching. They begin by creating a life chronicle and supplement it throughout the course by journals, letter-writing and stories. We, and other class members, respond to these journals and letters and encourage more thought, additional reading, further research and ongoing conversations with others. Autobiographical work is written and told in class, and each person writes a final paper in which he or she tells a life story, or a part of it, as a narrative.

When students come to graduate classes where they find stories of experience valued and validated, they express surprise. They see this valuing of their stories as diverging from what universities normally accept. The novelty of narrative and autobiographical writing attracts many individuals, among them people who have lived their lives on the margins. Individuals who have felt uncomfortable and silenced within our institutions often see narrative and storytelling as points of access into institutions where they had supposed they would be ignored.

But we note a tension because most students also expect to be treated according to the professional knowledge story they have heard of universities. It is a story in which the university and its teachers stand in expert relationship to the school and school teachers. Through the rites of passage towards a postgraduate degree, graduate students expect to be granted the status that their professional knowledge story tells them that it holds within universities. In most universities this story is confirmed both in undergraduate and most graduate courses.

In our graduate classes, and in others like them, while students are pleased to see their stories admitted to the university curriculum, they expect storytelling and narrative to be treated the same way any other element of the university curriculum is treated. For example, in our curriculum classes, students are pleased to see that their stories receive responses as part of the subject matter of the curriculum rather than as the sole focus on the theories and research of curriculum. But in the end the basic professional knowledge story does not change in that students wish and expect to participate in the professional knowledge landscape norms of the university. Following the norms in the professional knowledge landscape, students expect to become experts, to engage in knowledge production, to debate others, to separate criticism of the person and criticism of the ideas, to participate in social criticism, to critique school practices, to ferret out school ideologies, and to make expert prescriptions for improving practice.

We tried to set aside the tension for, like our students, we were caught up in the excitement of a new agenda for educational research and a new curriculum for teachers at the university. Like the people who came to work with us, we too saw ourselves as attracted to teaching against the grain, as questioning the taken-for-granted. But we could hardly help noticing that for many students their idea of what narrative and storytelling were about had been essentially shaped by their idea of the professional knowledge landscape of the university.

We share with others who have worked with teachers in this way a sense of amazement at teachers' profound feelings of validation of their work lives when their stories receive accommodation. We think this powerful feeling of liberation must account, at least in part, for the surge of interest in narrative and biography. The interest in narrative continues to grow despite the objections to its subjectivity, its failure to offer generalizations, and its lack of rigor as a satisfactory way of understanding schools either from an insider teacher perspective or from an outsider university and policy-making perspective. This sense of liberation and emancipation is important. We do not wish to minimize the importance of teachers creating narrative texts of their lives—that is, telling their stories. We see much educational value for each of us in doing so. As Robert Coles (1989) put it, "Their story, yours, mine—it's what we all carry with us on this trip we take, and we owe it to each other to respect our stories and learn from them" (p. 30). We see the creation of such autobiographical texts as constituting a narrative reflection on practice. This process of telling our stories is critical to educational development. People, including ourselves, see narrative and storytelling in our teaching and research as exciting, energizing and educational.

To return for a moment to our metaphor of the ridge with school teachers on one side and university teachers on the other, we saw much of educational value for both sides. The telling of, and responding to, teachers' stories and telling our own teaching and research stories as university teachers is educationally important on both sides of the ridge. But as we considered our own teaching and research, we wondered if telling stories was enough. We wondered if the telling of our stories could lead to an increasingly illuminated story that became a kind of reification, a kind of fixed sculpture of our story, captured and frozen in time. Telling our story would lead to a certain satisfaction, a sense of certainty in knowing it. We might find ourselves telling the same story again and again with no edge or tension for inquiry, for growth. As we thought about our own stories, we saw the possibility that what had seemed so illuminating in our first tellings might become "the" story of, and for, our lives. As teachers, we see how what might be an awakening in the short run could become a reification over time.

Meanwhile, we watched the literature fill with stories, and sometimes we felt inundated. Our wonders about whether stories were enough became a tension leading to new inquiries as we asked questions about what difference telling stories made to the tellers, to the listeners and to the institutions in which the stories were told and heard. Most importantly, for us, we began to wonder about the difference they made for people with whom we entered into educational relationships. We began thinking and writing about lives and education in terms of cultivations, awakenings and transformations, and phrased in these terms our questions become "How will we retell our stories with new insights?" and "How will we relive them with changed practices in our lives?" From the point of view of our imagined ridge, both university teachers and school teachers are engaged in the retelling of stories, and lives on both sides of the ridge will be affected.

What we now see happening in the rush to narrative and storytelling is that school teachers and university teachers actively pursue storytelling and become energized by it. One reading of this state of affairs is that education acquires a new buzzword complete with strategies and activities. Following the professional knowledge story of the universities as expert, narrative and storytelling could be turned into one more subject matter for school reform. For example, new storytelling curricula can be developed for workshop implementation. Story groups can be mandated for school professional development. Without fundamental changes in the professional knowledge story and in the professional knowledge landscapes on both sides of the ridge this is the likely outcome. Then, we imagine, the whole thing will soon fade out.

This possible outcome highlights the importance of asking new questions about telling stories and biography. So far we have argued that the greatest promise of narrative and storytelling is contained neither within a story nor in the criticism of stories, nor in answering such questions as what makes a good story and who owns it. We saw the educational promise of storytelling as emerging when storytelling becomes part of our inquiry into what it means to live an educated life and what conditions are educational. For us, the promise of storytelling emerges when we move beyond regarding a story as a fixed entity and engage in conversations with our stories. The mere telling of a story leaves it as a fixed entity. It is in the inquiry, in our conversations with each other, with texts, with situations, and with other stories that we can come to retelling our stories and to reliving them. We want to begin to reexamine our teaching in order to allow ourselves, and those who come to work with us, the possibility of meeting on the ridge. This meeting on the ridge, this engagement with each other, offers the possibility of re-storying the professional knowledge landscapes on both sides. The tension we noted earlier about storytelling in our graduate classes offers a starting point for this inquiry.

Retelling Personal Stories: Recognizing Social Stories
While we were caught up in the celebration of telling our stories, we became concerned that storytelling would be coopted into the taken-for-granted professional knowledge story of the university in expert relationship to schools. We feared that the tellings would become ends in themselves and would not lead to retellings of the individual and to the challenges to the social stories implicit in the retellings. Our goal is to

engage in retellings that might lead to different social narratives lived out on the professional knowledge landscapes in schools and universities.

Like our students, we were excited by the discovery of the power of storytelling to reveal nuances in their practices and in ours. In our teaching we overlooked what we had written in our research papers namely, that telling is a step to retelling and to reliving our stories. From our point of view as teachers, we neglected to take our students to the next step of other possible retellings. It was difficult for many students to make the transition from telling to retelling. We found enjoyment and insight for both our students and ourselves in the stories told, but we felt reluctant to push too hard to imagine new possible ways to retell the stories. But not to take the next step is to lose the potential for educative change for the individual and for the institution. We began to think again about the difficulties with retelling. But to appreciate them fully we had to remind ourselves of the difficulties of telling. While people by and large embrace storytelling, stories of self are risky for the teller. We know this from our classes where it is important to build trust. Trust becomes an important topic in storytelling settings. We also know the risk because we, and those who work with us, worry when our stories are written down. We feel less safe with the printed word than with the spoken word. The risk increases. When people outside the storytellers community read them, the tellers relinquish control over the context and interpretation.

But if telling stories is a hard task, retelling stories is even more difficult. Retelling requires a vivid imagination as people try to rethink their stories in the context of the stories of others with whom they interact. Class participants, in a kind of microcosm of inquiry more generally, need to explore their stories. Conversations that draw out the conditions under which stories were lived and told move through imaginative suggestions in order to allow the storyteller to retell a new story. Class participants need to join in this process in a spirit of inquiry and create an inquiry-oriented conversation that moves from the story told to the possibility of a retold story.

Summary

These are pressing questions. If we imagine the narrow ridge to be peopled with ourselves and our students, and if we persist with our questions about ways in which retelling and reliving stories contribute to educational growth, using stories in educational settings will be much more difficult for all of us. In our conversations on the ridge, we find little certainty. Every retelling of a story has its own idiosyncratic history. University teachers and school teachers alike who enjoy the pleasures of storytelling will find the pleasures of retelling more difficult to come by. Many will leave the ridge: Our students who wish to become embodiments of the professors they have imagined in their stories of the university's professional knowledge landscapes will leave; academics who tire of collecting teacher stories and find their fans dissipating as they try to engage in imaginative retellings will leave; individuals who build professional development workshops around storytelling and who are no longer in demand when teachers grow tired of telling their stories will leave.

We worry that storytelling may be dismissed soon as just a fad in educational studies. This possibility concerns us because we see potential in a conversation founded on stories both autobiographical and biographical and aimed at reimagining the professional knowledge landscapes of both schools and universities into healthier educational relationships. In the end, we imagine that stories will allow us to re-imagine schools, universities and other places that are more educative for children and for all of us. But if we fail to question storytelling or do nothing about the answers, nothing will change for education.

The authors gratefully acknowledge the support of the Social Sciences and Humanities Research Council of Canada in the preparation of this work.

Chapter Twenty One

Inquiry, Data and Understanding: A Search for Meaning in Educational Research

Lorin W. Anderson

I remember my first experience with educational research in the fall of 1966. I was a college senior. Dr. Jack Rossman, a psychology professor, had received an Elementary and Secondary Education Act (ESEA) grant for training undergraduates in the philosophy, design, conduct and interpretation of educational research, and I was one of a dozen seniors who participated in a year-long seminar Jack taught. He expected each of us to carry out original research and report on its results. Because my major was mathematics and I aspired at the time to be a high school mathematics teacher, I investigated the relationship between students' attitudes toward mathematics and their mathematics achievement. While my study was modest (almost as modest as the correlation between attitude and achievement), its impact on me was profound. I found something exciting about research, and the seeds of an educational researcher had been sown.

After spending four years teaching high school and junior high school mathematics, I began my doctoral studies at the University of Chicago. While my major field was called Measurement, Evaluation, and Statistical Analysis (MESA), I believed it was just another name for educational research. I acquired the research tools I needed in my courses and developed skills in their application during my two-year assistantship with Benjamin Bloom.

With my doctoral degree in hand, I accepted a position as an assistant professor at the University of South Carolina. Most of my colleagues possessed expertise in a single substantive area (for example, child or adolescent development, instructional design, sociology of education, philosophy of education). I did not. I was a researcher. In fact, one of my favorite stories about myself concerns my lack of expertise. Brian Rowan, whom I did not know at the time but who has since become a good friend, asked if I would serve as a site coordinator for a federally funded study of Chapter I (now, for the time being, Title I). I told him that while I was interested, I knew very little about Chapter I programs. He replied, "I know. That's why I called. I'm looking for someone who will be objective in what he sees, hears and reports."

I found myself different not only from both the substantive experts with whom I worked but from most of the research methodologists as well. Most of my methodology oriented colleagues were enamored of what I consider the "tools of research." They discussed the elegance of various statistical techniques. They argued over the relative merits of two- and three-parameter latent trait psychometric models. They truly cared whether you used an analysis of covariance or an analysis of variance with gain scores.

After a decade in the Department of Educational Psychology, I began to doubt whether I really belonged. I also began to wonder whether the MESA program from which I had graduated was really a program for training educational researchers. I realized that I had learned much more than the application of skills during my graduate assistantship; I had learned to think like an educational researcher. I had learned to pose questions and find answers to them using disciplined inquiry.

These realizations led me to consider what it meant to be an educational researcher, and more often than not a single question recurred: Why do educational researchers do research? I began to answer this question during a sabbatical leave seven years ago (Anderson and Burns, 1990), and I am now ready to provide a fairly elaborate response.

Educational researchers conduct research in order to understand some phenomenon—perhaps the relationship between aptitude and learning, the way in which teachers use language in the classroom, the culture of a school, or the life of an interesting educator. Researchers want to understand. This is the primary purpose of research. Once they gain new understanding, they may share it with others using a variety of recognized vehicles: paper presentations, journal articles, monographs and books. But if they disseminate their research, they do so for a different purpose. While some may choose to spread their understanding to achieve a certain status (for example, tenure and promotion, professional recognition), a far more important reason exists. Researchers have a professional responsibility to make their understanding public and to subject it to scrutiny and criticism.

Understanding, regardless of how one achieves it, is idiosyncratic. At the end of a study, the most a researcher can say is, "This is what *I* understand now." He or she then publishes the study to see how *others* react to this understanding. Do they it reject it? Worse yet, do they ignore it? Or, do they accept it, thereby acknowledging that the researcher has contributed to some common understanding of the phenomenon under investigation?

One of the major questions facing the researcher who intends to share understanding, then, is Who are these others? That is, who is my intended audience? In the pioneering days of educational research, there tended to be only one answer to this question—namely, members of the educational research community.[1] This community was small at the time. Its members often knew each other personally, they tended to operate within a common paradigm, and they shared a common language.

Over the past sixty years or so, the question of audience has become more difficult to answer and has assumed greater importance. The educational research "community" has become increasingly diverse and fragmented. In recent years this fragmentation has led to outright academic warfare (Gage, 1989). Increasingly, if a researcher presents findings to an audience that does not value the methods used in the study (for example, experiments or case studies), the data collection techniques (for example, tests or interviews), or the nature of the data themselves (for example, quantitative or qualitative data), the understanding is rejected out of hand.

Understanding Understanding

If the purpose of educational research is to foster understanding on the part of the researcher, we must understand
understanding. I owe my understanding of understanding
primarily to one person, John Carroll. Carroll (1985) differentiated among three terms: concepts, words and meanings.
Concepts are "abstracted and often cognitively structured
classes of 'mental' experience learned by [people] in the
course of their life histories" (p. 233). First kisses, birthday
parties and long weekends may be classified as "pleasant
experiences." The experiences that we place into a particular
class or category must share at least one common critical
attribute or defining feature. Typically, they share many
more.

Because concepts are grounded in personal experience,
these critical attributes or defining features may be perceptual,
intellectual or emotional. We may recognize a rock when we
see one (perceptual), we may know about the chemical proper-
ties of rocks (intellectual), or we may delight in collecting new
varieties of rocks (emotional). The perceptual and intellectual
attributes or features of concepts often receive an emphasis at
the expense of the emotional ones, particularly in the academic realm.

Many if not most concepts acquire names—that is, words
in a particular language that enable people to share both their
experiences and the way in which they classify or categorize
them. Words are understood when they are associated with one
or more concepts. Thus, we understand "dog" because we
associate it with our concept of dog, but we cannot understand
"jupe" because we cannot associate it with any concept.

Finally, meanings are shared concepts linked with common words. Or, in Carroll's words, "a 'meaning' of a word is,
therefore, a societally standardized concept, and when we say
that a word stands for or names a concept it is understood that
we are speaking of concepts that are shared among the
members of a *speech community*" (p. 240, emphasis mine).
Because concepts are initially idiosyncratic, misunderstandings
are inevitable. My concept of "young" may differ from your
concept of young because I am 51 and you are 21. So when I
use the word "young" I cannot necessarily assume that you

understand it the way I intend it. Misunderstanding, then, implies a lack of meaning.

Once formed, concepts do not exist in isolation. Because we have a myriad of experiences, we form a multitude of concepts. These concepts tend to relate to one another in a variety of ways. Some are parts of others, some subsume others, some precede others, some cause others. Our concepts and the relationships among them form our conceptual framework. We use this conceptual framework to make sense of new experiences. If a new experience fits into our conceptual framework, we assimilate it. If it does not, we may have to modify our conceptual framework in order to accommodate the new experience.

Conceptual Frameworks, Data and Educational Research
Like all other people, educational researchers have conceptual frameworks that affect what they find interesting or important, how they choose to study, and the sense they make of the results of their study. Using more technical wording, a researcher's conceptual framework influences the choice of research topic or problem, the selection of methods and techniques he or she uses to investigate the topic or address the problem, and his or her interpretation of the data—the term used in its broadest sense—collected during the investigation.

As researchers, our personalized, experientially-grounded conceptual frameworks determine what we choose to investigate. Earlier I mentioned that in my very first study I chose to investigate the relationship between attitudes toward mathematics and mathematics achievement because I wanted to be a mathematics teacher. Obviously, "mathematics" and "mathematics teacher" were key concepts in my conceptual framework at that time. I focused my dissertation research on the relationship between time spent learning and amount learned. I borrowed the conceptual framework underlying this study from John Carroll's (1963) model of school learning. I became intrigued with the possibility that one could define aptitude as the rate of learning (as Carroll defined it), rather than the more traditional view of aptitude as capacity for learning. In more recent years, I turned my attention to the education of economically disadvantaged children. While part of my interest in these children arose from the chance to study them Brian Rowan afforded me, a larger part came from growing up in a working class home near the iron mines of northern Minnesota.

There are two points to be made here. First, our conceptual framework defines "relevant" topics, issues and problems. Consequently, researchers operating within the context of different conceptual frameworks are likely to question the *relevance* of others' research. Second, because of the role that affect plays in our choice of topics and problems, researchers must guard against the possibility that our primary purpose will shift from increasing our understanding of some phenomenon to proving that our current understanding of the phenomenon is correct. The number of doctoral students who tell me that the purpose of their dissertation research is to "show that" or "prove that" has increased beyond my ability to count.

Our conceptual frameworks also influence our choice of research methods and techniques. Researchers with a grounding in science and mathematics tend to be more comfortable with studies that involve experimental designs and "high powered" statistical analysis. Those coming from the humanities, on the other hand, prefer naturalistic designs and narratives. The former group argues that their data are more precise; the latter that theirs are more meaningful. But what if, as a researcher, you want to be meaningful *and* precise. The zealots on either side would argue that you cannot have both; you must choose.

I find this argument disquieting. The methods and techniques used should be those that help you conduct your study in a way that allows you to gain the understanding you seek. If you want to understand the culture of a school, engage in ethnography. If you want to learn the life history of John Carroll, engage in biography. If you are interested in understanding the use of language in the classroom, engage in socio-linguistic research. If you want to know which approach to reading simultaneously optimizes reading achievement and attitude, engage in experimental psychological research.

While you can either match the purpose to the method or the method to the purpose, I choose and advocate the latter.

Why limit yourself to only those phenomena that can be understood through your favorite method and related techniques? Methods and techniques are means to ends; they are not ends in themselves. Consequently, while heated discussions of methods and techniques may be useful academic exercises, they do little to increase our understanding of what we study. In my lifetime I have heard more discussion of whether structured observation schedules or field notes should be used to study classrooms than I have about what we know about classrooms on which we can agree.

Because of the complexity of most phenomena—be they classrooms, typologies of children, or individuals with interesting life histories—the prudent researcher will become facile with as many methods and techniques as possible. Ignoring test data because they are quantitative can do nothing to increase understanding. Similarly, ignoring teachers' reports of violations of the requisite standardized conditions under which the tests were administered certainly raises questions about the validity of the data.

The argument I offer here is consistent with Cronbach's (1982) call for eclectic social science:

> What research styles and objectives follow from the intent to advance understanding? A mixed strategy is called for: censuses and laboratory experiments, managerial monitoring and anthropological *Einfuhlung*, mathematical modeling and unstructured observation. A few maxims can be offered even for eclectic social science (p. 73).

Finally our conceptual framework determines the sense we make of the data we gather; it aids in our interpretation. Interpretation is an essential part of all research. A quantitative researcher must know what a mean of 57.5 means. An ethnographer needs to understand the significance of a particular behavior within a particular culture. Biographers too must make interpretations. Leon Edel (1981) makes this point succinctly:

> There are biographies that are mere compendiums. . . . A compendium is like a family album; a series of pictures, selections from an archive. The biographer producing such a

work often pretends that he is allowing the character to speak for himself or herself. This is an ingenuous way of avoiding biographical responsibility. That responsibility involves not only accumulating and offering facts; it entails the ability to interpret these facts in light of all that the biographer has learned about his subject (p. 18).

Since the interpretation made depends on both the evidence considered and the conceptual framework brought by the researcher to the evidence, interpretations by their very nature are idiosyncratic. When biographer Honor Moore at the 1996 AERA conference was asked about her interpretations in her recently released work, *The White Blackbird* (Moore, 1996), she exclaimed, "Yes, isn't it glorious. It's my interpretation. If people don't like it, they can write their own." Sharing interpretations is critical to the developed of shared meaning.

The Vanishing Research Community
You have probably noticed the theme of community in promoting and enhancing understanding that runs through this essay. Communities allow us to develop shared understanding. Through their language systems, they also help us communicate our understanding with one another.

Ample evidence suggests that the educational research community has become increasingly diverse and divisive over the recent decades. Some even may question the importance of community, arguing instead that understanding by its very nature is and must remain idiosyncratic. Furthermore, the process of sharing interferes with the need of individuals to discover and construct "meaning" in their lives.

This use of the word "meaning" is inconsistent with Carroll's (1985) definition. In Carroll's conceptual framework, meaning is societally standardized. This difference of interpretation may highlight the real problem inherent in the research community at present. *We have far too much understanding and far too little meaning.*

How do we go about regaining our concern for meaning and meaningful dialogue on critical topics and problems? Adopting Cronbach's (1982) eclectic approach might be a good start. But how do we do that? I see two possibilities. The first is to get researchers operating within different conceptual frameworks and from different research traditions to work together on critical topics and problems. Since, however, conceptual frameworks influence what we believe to be important, this solution may be difficult to achieve, at least at first.

The second possibility is to begin with researchers who already have an eclectic orientation. One group that comes to mind is educational biographers—those researchers who live between the humanities and the social sciences. Educational biographers tend to have differing conceptual frameworks, use a wide variety of methods and techniques, and have as their primary goal increased understanding. If we select this option, however, educational biographers will have their work cut out for them. The schisms among tribes of researchers run deep and are opened as much by emotion as by intellectual differences. Yet, I believe that reconciliation is possible if two conditions are met.

First, we have a real need to shift the discussion away from ideology and methodology towards substance. The fundamental question underlying our dialogue must be "What have we learned about X?" where X could be improving learning conditions, making better use of existing resources or living better lives. Just like common enemies, these common "needs to know" promise to unite us. When researchers work on common problems, the diversity among them becomes beneficial rather than divisive. We are also better able to move beyond idiosyncratic understanding to shared meaning.

Second, we have an equally great need to emphasize quality in research. There are good and poor surveys, good and poor experiments, good and poor ethnographies and good and poor biographies. Unfortunately, our educational research community has fallen down in matters of quality. We now consider all voices equally important, all narratives of equal merit, all interpretations worthy of consideration. Biographers must be willing to judge the quality of their own work as well as the quality of the work of their peers. In their own work, they must be able to determine what is factual and noteworthy, put the pieces together into some kind of whole, and then go below the surface to gain and share insights of the deeper meaning of the life being examined. They must also hold other biographers to these standards of quality. The biographer's willingness to emphasize quality and to argue, discuss and question brings new dimensions, new discourse, new communities together. Ultimately, this may provide a common bond that unites researchers across research traditions and conceptual frameworks.

A Postscript
I recently published a short article (1996b) entitled, "If You Don't Know Who Wrote It, You Won't Understand It: Lessons Learned from Benjamin S. Bloom." It was my third adventure into biography (Anderson, 1988, 1996a). I expanded the thesis, evident in the title, this way:

> It should come as no surprise that knowing something about people helps us understand their work. . . . Nonetheless, we in education often forget this simple point. We do not read multiple books and articles written by a single author to determine the author's point of view and to understand how that point of view changes over time. Rather, we tend to read everything in isolation. As a consequence, we seldom have a context, either personal or historical, for interpreting what we read (p. 85).

As a long-time researcher and neophyte biographer, I am both intrigued with the possibilities of biography and interested in its future role in educational research. Ideally, biography will provide the glue we need to become a research community once more.

Note
1. Lee Cronbach and Pat Suppes (1969) suggested that the period from 1900 to 1930 was the heyday of empiricism. Major advances in statistical theory, testing and assessment, and survey research were made during these decades.

Epilogue

> The problem with the power of biography to attract students is
> that most of these neophyte biographers have had little or no
> acquaintance with the nature of biography. An often simplistic
> belief that anybody can write good biography results in too
> many gray, soggy, lifeless chronicles.
> Edward Beauchamp (1990, p. 2)

I too was attracted by the power of biography and, while
noticing the many pervasive influences of biographical
inquiry in education, was enthralled by the self-examination
of the biographer—what ultimately serves to integrate
researcher with subject. Yet, Edward Beauchamp's assessment
in "Education & Biography in the Contemporary United
States" (an introduction to *Biography: An Interdisciplinary
Quarterly*) was all too painfully true—mere enthusiasm leads
to such lifeless chronicles. This 1990 state-of-the-field essay
served to accelerate my efforts to gather documents for an
archives of biographical materials in education.

As curator of a museum, I saw an opportunity to provide a
conceptual place—a space to explore the arena of biographical inquiry—and to bring together "adventurous company," individuals driven by curiosity, knowledge and com-
passion. Bibliographies of biographical theory were compiled;
a research library was procured. I developed a seminar in
biographical research, and Museum of Education gatherings
—conferences and endowed lectures—and AERA Biographical and Archival Research SIG (Special Interest Group)
sessions were scheduled where educational biographers and
researchers could discuss documentary, interpretive and

literary aspects of their work. While the "power of biography" did indeed attract students and colleagues, I wished to address directly the simplistic belief, as Beauchamp notes, "that anybody can write good biography." Yet, I wished not to compile, as an antidote to such a belief, a list of biographical techniques or a compendium of biographers' skills and approved practices.

Instead, I contacted major contemporary biographers throughout the United States—many were academics from the humanities but more worked as independent scholars and professional writers. This was a conscious effort to bring together cultures and, as a curator, part of an acquisitions program to stage a permanent exhibition of biographers' statements and position papers. My intent was to invite individuals equipped to offer advice to the "neophyte biographer"—namely, the educator versed in quantitative or qualitative research methods who has never engaged in biographical work. I hoped their statements would reveal a wide array of perspectives and points of view. I was, however, concerned whether active biographers would take the time to respond to a museum of education, an archival entity often far removed from the biographer's sphere. Louise DeSalvo, the distinguished biographer whose works include *Conceived with Malice* (1994) and *Virginia Woolf: The Impact of Childhood Sexual Abuse on Her Life and Work* (1989), was the first to respond to my initial invitation. The kindness and thoughtfulness that she extended to the Museum's acquisition project reaffirmed my resolve to prepare this collection and confirmed my belief that a compendium of techniques was needless and unnecessary.

While we all have hopes for biography's role in education, this collection should conclude in the spirit of the biographer's adventure and excitement. For biographical context I quote from DeSalvo's (1996) recently released memoir, *Vertigo*:

> I got into Woolf scholarship quite by accident. (Or so I thought at the time.) When I was in graduate school at New York University, I took a course with the Woolf scholar Mitchell Leaska. . . . I was enthralled with his classes. . . . I

changed my mind about what I would be doing with my scholarly life in the moments it took him to read to us from Woolf's earlier version of *The Years*. Here was a more political, less guarded Woolf.

I hadn't known that earlier versions of literary texts were available. It hadn't occurred to me that one could study how an author created a novel and learn about the writing and revision process. It sounded like detective work. It was meticulous. It required stamina. Drive. It was exciting. I too would be working with manuscripts. I think I understood subconsciously that I required a grand consuming passion in life. (pp. 221-222)

In this spirit we conclude *Writing Educational Biography* by turning to Louise DeSalvo's advice to the aspiring biographer. I hope our collection will serve as a beginning—as a micrologos—for those who wish to explore the possibilities of biographical research in education.

Advice to Aspiring Educational Biographers

Louise DeSalvo

What advice can I possibly offer the aspiring biographer that
would help him or her embark on a journey of inquiry into
the meaning of another person's life? Most importantly, that,
if it is your predilection, you unashamedly bring whatever you
are concerned with in your life into the arena of your work, to
enrich and deepen your understanding of someone else's life,
to create an ongoing dialectic between your life and your
work in which your work enables you to understand your life
better and your life enables you to understand your subject's
life better. When I began my work on Virginia Woolf as an
incest survivor, I had reached a stage in my life where I
suddenly became occupied with thinking about the condition
of childhood. My children were grown, and because I was
beyond the day-to-day tasks that child rearing brings, I had
time to reflect on my childhood, and that of my children.

In this context I wanted to find out what kind of childhood Virginia Woolf had, and to explore this issue, I decided
to write a book about Virginia Woolf and childhood that
would examine her life as a child, and her depiction of
childhood in her novels. I did not, at the outset, know I would
be writing a book about Virginia Woolf as an incest survivor.

What I discovered immediately was that narrowing my
focus was fruitful, for it provided me with a way of learning
much more about Woolf throughout her life than if I had tried
to write a standard "birth to death" biography, which frankly
I was never interested in writing. So I would urge the begin-

ning biographer to focus on "the story" they want to tell about their subject's life, and to leave the rest to someone else. I, for one, read biography not to find out all the facts about that person's life—what she did, wore and ate; where she lived; and whom she loved. I wanted to know what the biographer makes of the subject's life. I'm much more interested in the biography that tells why the biographer thinks the subject did what she did, wore and ate; why she chose to live where she lived; and how she loved—what the acts of love, of work, say, meant to her and why. That is to say, I am interested in the biographer's interpretation of the meaning of the trajectory of a person's life. So, I would ask the aspiring biographer to ask herself or himself to be clear about why a reader would be interested in this life; in what ways the reading of this life would be useful to a non-specialist "common reader." To me, all the truly great biographies provide a reader with an abiding sense of the miracle human beings accomplished as they struggle to make and find meaning in their lives. This is why I read biography: to support my hope that members of the human race can sometimes lead worthwhile lives. I want to find out how they did it. This is why I write people's lives: to illuminate the process by which creative people make their lives worthwhile through their work.

I would urge the aspiring biographer, too, to try to crawl into the psychic space their subject inhabited. I am always irritated when a biographer takes a "holier-than-thou" attitude—when he or she condescends to the subject, or becomes overly critical of a subject's choices. These seem to me to be defensive postures; the biographer is afraid of imagining what it must have been like to feel as the subject felt. This became evident to me when I found it necessary to discover what the emotional landscape of Woolf's family was like and what kind of household she was born into. Her father wrote to her mother a set of letters when Woolf was a baby and young child that reveal a household in chaos, her mother severely overworked and depressed, her father rarely home, and one of Woolf's half-sisters being treated in an excessively harsh and cruel manner. When I read those letters, and tried to imagine what it must have been like to live in that household and to see your half-sister locked away in another part of the house for supposed misbehavior, I learned that this so-called scholarly task involved taking great emotional risks necessary to an understanding of Woolf's life. Other biographers, I came to believe, had not permitted themselves to do this work and so had missed the pathos, the emotional neglect and deprivation that had been important features of Virginia Woolf's infancy and childhood. Therefore, my advice to beginning biographers is to understand that charting the emotional life of a subject is more than just work for the mind; it is work that demands that the biographer use all the intellectual and emotional resources he or she can command.

Now I want to say something about the work. Most biographers I know at some point feel overwhelmed by the immense quantity of material they have to find, read, interpret and try to understand. The urge to work constantly, to bury oneself in one's work so that it will one day be finished persists. I would suggest that the beginning biographer keep office hours, and keep the work from spilling over into the rest of life, to find creative ways to deal with the feeling of being overwhelmed, and to resist adopting a life that is nothing but work. Otherwise—and this is a real occupational hazard—you will find that, in writing your subject's life, you have lost *your* life, that you have become a shadow with nothing in your own life but the life of your subject.

On a lighter note, remember too that few people in your life will find your subject as fascinating as you do. Friends of mine cannot understand, for example, how I can stay married to a man who has never read a word of Virginia Woolf when I have worked on her since 1975. It's simple, I tell them. Why should I expect him to be fascinated by Woolf when I admire but am not fascinated by his work? I stay with him for the same reason he stays with me: We share a life beyond our work, though our work is extremely important to each of us. And so, my final bit of advice is occasionally to resist the urge to begin dinner table conversation with yet another anecdote about a recent biographical discovery. Connect with the people you love at some other level: a shared love of movies, say, or pasta. Try to continue to be a human being, not just a pencil-pushing scribe as you try to write someone's life. I can assure you through my experience, that sometimes it's not easy.

Bibliography

Allende, I. (1994). *Paula*. New York: HarperCollins.

Alpern, S., J. Antler, E. I. Perry, & Scobie, I. W. (Eds.) (1992). *The Challenge of Feminist Biography*. Urbana, Illinois: University of Illinois Press.

American Council on Education. (1983). *American Universities and Colleges* (12th ed.). New York: Walter de Gruyter.

Anders, L. (1991). Personal interview with E. Epps, December 20.

Anderson, L. W. (1988). Benjamin Bloom: His Research and Influence on Education, *Teaching Education, 2* (1), pp. 54-58.

Anderson, L. W. (1996a). Benjamin Bloom, Values and the Professoriate, in *Teachers and Mentors*, edited by C. Kridel, et al. New York: Garland Publishing, pp. 45-54.

Anderson, L. W. (1996b). If You Don't Know Who Wrote It, You Won't Understand It: Lessons Learned from Benjamin S. Bloom, *Peabody Journal of Education, 71* (1), pp. 77-87.

Anderson, L. W. & Burns, R. B. (1990). The Role of Conceptual Frameworks in Understanding and Using Classroom Research, *South Pacific Journal of Teacher Education, 18* (1), pp. 5-18.

Andrews, W. L. (Ed.) (1993). *African American Autobiography*. Englewood Cliffs, NJ: Prentice Hall.

Antler, J. (1986). *Lucy Sprague Mitchell*. New York: Yale University Press.

Appleby, J., Hunt, L., & Jacob, M. (1994). *Telling the Truth about History*. New York: W. W. Norton & Co.

Ascher, C. (1984). On "Clearing the Air": My Letter to Simone de Beauvoir, in *Between Women* edited by C. Ascher, L. DeSalvo & S. Ruddick. Boston: Beacon Press, pp. 85-103.

Ascher, C., DeSalvo, L., & Ruddick, S. (Eds.) (1984). *Between Women*. Boston: Beacon Press.

Austin, M. (1932). *Earth Horizon*. Boston: Houghton Mifflin Company.

Ayers, W. (1990). Small Heroes: In and Out of School with 10-year-old City Kids. *Cambridge Journal of Education, 20* (3), pp. 269-278.

Barkan, M. (1952). The Conference on Interdisciplinary Research into Implications of Creative Experience in the Arts. Ross Mooney Papers, Museum of Education, University of South Carolina.

Barksdale, M. (1993). Review of W. Urban's *Black Scholar*, *N.C. Historical Review, 70* (2), p. 221.

Barlow, N. (Ed.) (1933). *Charles Darwin's Diary of the Voyage of the H.M.S. Beagle*. Cambridge: Cambridge University Press.

Barlow, N. (Ed.) (1946). *Charles Darwin and the Voyage of the Beagle*. New York: Philosophical Library.

Barlow, N. (Ed.) (1958). *The Autobiography of Charles Darwin 1809-1882*. London: Collins.

Barlow, N. (Ed.) (1967). *Darwin and Henslow*. Berkeley: University of California Press.

Barth, J. (1994). Ad infinitum: A Short Story, *Harper's, 288*, pp. 65-68.

Batchelor, J. (Ed.) (1995). *The Art of Literary Biography*. Oxford: Clarendon Press.

Bateson, M. C. (1989) *Composing a Life*. New York: The Atlantic Monthly Press.

Beauchamp, E. (1990). Education & Biography in the Contemporary United States: An Introduction, *Biography, 13* (1), pp. 1-5.

Behar, R. (1993). *Translated Woman: Crossing the Border with Esperanza's Story*. Boston: Beacon Press.

Benson, P. (Ed.) (1993). *Anthropology and Literature.* Chicago: University of Illinois Press.

Bergland, B. (1994). Postmodernism and the Autobiographical Subject, in *Autobiography and Postmodernism,* edited by K. Ashley & L. Gilmore. Amherst: The University of Massachusetts Press, pp. 130-166.

Bernstein, C., & Woodward, B. (1974). *All the President's Men.* New York: Simon and Schuster.

Bernstein, R. (1992). *The New Constellation.* Cambridge, MA: The MIT Press.

Blumenfeld-Jones, D., Stinson, S., & Van Dyke, J. (1990). An Interpretive Study of Meaning in Dance, *Dance Research Journal, 22* (2), pp. 13-22.

Bollas, C. (1995). *Cracking Up the Work of Unconscious Experience.* New York: Hill and Wang.

Bowen, C. D. (1959). *Adventures of a Biographer.* Boston: Little, Brown, & Co.

Bowen, C. D. (1966). *Miracle at Philadelphia.* Boston: Little, Brown, & Co.

Bowen, C. D. (1968). *Biography.* Boston: Little, Brown, & Co.

Bowen, C. D. (1986). The Biographer's Relationship with his Subject, in *Biography as High Adventure,* edited by S. B. Oates. Amherst: University of Massachusetts Press, pp. 65-69.

Branom, F. K. (1932). *New Pictorial Atlas of the World.* Chicago: Reilly & Lee.

Bruner, J. (1986). *Actual Minds, Possible Worlds.* Cambridge, Mass: Harvard University Press.

Bruner, J. (1990). *Acts of Meaning.* Cambridge, Mass: Harvard University Press.

Buber, M. (1957). *Pointing the Way.* New Jersey: Humanities Press International

Buckley, J. J., Jr. (1972). Review of *The Water Is Wide, America, 127* (7), p. 181.

Bullough, R. V., Jr. (1981). *Democracy in Education: Boyd H. Bode.* Bayside, NY: General Hall.

Bullough, R. V., Jr. (1989). *First Year Teacher.* New York: Teachers College Press.

Bullough, R. V., Jr. & Baughman, K. (1995a). Inclusion: A View from the Classroom, *Journal of Teacher Education, 46* (2), pp. 85-93.

Bullough, R. V., Jr. & Baughman, K. (1995b). Narrative Reasoning and Teacher Development: A Longitudinal Study. Paper presented at the annual meeting of AERA, San Francisco.

Bullough, R. V., Jr. & Baughman, K. (1997). *A Teacher's Journey: First Year Teacher Revisited.* New York: Teachers College Press.

Bullough, R. V., Jr. with Baughman, K. (1993). Continuity and Change in Teacher Development: First Year Teacher after Five Years, *Journal of Teacher Education, 44* (2), pp. 86-95.

Bullough, R. V., Jr. & Gitlin, A. (1995). *Becoming a Student of Teaching.* New York: Garland Publishing.

Bullough, R. V., Jr., Knowles, J. G., & Crow, N. A. (1991). *Emerging as a Teacher.* New York: Routledge.

Butchart, R. (1986). *Local Schools.* Nashville, TN: American Association for State and Local History.

Butchart, R. (1993). Review of W. Urban's *Black Scholar, Pedagogical Historica, 29* (2), pp. 569-570.

Capote, T. (1965). *In Cold Blood.* New York: Random House.

Carroll, J. B. (1963). A Model of School Learning, *Teachers College Record, 64,* pp. 723-733.

Carroll, J. B. (1985). Words, Meanings, and Concepts, in *Perspectives on School Learning,* edited by L.W. Anderson. Hillsdale, NJ: Lawrence Erlbaum Associates.

Carter, K. (1993). The Place of Story in the Study of Teaching and Teacher Education, *Educational Researcher, 22* (1), pp. 5-12, 18.

Castenell, Jr., L. A. & Pinar, W. F. (Eds.) (1993). *Understanding Curriculum as Racial Text.* Albany: State University of New York Press.

Cattermole, M. & Wolfe, A. (1987). *Horace Darwin's Shop.* Bristol: Adam Hilger.

Clandinin, D. J. & Connelly, F. M. (1994). Personal Experience Methods, in *Handbook of Qualitative Research,* edited by N. K. Denzin & Y. S. Lincoln. Thousand Oaks, CA: Sage Publications, pp. 413-427.

Clandinin, D. J. & Connelly, F. M. (1995). *Teachers' Professional Knowledge Landscapes*. New York: Teachers College Press.

Clandinin, D. J. & Connelly, F. M. (1996). Teachers' Professional Knowledge Landscapes, *Educational Researcher, 25* (3), pp. 24-30.

Clifford, G. J. (1975). Saints, Sinners, and People: A Position Paper on the Historiography of American Education, *History of Education Quarterly, 15*, pp. 257-272.

Clifford, G. J. & Guthrie, J.W. (1988). *Ed School*. Chicago: University of Chicago Press.

Clifford, J. L. (1970). *From Puzzles to Portraits: Problems of a Literary Biographer*. Chapel Hill: University of North Carolina Press.

Coetzee, J. M. (1986). *Foe*. New York: Viking Penguin.

Cogswell, R. (1992). *Copyright Law for Unpublished Manuscripts and Archival Collections*. Dobbs Ferry, NY: Glanville Publishers.

Coit, M. L. (1950). *John C. Calhoun, American Portrait*. Boston: Houghton Mifflin.

Coles, R. (1989). *The Call of Stories*. Boston: Houghton Mifflin.

Connelly, F. M. & Clandinin, D. J. (1990). Stories of Experience and Narrative Inquiry, *Educational Researcher, 19* (5), pp. 2-14.

Conroy, P. (1972a) *The Water Is Wide*. Boston: Houghton Mifflin Co.

Conroy, P. (1972b). Conrack, You're Crazy, *Life, 72* (21), pp. 55-72.

Conway, J. K. (1990). *Road from Coorain*. New York: Random House.

Conway, J. K. (1992). *Written by Herself*. New York: Random House.

Cook, B. W. (1978). *Crystal Eastman on Women and Revolution*. New York: Oxford University Press.

Cook, B. W. (1984). Biographer and Subject: A Critical Connection, in *Between Women: Biographers, Novelists, Critics, Teachers and Artists Write About Their Work on Women*, edited by C. Ascher, L. DeSalvo, & S. Ruddick. New York: Routledge, pp. 397-411.

Cook, B. W. (1992). *Eleanor Roosevelt, vol. I, 1884-1933.* New York: Viking.

Cook, B. W. (in press). *Eleanor Roosevelt, vol. II.* New York: Viking.

Cooper, J. F. (1826/1986). *The Last of the Mohicans.* New York: Viking Penguin.

Cronbach, L. J. (1982). Prudent Aspirations for Social Inquiry, in *The Future of the Social Sciences*, edited by L. Kruskal. Chicago: University of Chicago Press.

Cronbach, L. J. & Suppes, P. (Eds.) (1969). *Research for Tomorrow's Schools.* New York: Macmillan.

Delpit, L. (1988). The Silenced Dialogue: Power and Pedagogy in *Educating Other People's Children, Harvard Educational Review, 38* (3), pp. 280-298.

Delpit, L. (1996). I Just Want to Be Myself, in *City Kids/City Teachers*, edited by W. Ayers & P. Ford. New York: The New Press.

Denzin, N. (1989). *Interpretive Biography.* Thousand Oaks, CA: Sage Publications.

Denzin, N. & Lincoln, Y. (Eds.) (1994). *Handbook of Qualitative Research.* Thousand Oaks, CA: Sage.

DeSalvo, L. (1989). *Virginia Woolf: The Impact of Childhood Sexual Abuse on her Life and Work.* Boston: Beacon Press.

DeSalvo, L. (1994). *Conceived with Malice.* New York: Dutton.

DeSalvo, L. (1996). *Vertigo: A Memoir.* New York: Dutton.

Dewey, J. (1916). *Democracy and Education.* New York: Macmillan.

Doll, M. (1995). *To the Light House and Back.* New York: Peter Lang.

Doll, W. E., Jr. (1993). *A Post-Modern Perspective on Curriculum.* New York: Teachers College Press.

Ducharme, E. R. (1993). *The Lives of Teacher Educators.* New York: Teachers College Press.

Dykhuizen, G. (1973). *The Life and Mind of John Dewey.* Carbondale, IL: Southern Illinois University Press.

Edel, L. (1959). *Writing Lives: Principia Biographica.* New York: W. W. Norton.

Edel, L. (1981). The Figure Under the Carpet, in *Telling Lives: The Biographer's Art*, edited by M. Pachter. Philadelphia: Univ. of Pennsylvania Press, pp. 16-34.

Ellsworth, E. (1989). Why Doesn't This Feel Empowering? Working Through the Repressive Myths of Critical Pedagogy, *Harvard Educational Review, 59* (3), pp. 297-324.

Ellsworth, E. (1993). Claiming the Tenured Body, in *The Center of the Web: Women and Solitude*, edited by D. Wear. Albany, NY: State University of New York Press, pp. 63-74.

Epps, E. (1993). Pat Conroy and the Daufuskie Island School (Doctoral Dissertation, University of South Carolina, Columbia, SC).

Epstein, J. (1985). *Plausible Prejudices: Essays on American Writing*. New York: W.W. Norton & Company.

Epstein, W. (Ed.) (1991). *Contesting the Subject*. West Lafayette, IN: Purdue University Press.

Erikson, E. (1958). *Young Man Luther*. New York: Norton.

Erikson, E. (1975). *Life History and the Historical Moment*. New York: Norton.

Fay, B. (1987). *Critical Social Science*. Ithaca: Cornell University Press.

Finkelstein, B. (Ed.) (1979). *Regulated Children/Liberated Children: Education in Psychohistorical Perspective*. New York: The Psychohistory Press.

Finkelstein, B. (1989). Conveying Messages to Women: Higher Education and the Teaching Profession in Historical Perspective, *American Behavioral Scientist, 32* (6), pp. 680-699.

Finkelstein, B. (1990). Perfecting Childhood: Horace Mann and the Origins of Public Education in the United States, *Biography, 13* (1), pp. 6-21.

Finkelstein, B. (1992) Education Historians as Mythmakers, in *Review of Research in Education*, edited by G. Grant. Washington, D.C.: American Education Research Association, Volume 18, pp. 255-297.

Finkelstein, B. (1994). Life at the Margins of Possibility, *American Studies Yearbook, 16* (2), pp. 1-10.

Flaubert, G. (n.d.). *Madame Bovary: A Story of Provincial Life*. New York: Rarity Press.

Fleming, M. & McGinnis, J. (Eds.) (1985). *Portraits: Biography and Autobiography in the Secondary School*. Urbana, IL: National Council of Teachers of English.

Franklin, B. (1993). Review of W. Urban's *Black Scholar*, *American Journal of Education, 101* (3), pp. 324-327.

Franklin, V. P. (1993). Review of W. Urban's *Black Scholar*, *American Historical Review, 98* (3), p. 954.

Friedlander, P. (1975). *The Emergence of a UAW Local: 1936-1939*. Pittsburgh: University of Pittsburgh Press.

Frisch, M. (1994). *A Shared Authority*. Albany, NY: State University of New York Press.

Gage, N. L. (1989). The Paradigm Wars and Their Aftermath, *Educational Researcher, 18* (7), pp. 4-10.

Garraty, J. (1957). *The Nature of Biography*. New York: Knopf.

Geertz, C. (1988). *Works and Lives: The Anthropologist as Author*. Stanford, CA: Stanford University Press.

Genovese, E. (1968). *In Red and Black: Marxian Explorations in Southern and Afro-American History*. New York: Pantheon Books.

Gilmore, L. (1994). *Autobiographics: A Feminist Theory of Women's Self-Representation*. Ithaca: Cornell University Press.

Giroux, H., & McLaren, P. (1986). Teacher Education and the Politics of Engagement: The Case for Democratic Schooling, *Harvard Educational Review, 56* (3), pp. 213-238.

Glass, J. M. (1993). *Shattered Selves: Multiple Personality in a Postmodern World*. Ithaca: Cornell University Press.

Goldstein, P. (1994). *Copyright's Highway: From Gutenburg to the Celestial Jukebox*. New York: Hill and Wang.

Goodson, I. F., & Walker, R. (1991). *Biography, Identity and Schooling*. London: Falmer Press.

Graff, H. J. (1995). *Conflicting Paths: Growing up in America*. Cambridge, MA: Harvard University Press.

Grealy, L. (1994). *Autobiography of a Face*. Boston: Houghton Mifflin.

Greene, M. (1995). *Releasing the Imagination*. San Francisco: Jossey-Bass.

Grumet, M. (1988). *Bitter Milk: Women and Teaching*. Amherst: The University of Massachusetts Press.

Grumet, M. (1990). Retrospective: Autobiography and the Analysis of Educational Experience, *Cambridge Journal of Education, 20* (3), pp. 277-282.

Hannabuss, S. & Marcella, R. (1993). *Biography and Children*. London: Library Association Publishing.

Hartman, M. (1972). Review of *The Water Is Wide*, *Library Journal, 97* (13), pp. 2388-2389.

Haskins, J. (1972). Rural Education Sea Islands Style, *New York Times Book Review*, September 24, p. 10.

Havighurst, R. J. (Ed.) (1971). *Leaders in American Education, 70th Yearbook of the National Society for the Study of Education*. Chicago: University of Chicago Press.

Hazo, S. (1996). Fear of Feeling, *Poets & Writers, 24*(4), pp. 26-31.

Hedrick, J. B. (1994). *Harriet Beecher Stowe*. New York: Oxford University Press.

Heilbrun, C. G. (1988). *Writing a Woman's Life*. New York: W. W. Norton & Co.

Hill, M. R. (1993). *Archival Strategies and Techniques*. Newbury Park, CA: Sage Publications.

Hillman, J. (1983). *Interviews*. New York: Harper & Row.

Horowitz, H. L. (1994). *The Power and Passion of M. Carey Thomas*. New York: Basic Books.

Horton, T. (1992). Moses Waddel: Nineteenth-Century South Carolina Educator (Doctoral Dissertation, University of South Carolina, Columbia, SC).

Huebner, D. (1995). Education and Spirituality, *JCT, 11* (2), pp. 13-34.

Hymes, J. (1991). Personal interview (telephone) with T. Reid, Sept. 2.

Iles, T. (Ed.) (1992). *All Sides of the Subject: Women and Biography*. New York: Teachers College Press.

Institute of Child Behavior and Development: 50 Years of Research, 1917-1967. (1967). Iowa City: University of Iowa.

Iowa Child Welfare Research Station: State University of Iowa, the 40th Anniversary, 1917-1957. (1959). *Monographs of the Society for Research in Child Development, serial no. 74, 24* (2).

Jacobs, L. (1991). Personal interview (telephone) with T. Reid, July 14.

Jalongo, M. R. & Isenberg, J. P. (1995). *Teacher's Stories: From Personal Narrative to Professional Insight*. San Francisco: Jossey-Bass.

Johnson, C. (1982). Risks in the Publication of Fieldwork, in *Ethics of Social Research*, edited by J. Sieber. New York: Springer-Verlag.

Kaplin, J. (1980). *Walt Whitman: A Life*. New York: Simon and Schuster.

Kazin, A. (1979). The Self as History: Reflections on Autobiography, in *Telling Lives: The Biographer's Art*, edited by M. Pachter. Philadelphia: University of Pennsylvania Press, pp. 74-89.

Kearns, D. (1981). Angles of Vision, in *Telling Lives: The Biographer's Art*, edited by M. Pachter. Philadelphia: University of Pennsylvania Press, pp. 91-103.

Kendall, P. M. (1965/1986). *The Art of Biography*. New York: W.W. Norton.

Klaus, C. H. (1994). The Chameleon "I": On Voice and Personality in the Personal Essay, in *Voices on Voice: Perspectives, Definitions, Inquiry*, edited by K. B. Yancey. Urbana, IL: National Council of Teachers of English, pp. 111-129.

Klohr, P. (1996). Laura Zirbes: A Teacher of Teachers, in *Teachers and Mentors*, edited by C. Kridel, et al. New York: Garland Publishing, pp. 139-145.

Krell, K. (1972). Daufuskie: The Island Where "Folks Are Well Knit Together," The [Columbia, S.C.] State, 11/19, pp. 1-B, 10-B.

Kridel. C., Bullough, R. V., & Shaker, P. (Eds.) (1996). *Teachers and Mentors*. New York: Garland Publishing.

Lane, L. (1842). Narrative of Lunsford Lane, formerly of Raleigh, NC. Boston.

Langness, L. & Frank, G. (1981). *Lives: An Anthropological Approach to Biography*. Novato, CA: Chandler & Sharp Publishers, Inc.

Lather, P. (1995). The Validity of Angels: Interpretive and Textual Strategies in Researching the Lives of Women with HIV/AIDS, *Qualitative Inquiry, 1* (1), pp. 41-68.

Lazerson, M. (1984). Teachers Organize: What Margaret Haley Lost, *History of Education Quarterly, 24*, pp. 261-270.

LeClercq, A. W. (1993). *Unpublished Materials: Libraries and Fair Use*. Washington, D.C.: Association of Research Libraries.

Ledoux, D. (1993). *Turning Memories into Memoirs*. Lisbon Falls, ME: Soleil Press.

Levine, L. W. (1977). *Black Culture and Black Consciousness: Afro-American Folk Thought from Slavery and Freedom*. New York: Basic Books.

Lewis, D. L. (1993). *W.E.B. DuBois: Biography of a Race*. New York: Henry Holt and Company.

Lewis, M. (1990). Interrupting Patriarchy: Politics, Resistance, and Transformation in the Feminist Classroom, *Harvard Educational Review, 60* (4), pp. 467-488.

Lomask, M. (1986). *The Biographer's Craft*. New York: Harper & Row, Publishers.

Lortie, D. (1975). *School-teacher: A Sociological Study*. Chicago: University of Chicago Press.

Lykes, R. W. (1975). *Higher Education and the United States Office of Education, 1867-1953*. Washington, DC: U.S. Office of Education.

McCarthy, C. (1997). The Uses of Culture: Canon Formation, Postcolonial Literature and the Multicultural Project, in *Curriculum: New Identities in/for the Field*, edited by W.F. Pinar. New York: Garland.

McLaren, P. (1989). *Life in Schools: An Introduction to Critical Pedagogy in the Foundations of Education*. New York: Longman.

McLaren, P. & Hammer, R. (1989). Critical Pedagogy and the Postmodern Challenge: Toward a Critical Postmodernist Pedagogy of Liberation, *Educational Foundations, 3* (3), pp. 29-62.

McPhee, J. (1967). *Oranges*. New York: Farrar, Straus & Giroux.

McPhee, J. (1970). _The Crofter and the Laird_. New York: Farrar, Straus & Giroux.

McPhee, J. (1990). _Looking for a Ship_. New York: Farrar, Straus & Giroux.

Mailer, N. (1968). _The Armies of the Night: The Novel as History, History as a Novel_. New York: New American Library.

Mailer, N. (1979). _The Executioner's Song: A True Life Novel_. Boston: Little, Brown.

Mann, M. P. (1867). _Thoughts Selected from the Writings of Horace Mann_. Boston: H.B. Fuller and Company.

Mann, M. P. (1891). _Life and Works of Horace Mann_. Boston: Marsh and Capon.

Marder, H. (1993). The Biographer and the Angel, _The American Scholar, 62_, pp. 221-231.

Mariani, P. (1984). _A Usable Past_. Amherst: University of Massachusetts Press.

Marshall, B. K. (1992). _Teaching the Postmodern: Fiction and Theory_. New York: Routledge.

Meath-Lang, B. (1990). The Dialogue Journal, in _Students and Teachers Writing Together_, edited by J. Kreeft-Peton. Alexandria, VA: TESOL Pub.

Meier, A. (1963). _Negro Thought in America, 1880-1915: Racial Ideologies in the Age of Booker T. Washington_. Ann Arbor: University of Michigan Press.

Meier, A. & Rudwick, E. (1986). _Black History and the Historical Profession, 1915-1980_. Urbana and Chicago: University of Illinois Press.

Mereoney, G.M. (1991). _Inseparable Loyalty: A Biography of William Bull_. Norcross, GA: Harrison Co.

Meyer, A. L. (1967). Laura Zirbes: In Memoriam, _ACEI Branch Exchange, 36_ (1), 36-H-I.

Miller, J. L. (1982). The Sound of Silence Breaking: Feminist Pedagogy and Curriculum Theory, _JCT, 4_ (1), pp. 5-11.

Miller, J. L. (1990). _Creating Spaces and Finding Voices: Teachers Collaborating for Empowerment_. Albany, NY: State University of New York.

Mills, C. W. (1959). _The Sociological Imagination_. New York: Oxford University Press.

Moore, H. (1996). _The White Blackbird_. New York: Viking.

Morrison, T. (1987). The Site of Memory, in *Inventing the Truth: The Art and Craft of Memoir*, edited by W. Zinsser. Boston: Houghton Mifflin Co, pp. 101-124.

Munro, P. (1992). Teaching as "Women's Work": A Century of Resistant Voices. Paper presented at the annual meeting of AERA, San Francisco.

Munro, P. (1993). Continuing Dilemmas of Life History Research, in *Theory and Concepts in Qualitative Research: Perspectives from the Field*, edited by D. Flinders & G. Mills. New York: Teachers College Press, pp. 163-181.

Munro, P. (1996). Resisting "Resistance": Stories Women Teachers Tell, *JCT, 12* (1), pp. 16-28.

Myerhoff, B. (1978). *Number Our Days*. New York: Dutton/ Meridian.

Namier, L. (1962). Function of the Historian, in *Biography as an Art*, edited by J.L. Clifford. New York: Oxford University Press.

Oates, S. B. (1982). *Let the Trumpet Sound: The Life of Martin Luther King, Jr.* New York: Harper & Row.

Oates, S. B. (Ed.) (1986). *Biography as High Adventure*. Amherst: University of Massachusetts Press.

Oates, S. B. (1991). *Biography as History*. Waco, Texas: Mankham Press Fund.

O'Brien, S. (1987). *Willa Cather: The Emerging Voice*. New York: Oxford University Press.

Ort, L. (1991a). Personal interview (telephone) with with T. Reid, July 19.

Ort, L. (1991b). Personal interview (telephone) with with T. Reid, July 29.

Pachter, M. (Ed.) (1981). *Telling Lives: The Biographer's Art*. Philadelphia: University of Pennsylvania Press.

Pagano, J. (1990). *Exiles and Communities: Teaching in the Patriarchal Wilderness*. Albany, NY: State University of New York Press.

Patterson, L. R. & Lindberg, S. W. (1991). *The Nature of Copyright: A Law of Users' Rights*. Athens, GA: University of Georgia Press.

Perle, E. G. (1992). *Fifth Annual U.S. Copyright Office Speaks: Contemporary and Intellectual Property Issues.* Englewood Cliffs, NJ: Prentice Hall.

Peters, C. (1995). Secondary Lives: Biography in Context, in *The Art of Literary Biography*, edited by J. Batchelor. Oxford: Clarendon Press, pp. 43-56.

Pinar, W. & Reynolds, W. (Eds.). (1992). *Understanding Curriculum as Phenomenological and Deconstructed Text.* New York: Teachers College Press.

Pinar, W., Reynolds, W., Slattery, P., & Taubman, P. (1995). *Understanding Curriculum.* New York: Peter Lang.

Plath, S. (1971). *The Bell Jar.* New York: Harper & Row.

Plath, S. (1975). *Letters Home: Correspondence, 1950-1963.* New York: Harper & Row.

Polkinghorne, D.E. (1988). *Narrative Knowing and the Human Sciences.* Albany: State University of New York Press.

Powell, M. E. (1992). Personal interview with E. Epps, November 13.

Preschool Laboratories at the Iowa Child Welfare Research Station. (1929). in *Preschool and Parental Education, 28th Yearbook of the National Society for the Study of Education, Part I*, edited by G. M. Whipple. Bloomington, IL: Public School Publishing Co, pp. 211-217.

Rampersad, A. (1991). Conversation with Arnold Rampersad, in *Life into Art*, edited by G. P. Mandell. Fayetteville: University of Arkansas Press.

Raverat, G. (1952). *Period Piece: A Cambridge Childhood.* London: Faber and Faber.

Reid, T. (1991). Laura Zirbes: Forerunner of Restructuring, *Childhood Education, 68*, pp. 98- 102.

Reid, T. (1993). Towards Creative Teaching: The Life and Career of Laura Zirbes (Doctoral Dissertation, University of South Carolina, Columbia, SC).

Reynolds, K. (in press). *Visions and Vanities: John Andrew Rice and the Black Mountain College Experiment.* Baton Rouge, LA: Louisiana State University Press.

Rice, J. A. (1937). Fundamentalism and the Higher Learning, *Harpers Monthly Magazine, 174*, pp. 587-597.

Rice, J. A. (1967). Personal interview with M. Duberman, June 10.

Rich, A. (1978). Origins and History of Consciousness, in *The Dream of a Common Language*, edited by A. Rich. New York: W. W. Norton & Co., pp. 7-9.

Rich, A. (1979). *On Lies, Secrets, and Silence*. New York: Norton.

Richardson, L. (1994). Writing: A Method of Inquiry, in *Handbook of Qualitative Research*, edited by N. Denzin & Y. Lincoln. Thousand Oaks, Sage, pp. 516-529.

Richardson, L. (1996). Ethnographic Trouble, *Qualitative Inquiry, 2* (2), pp. 227-229.

Rodriguez, R. (1982). *Hunger of Memory*. New York: Bantam.

Rollyson, C. (1992). *Biography: An Annotated Bibliography*. Pasadena, CA: Salem Press.

Roosevelt, E. (1937). *This Is My Story*. New York, London: Harper & Brothers

Roosevelt, E. (1949). *This I Remember*. New York: Harper & Brothers.

Roosevelt, E. (1961). *Autobiography*. New York: Harper.

Rorty, R. (1991). A Paradigm for Intellectuals, *The New Leader*, 5/20, pp. 13-15.

Rose, P. (1984). *Parallel Lives*. New York: Knopf.

Ross, D. (1972). *G. Stanley Hall: the Psychologist as Prophet*. Chicago: University of Chicago Press.

Ross, V. (1991). Too Close to Home: Repressing Biography, Instituting Authority, in *Contesting the Subject*, edited by W. H. Epstein. West Lafayette, IN: Purdue University Press, pp. 135-165.

Rossiter, M. (1982). *Women Scientists in America: Struggles and Strategies to 1940*. Baltimore: Johns Hopkins Press.

Ruddick, S. (1984). New Combinations: Learning from Virginia Woolf, in *Between Women*, edited by C. Ascher, L. DeSalvo & S. Ruddick. Boston: Beacon Press, pp. 137-159.

Ryan, A. (1995). *John Dewey and the High Tide of American Liberalism*. New York: W. W. Norton & Co.

Salvio, P. (1990). Transgressive Daughters: Student Autobiography and the Project of Self-Creation, *Cambridge Journal of Education, 20* (3), pp. 283-290.

Sanchez, G. (1993). *Becoming Mexican American*. New York: Oxford University Press.

Schubert, W. & Ayers, W. (Eds.) (1992). *Teacher Lore: Learning from Our Own Experience*. New York: Longman.

Shields, C. (1994). *The Stone Diaries*. New York: Viking.

Shostak, M. (1981). *Nisa: The Life and Words of a !Kung Woman*. New York: Vintage Books.

Shulman, L.S. (1986). Paradigms and Research Programs in the Study of Teaching: A Contemporary Perspective, in *Handbook of Research on Teaching*, edited by M.C. Wittrock. New York: Macmillan, 3rd ed., pp. 3-36.

Simmons, E. (1992). Personal communication (letter) to E. Epps, September 29.

Simms, W. G. (1854). *The Scout; or, The Black Riders of the Congaree*. New York: Redfield.

Sklar, Z. (1992). Telephone interview with E. Epps, October 20.

Smith, L. G. & Smith, J. K. (1994). *Lives in Education*. New York: St. Martin's Press.

Smith, L. M. (1994). Biographical Method, in *Handbook of Qualitative Research*, edited by N. Denzin & Y. Lincoln. Newberry Park, CA: Sage Publications, pp. 286-305.

Smith, L. M. (In process). *Nora Barlow and the Darwin Legacy*. Ames, Iowa: Iowa State University Press.

Smith, L. M., Dwyer, D. C., Prunty, J. J., & Kleine, P. F. (1988). *Innovation and Change in Schooling: History, Politics, and Agency*. London: The Falmer Press.

Smith, L. M., Kleine, P., Prunty, J., & Dwyer, D. (1986). *Educational Innovators: Then and Now*. London: Falmer Press.

Smith, L. M., Prunty, J. J., Dwyer, D. C., & Kleine, P. F. (1987). *The Fate of an Innovative School: The History and Present Status of the Kensington School*. London: Falmer Press.

Society of American Archivists. (1992). Code of Ethics. Washington: S.A.A.

Stameshkin, D. M. (1993). Review of W. Urban's *Black Scholar*, *History of Education Quarterly, 33* (2), pp. 250-252.

Stanton, E. C. (1898). *Eighty Years and More: Reminiscences, 1815-1897*. New York: Shocken Books reprint, 1971.

Stern, D. (1995) *Teaching English So It Matters*. San Francisco: Corwin.

Stewart, J. (1989). *Drinkers, Drummers and Decent Folk: Ethnographic Narratives of Village Trinidad*. Albany: State University of New York.

Strong, William S. (1993). *The Copyright Book: A Practical Guide*. Cambridge, Massachusetts: MIT Press.

Taylor, H. (1973). Introduction, in *The Life and Mind of John Dewey* by G. Dykhuizen, Carbondale, IL: Southern Illinois University Press, pp. xiii-xxv.

Terkel, S. (1970). *Hard Times: An Oral History of the Great Depression*. New York: Pantheon Books.

Thomas, D. (1993). Treasonable or Trustworthy Text: Reflections on Teacher Narrative Studies, *Journal of Education for Teaching, 19* (3), pp. 214-221.

Tomalin, C. (1991). *The Invisible Woman: The Story of Nelly Ternan and Charles Dickens*. New York: Knopf.

Tsing, A. L. (1993). *In the Realm of the Diamond Queen*. Princeton, NJ: Princeton University Press.

Urban, W. J. (1982). *Why Teachers Organized*. Detroit: Wayne State University Press.

Urban, W. J. (1992). *Black Scholar: Horace Mann Bond, 1904-1972*. Athens and London: University of Georgia Press.

Utterback, R. (1991). Personal interview (telephone) with T. Reid,, July 14.

Vandiver. F. E. (1983). Biography as an Agent of Humanism, in *The Biographer's Gift: Life Histories and Humanism*, edited by J. F. Veninga. College Station: Texas A & M University Press, pp. 3-20.

Van Manen, M. (1994). Pedagogy, Virtue, and Narrative Identity in Teaching, *Curriculum Inquiry, 24* (2), pp. 135-170.

Veninga, J. F. (1983). *The Biographer's Gift*. College Station, TX: Texas A&M University Press.

Vidich, A. J., & Bensman, J. (1968). *Small Town in Mass Society*. Princeton, NJ: Princeton University Press.

Vourvoulias, B. (1996). Horizontal Lines to Other Worlds: An Interview with Kenzaburo Oe, *Poets and Writers, 24* (1), pp. 50-59.

Wagner-Martin, L. (1982). *Ellen Glasgow: Beyond Convention.* Austin: University of Texas Press.

Wagner-Martin, L. (1987). *Sylvia Plath: A Biography.* New York: Simon and Schuster.

Wagner-Martin, L. (1988). *Sylvia Plath: The Critical Heritage.* New York: Routledge.

Wagner-Martin, L. (1994). *Telling Women's Lives: The New Biography.* New Brunswick: Rutgers University Press.

Wagner-Martin, L. (1995). *Favored Strangers: Gertrude Stein and Her Family.* New Brunswick: Rutgers University Press.

Walsh, W. (1989). Interview: Pat Conroy, *Other Voices, 11*, pp. 200-218.

Ward, J. W. (1970). *Andrew Jackson, Symbol for an Age.* New York: Oxford University Press.

Weedon, C. (1987). *Feminist Practice and Poststructuralist Theory.* New York: Basil Blackwell, Inc.

Weems, M. L. (1824; 1976). *Life of Francis Marion.* Charleston: Tradd Street Press.

West, J. (1945). *Plainville, U.S.A.* New York: Columbia University Press.

Westbrook, R. B. (1991). *John Dewey and American Democracy.* Ithaca, NY: Cornell University Press.

Whyte, W. E. (1955). *Street Corner Society.* Chicago: University of Chicago Press.

Willingham, R. M., Jr. (1980). Pat Conroy, in *Dictionary of Literary Biography, Vol. 6: American Novelists since World War II*, edited by J.E. Kibler, Jr. Detroit: Gale Research Co, pp. 55-58.

Wilson, R. (1991). Producing American Selves: The Form of American Biography, in *Contesting the Subject*, edited by W. H. Epstein. West Lafayette: Purdue University Press, pp. 167-192.

Wolcott, H. (1996). *The Art of Fieldwork.* Walnut Creek, CA: AltaMira Press.

Woolf, V. (1967). The Art of Biography, in *Collected Essays by Virginia Woolf: vol. 4.* London: The Hogarth Press, pp. 221-228.

Wolff, G. (1981). Minor Lives, in *Telling Lives*, edited by M. Pachter. Philadelphia: University of Pennsylvania Press, pp. 56-72.

Works Progress Administration, Slave Narratives of the Nineteenth Century, unpublished manuscripts compiled after the Civil War by agents of the W.P.A.

Yin, R. K. (1989). *Case Study Research: Design and Methods*. Newbury Park, CA: Sage.

York, L. (1987). Pat Conroy's Portrait of the Artist as a Young Southerner, *The Southern Literary Journal, 19* (2), pp. 34-46.

Yow, V. R. (1994). *Recording Oral History*. Thousand Oaks, CA: Sage Publications.

Zirbes, L. (1958). The In-service Education of Teachers, *California Journal of Elementary Education, 26*, pp. 205-219.

Zirbes, L. (1959). *Spurs to Creative Teaching*. New York: G. P. Putnam's.

Zirbes, L. (1962). The Challenge of Changing Values. College Park, MD: ACEI Archives. Taped speech given to the ACEI Study Conference in Indianapolis.

Contributors

Lorin W. Anderson is the Distinguished Carolina Professor of Education at the University of South Carolina, Columbia.

William Ayers is Professor of Curriculum and Instruction at the University of Illinois, Chicago and Co-chair of the Small Schools Workshop, Chicago.

Robert V. Bullough, Jr. is Professor of Educational Studies at the University of Utah.

D. Jean Clandinin is Professor of Education and Director of the Centre for Research for Teacher Education and Development at the University of Alberta, Edmonton.

Geraldine Joncich Clifford is Emeritus Professor of Education at the University of California, Berkeley.

F. Michael Connelly is Professor of Education and Director of the Joint Centre for Teacher Development at the Ontario Institute for Studies in Education and the University of Toronto.

Blanche Wiesen Cook is Professor of History and Women's Studies at John Jay College and The Graduate Center, CUNY.

Louise DeSalvo is Professor of English at Hunter College.

Edwin C. Epps is Co-director of the South Carolina Writing Project at the University of South Carolina, Spartanburg.

Barbara Finkelstein is Professor of Education in the Department of Educational Policy, Planning, and Administration at the University of Maryland, College Park.

Corrine E. Glesne is an Associate Professor of Education and Associate Dean of the College of Education and Social Services at the University of Vermont.

Herbert J. Hartsook is Curator of the Modern Political Collection, South Caroliniana Library, University of South Carolina, Columbia.

Thomas B. Horton is an Instructor of History at The Porter-Gaud School, Charleston, South Carolina.

Philo Hutcheson is an Assistant Professor of Higher Education in the Department of Educational Policy Studies at Georgia State University.

Craig Kridel is Professor of Curriculum and Foundations and Curator of the Museum of Education at the University of South Carolina, Columbia.

Janet L. Miller is Professor of Education in the Department of Interdisciplinary Studies at National-Louis University.

Anne E. Pautz is a Visiting Assistant Professor of Education in the Department of Curriculum & Instruction at Oklahoma State University.

William F. Pinar is the St. Bernard Parish Alumni Endowed Professor of Education at Louisiana State University.

Tony Reid is Principal of the Hansen Elementary School in Cedar Falls, Iowa.

Katherine C. Reynolds is an Assistant Professor of Higher Education at the University of South Carolina, Columbia.

Louis M. Smith is Emeritus Professor of Education at Washington University.

Lynda Anderson Smith is a District Administrator in the Pitt County Schools, Greenville, NC.

Wayne J. Urban is the Regents' Professor of Educational Policy Studies and Professor of History at Georgia State University.

Linda C. Wagner-Martin is the Hanes Professor of English and Comparative Literature at the University of North Carolina, Chapel Hill.

Alan Wieder is an Associate Professor of Educational Foundations at the University of South Carolina, Columbia.

Index